The Race To Be Myself

CASTER SEMENYA

The Race To Be Myself

1 3 5 7 9 10 8 6 4 2

#Merky Books
20 Vauxhall Bridge Road
London SW1V 2SA

#Merky Books is part of the Penguin Random House group of companies
whose addresses can be found at global.penguinrandomhouse.com.

First published in the US by W. W. Norton & Company in 2023
First published in the UK by #Merky Books in 2023

www.penguin.co.uk

A CIP catalogue record for this book is available from the British Library.

ISBN 978–1–529–18636–9 (hardback)

Book design by Lovedog Studio

Printed and bound in Great Britain by Clays Ltd, Elcograf S.p.A.

The authorised representative in the EEA is Penguin Random House Ireland,
Morrison Chambers, 32 Nassau Street, Dublin D02 YH68

www.greenpenguin.co.uk

MIX
Paper | Supporting
responsible forestry
FSC® C018179

Penguin Random House is committed to a
sustainable future for our business, our readers
and our planet. This book is made from Forest
Stewardship Council® certified paper.

*For those who are born different
and feel they don't belong in this world,
it is because you were brought here
to help create a new one.*

CONTENTS

Prologue   1

PART I
THE BEGINNING

Chapter 1   GOD MADE ME   13

Chapter 2   A DIFFERENT KIND OF GIRL   18

Chapter 3   I AM NOT AFRAID   30

Chapter 4   HUNTING WITH BOYS   40

Chapter 5   THE CHANGE   51

Chapter 6   THABISO   60

PART II
THE RISE

Chapter 7   WHERE I BELONG   73

Chapter 8   THEY SAW ME RUN   83

Chapter 9   ON THE WAY UP   93

Chapter 10   A HIGHER EDUCATION   103

Chapter 11   THE TROUBLES BEGIN   118

Chapter 12   BERLIN   131

PART III
THE AWAKENING

Chapter 13   NOT WOMAN ENOUGH   155

Chapter 14   *YOU* MAGAZINE   167

Chapter 15   THE NOTHINGNESS   173

Chapter 16   HOPE   184

Chapter 17   THE COMEBACK   196

Chapter 18   LOVE AND HAPPINESS   207

PART IV
THE REDEMPTION

Chapter 19   ROAD TO LONDON 2012   221

Chapter 20   GOLD IN RIO   241

Chapter 21   RETURN OF THE IAAF   260

Chapter 22   INSIDE THE COURT   274

Chapter 23   THE AFTERMATH   289

Epilogue   THE COBRA   301

Acknowledgments   307

The Race To Be Myself

PROLOGUE

I AM MOKGADI CASTER SEMENYA. I AM ONE OF THE greatest track & field athletes to ever run the 800-m distance. I've won two Olympic gold medals and three world championships, along with dozens of Diamond League meets, and went unbeaten for almost four years. Unfortunately, it is not what I have achieved on the track that has likely brought me to your attention.

Much has been written about me in virtually every major international outlet in the world since I came into the public's eye in 2009, and most of it is outright lies or half-truths. I have waited a long time to tell my story. For more than a decade I have preferred to let my running do the talking. After what has happened to me, it felt easier that way.

In 2019, the International Association of Athletics Federation (now World Athletics) banned me from running my favored 800-m event, along with the 400-m and the 1500-m distances. My last IAAF-sanctioned 800-m race was on June 30, 2019, when I won the Diamond League Prefontaine Classic at Stanford University. I was not banned because I was caught doping or cheating. Rather, I am no longer allowed to run those distances because of a biological condition I was born with and that I refuse to take unnecessary drugs to change.

I have what is called a difference in sex development (DSD), an umbrella term that refers to the varying genetic conditions where an embryo responds in a different way to the hormones that spark the development of internal and external sexual organs. To put it simply, on the outside I am female, I have a vagina, but I do not have a uterus. I do not menstruate and my body produces an elevated amount of testosterone, which gives me more typically masculine characteristics than other women, such as a deeper voice and fewer curves. I cannot carry a child because I don't have a womb but, contrary to what many people think, I do not produce sperm. I can't biologically contribute to making new life. I did not know any of this about my body until soon after August 2009, when I won the gold medal in the 800-m race at the World Championships in Berlin, Germany. I was only eighteen years old and had been subjected to invasive and humiliating gender confirmation tests without my consent just prior to the race. What followed was a media firestorm that continues to this day.

People believed all sorts of insanity about me—that I was a boy who managed to hide his penis all the way to the world championships, that I was paid to have my penis removed so South Africa could bring home a medal in the women's category, that I was a hermaphrodite forced to run as a girl for political gain. Journalists descended into my village and every school I'd ever attended. My parents and siblings, friends, and teachers, were harassed with calls and by visitors, day and night. I can still hear my mother wailing desperately as she tried to explain to perfect strangers that I was born a girl, and that I was her little girl, and why was all of this happening?

I have never spoken in detail about what happened during this time of my life but I am now ready to do so. It is said that silence will not protect us. From the moment I stepped on to the track for the final meet in Berlin on August 19, 2009, I have been vilified and persecuted. My accomplishments since have been celebrated, yes, but it is hard to think of another athlete at the elite level who has endured as much scrutiny and psychological abuse from sports governing bodies, other competitors, and the media as I have. It has affected me in ways I cannot describe, although I will try. And while I have faced significant hardships throughout my life, I want to make clear that my story is not one of pain and torment, but rather about hope, self-confidence, and resilience.

I am still standing; I am still here. What has been said about me in the media is not who I really am. I've heard myself described as "surly," "rude," "shy," "stoic," "dignified," and "superhuman." All those things may seem true, at times. I'm also quite charming and funny, and I've been said to have a biting wit. Like every human, I am many things—a proud Black woman from Limpopo, a rural province in the northernmost part of South Africa, a daughter, a sister, a wife, and now I am a mother to two baby girls: Oratile, who was born in 2019, and Oarabile, who was born in 2021. I feel and I hurt just like a regular person, although I am not considered by science or some people to be a regular woman.

The scientific community has labeled my biological makeup as "intersex," and I am now one of, if not the, most recognizable intersex person in the world. The truth is I don't think of myself that way. I want everyone to understand that despite my condition, even though I am built differently than other women, I am a woman. Of course, growing up I knew I looked and behaved differently from many of my peers, but my family, my community, and my country accepted me as I was and never made me feel like an outsider. The beauty of my childhood was that I never felt othered or unwanted—this is the source of my strength. I have never questioned who I am.

And I am a runner. I love running with all of my heart. It is one of those things that just makes sense to me. Runners at every level know what I mean when I say running makes me feel free but also grounds me. It is like meditating for me—it centers me. There's this thing that happens every time I get to the starting line of a race. My mind goes completely silent. I hear nothing, except my own breathing. I see nothing, except the track in front of me. Some people call this the zone, where the line between nothing and everything no longer exists—we are simultaneously in and out of our bodies.

I think it's important to talk about lines. We humans are obsessed with them. There are starting lines and finish lines, there are the lines we draw around ourselves that tell others where to stop, where they are not wanted, and there are the lines that define what kind of human we are—our race, our gender, our sexuality. Most people are content to walk the line as it is drawn, to be defined by it, to stay in their place. I am not one of those people. I never have been. The biological makeup of my body, the way I look on the outside and the way I live my life, is a crossing of lines in many people's minds. The way I look may be what brought me to the IAAF's attention in the first place. According to Sebastian Coe, the current president of the IAAF, there is no line more important, no line more worth protecting than the difference between men and women in sports competition. As you will see in my story, that line is hard to define, and it keeps moving depending on who is doing the defining. I have been banned from running because women are a "protected class" in athletics, and women with differences in sexual development are considered a threat to the line between genders.

I sometimes remind myself of how blessed I am to be where I am today. Not that many years ago, the sports governing body of my own country of South Africa wouldn't have allowed me to run in the Olympics because I am Black. I was born in 1991, just a few years before the first democratic elections in 1994 would finally begin to unravel that insidious and dehumanizing system of government that defined people and even ripped families apart based on the color of their skin and other physical features. My parents, older siblings, and extended family lived through this time. They were not allowed to travel or live where they wanted; some were forcibly relocated. Black people didn't have access to higher education. And unlike me, so many great Black athletes never got a chance. There is still so much trauma in our communities from the brutality of apartheid. I carry that history of discrimination and resistance and the yearning for freedom within me; they are there in everything I do.

As a young girl, I heard Nelson Mandela, the beloved leader of our country and icon of freedom and resistance around the world, speak about sports as having "the power to inspire . . . the power to unite people in a way that little else does. . ." And I loved sports. I knew from a young age that I wanted to be known and appreciated for my physical talents. My siblings thought I was crazy when, as an eight-year-old girl, I would point up to the skies and say, "One day, it will be me on that plane." Of course, in those days I believed I was going to be a famous soccer player and travel with our national team, Bafana Bafana. No notable athletes had ever come out of our small village, and people were more concerned with surviving than dreaming. I had no real reason to believe in my eventual success, but I was sure I was going to make it.

Well, this girl child ran so fast that people insisted no girl could possibly run that fast. Unless, the rumors went, I wasn't really a girl. Or maybe I *was* a girl, but one whose coaches had pumped her full of drugs that turn women into men anyway. After all, the media said, I had "come out of nowhere" to win. The point seemed to be that I did not belong at the world championships and that my win had to be because I was cheating in some form or other. Sports and entertainment commentators discussed my facial features, the size of my arms and legs and breasts, the muscles in my abdomen. They would zoom in on pictures of my crotch and wonder what could possibly be going on between my legs. I would say I was being treated like an animal, but I grew up tending to my family's livestock, and we treated them with more respect than that.

I'm aware that Black women's bodies in general have been objectified and treated as spectacles. The most well-known historical example is Saartjie Baartman, a fellow South African brought to Europe where she was put on display in circus-like exhibits for a paying audience in the 1800s. Her body's proportions were considered abnormal by Western standards. After her death in 1815 at the age of twenty-five, her genitals were cut from her body, preserved, and displayed along with her skeleton in a French museum until 1974. The circumstances of her death aren't clear, but it is said she died of disease, far from the comfort of her people and homeland. Nelson Mandela had Saartjie's remains repatriated once he was in power, and she was finally laid to rest in the country of her birth in 2002.

At times, it seems not much has changed from Saartjie's days. We only have to look at the way women like Michelle Obama and Serena Williams have been treated by today's media and parts of society. They have been called monkeys, accused of being men. Every part of their body, their musculature, their facial features, have been openly derided and insulted. Black women have always been held to some standard of beauty and femininity that makes us something other than women.

I am a tall, dark-skinned, African woman with well-defined muscles, a deep voice and not a lot up on top. I know I look like a man. I know I sound like a man and maybe even walk like a man and dress like one, too. But I'm not a man. I've made no secret of preferring to play soccer and baseball and basketball with boys and hanging out with them when I was growing up. In my village, boys were playing the sports I wanted to play, and my parents didn't stop me from doing what made me happy. I was accepted, but it didn't mean people didn't see that I was different. Like I used to say to would-be bullies, "You think I look like a boy? So what? What are you going to do about it?" One thing about me is that I've never tolerated bullying—of myself or others in my presence. If the situation escalated, I'd let my fists do the rest of the talking. Playing sports and having muscles and a deep voice make me less feminine, yes. I'm a different kind of woman, I know. But I'm still a woman. Growing up, my family and friends just understood I was what the Western world calls a "tomboy."

I WAS EIGHTEEN years old and had just run in the biggest race of my life when Pierre Weiss, the IAAF's general secretary, cruelly said to the media, "It is clear she is a woman. But maybe not 100 percent."

The IAAF and the International Olympic Committee have been gender-testing women in various ways since the beginning of organized competition, but by the time I won my first World Championship in 2009, there was no uniform test required for all women athletes. Rather, there was an arbitrary policy that anyone (say, an envious coach or athlete) could anonymously report their suspicion that an athlete wasn't the gender they claimed. If the IAAF chose to do so, that female athlete would have to prove themselves through a battery of invasive psychological, gynecological, and endocrinal tests. Women in my position have attempted to and even killed themselves. Many more have just left athletics out of fear and shame.

Like me, other women caught in the IAAF's gender investigations had no idea about their condition. The only solutions offered are medically unnecessary and potentially harmful. The diagnosis not only ends their dreams of running on the international stage and a way of helping their families, but depending on where they live in the world, a medical determination may also have more severe consequences. Rumors arising from an IAAF investigation may end their dreams of building a family or lead to them being ostracized by their communities or injured or worse. It is hard to explain the psychological violence of having your gender identity questioned or ripped away, of feeling rejected by society. I'm sure the IAAF thought I would be one of the ones who just went away.

They were wrong. It is not in my nature to give up. Like I said, I don't like bullies.

Many people thought I would never run again after the 2009 debacle. That I would go back to my village and live the rest of my days as best I could. Well, I have achieved more than many thought possible, although the circumstances of my success have caused me great mental and physical injury, and my refusal to bow my head to the IAAF's regulations on testosterone limits for women has hobbled what future I have left in athletics. In some ways, I know my time as a competitor is coming to an end. It is an eventuality that every athlete must confront. I am now thirty-two years old. As someone who works with their body, I know that no one can outrun time.

I feel that the IAAF has confiscated a large part of my life. I've spent as much time fighting them as I have training and racing. They have stolen years of performances not only from me but also from the audience—their joy at seeing me on the track over the years, win or lose, has brought me joy. The blow of every insult hurled at me has been softened by the love and admiration of people who watch me run.

I dreamt of defending my gold medal at the Tokyo 2020 Olympics. I'd appealed the IAAF's reinstatement of testosterone regulations to the Court of Arbitration for Sport in 2018 and hoped its members would see things our way in time for me to compete. They did not. We tried again with the Swiss Supreme Court and unfortunately lost again. But the fight is not over yet. As I write this, my lawyers are challenging the ruling at the European Court of Human Rights. We hope they agree perfectly healthy women should not have to undergo surgeries or take drugs that alter their natural bodies to compete; this is a barbaric infringement on our human dignity. The World Medical Association and the United Nations Humans Right Council have both publicly condemned the IAAF's decision.

By now, it is no secret that when the IAAF sidelined me for

almost a year after I won gold in 2009, I was so desperate to get back on the track, to fulfill my dreams and help my family, that I did take medication to lower my testosterone level. It was the only way. I took the drugs for years. The side effects were horrible. During those years, I ran despite feeling sick, and I ran while injured. I've had some great running years and some terrible ones. Contrary to what some think, I've never thrown a race to appear slower than my competitors and, unlike a few I've run against, I've never taken illegal substances to gain an edge. I am a pure athlete, win or lose. I've worked hard throughout my life, sacrificed time with my loved ones, sacrificed many normal life experiences, in order to have the privilege and opportunity to do what I love.

I was lucky to be born with these special talents—my mind has a special ability to focus, my body can stand the pain and exhaustion of endless training. It's not the testosterone in my body that makes me great, it's my ambition, perseverance, and faith in myself. Every time I've been knocked down, I get back up. Every setback has made me stronger.

I am not a scientist. I am not here to deliver a lecture on human biology. I am not here to prove my humanity—*that* has been granted to me by God. It is true we athletes tend to think in simple ways—win or lose, train hard and try again the next day. My world has always been very black and white and, I admit, very small. I have traveled all over the world and never explored the outside of a hotel or a race track. It had to be that way so that I could endure the physical and mental requirements of elite athletics, especially given the situation I was shoved into after Berlin in 2009.

"I DON'T HAVE TIME for nonsense," I have replied to the journalists who've approached me about the "gender issue" throughout the years. And I mean it. Because that's how I've always seen it. Nonsense and stupidity and ignorance. I'm here to run and put on a show. That was the totality of my job. But the way I was treated by the IAAF and the media, and the way I have carried myself despite it all, has catapulted me beyond athletics. I have become a human rights icon in many people's eyes. I will miss running my beloved 800- and 1500-m distance races, but I know I can never again put my body through what I did in order to compete, and I hope no other girl has to.

I accept and love myself just the way I am. I always have and I always will. God made me. I am fortunate to have had a family who never tried to change me, and a country that wrapped its arms around me and fought for my right to run. There is always a sadness to the end of an era, but I will run as long as my body allows me to. When I can no longer run, either because of time or more regulations targeting people like me, you will still see me on the track supporting the coming generations.

I am a proud South African woman born in a tiny village to people who loved me. They have survived more humiliations than I could possibly know. It is from them that I know about maintaining dignity in the face of oppression. It is my hope that by telling my truth, I inspire others to be unafraid, to love and accept themselves. May this story contribute to a more tolerant world for us all.

PART I

THE BEGINNING

Chapter 1

GOD MADE ME

I'M RUNNING HARD AND FAST. THE GROUND HAS cracks everywhere, and I keep tripping. I am climbing over metal fences and floating and then falling and pushing up with my body and floating again. My feet are caked with dirt, and they are also wet. Sometimes they hurt, but the pain goes away. I am happy. I feel free. No one can catch me. My mother and sisters try, but I'm too fast for them. I believe this is the first time I felt like "me." That I was a person, separate from the people and things around me. It is my earliest memory. I was around two years old.

My mother says I was an early walker. I took my first steps at seven months. From there, it seemed like I was flying from one place to the next. My feet were always bleeding because the floor of my parents' home was made of rough cement. It was easy for a toddler to stumble and fall. My legs and knees were always scratched and bruised. They said I wouldn't cry when I fell, I'd just get up and keep going. And I was strong. If my older siblings wanted to take something away from me, they'd have to work hard to pry it out of my tiny hands. Even as a toddler, I was fierce. My mom said she knew I was something special right from the start.

I was born to Dorcas and Jacob Semenya on January 7, 1991, in a rural village called Ga-Masehlong, located in what is today called Limpopo, the northernmost province of South Africa. Our village is small and remote; only about a thousand people lived there. There was a time when it couldn't be found on Google Maps. There is only one road that leads into the village. If you were driving from the city of Polokwane, capital of the Limpopo province, you'd drive about 60 kilometers northwest on the only main road, and then make a left and head into nothing but open sky, wilderness, and dirt tracks. Eventually, you would arrive at a tree that holds a sign with our village's name on it.

We had eight main streets, which sat parallel to each other. Mostly there were homes on rectangular plots of land and a few shops, what we call "spaza" or "tuck" shops, convenience stores that sold basic household items and snacks and drinks. Anyone could put up a spaza shop; many were in people's homes. We had one liquor store, a supermarket, and a primary school. And of course, we had a church. Our small church was part of the Zion Christian Church family, the largest in South Africa. The church was the hub of the village, and you'd find almost everybody gathered there on Sundays, and sometimes during the week, singing, dancing, and calling out to God and his Son. Many of the working-age people left during the day to work as farmers and laborers and domestic workers in towns and cities or in the larger neighboring villages.

I've often described my village as a "dusty, dusty place." And it was that. The flat dry land surrounding the homes seemed like it could go on forever. It was dotted with baobab and jacaranda trees, bushes, brambles and thorns. You could see mountains in the distance. There wasn't much to do there except survive. When I was growing up, the houses were made of mud and stone. Some folks built their roofs with corrugated tin, and others used tightly woven dried grass or thatch. There was wire fencing around many of the homes to keep in the cows and goats and sheep, although the animals would also roam freely around the village. Everyone in the village knew each other, and kids were allowed to roam freely, too. We call the wilderness surrounding our village "the bush," and it's where I spent most of my childhood.

My mom had been a teacher in her youth, but once she married my father, he preferred that she stay home. My mom still wanted to contribute financially to our family, so she opened a spaza shop in our yard. She sold a little of everything, mostly foodstuffs like raw cuts of meat and fish and sweets from the back of our home. During the week, she would also take some merchandise to our school and sell to students during lunchbreaks. She'd have candy and fresh-baked bread with raisins. I used to love the sweet bread, but I didn't like the raisins, so I would pick them and throw them on the ground. My mother didn't like that I wasted perfectly good food. When they were home, my sisters would help my mom. When I got older, I helped my mom sell, too. My mother was beautiful, with rich brown skin and a rounded face and curves that made others stop and look. Like most of the women in my family, she was not tall, but she carried herself with a dignity that made her seem much taller. My mom was very motherly, by which I mean patient, kind, and protective. I inherited her easy, wide smile. She was tough, too—not a woman you wanted to cross.

My father worked as a municipal gardener in Pretoria, a city about 310 kilometers from our village. The work kept him away from home a lot. He'd be gone sometimes for months at a time and come back for holidays or when he was given a break. I loved my mom with all my heart but I was what they call a "daddy's girl." I missed him terribly when he would go off to the big city. I remember he would come home and I would run to him and hug him for a long time. He'd pick me up and spin me around and around. Most would say I inherited my height, facial features, and disposition from my father, who was thin and long-limbed but muscular, with sharp cheekbones. He, too, had a big smile. My dad could come off as shy and reserved, but he was also a jokester, and it seemed you could hear his laughter from miles away.

My mother gave birth to me at WF Knobel Hospital, the closest hospital to our village. I am the fourth child of six children, five girls and one boy. My eldest sister, Wenny, was born in 1980, and then Nico was born in 1985, followed by Olga, born in 1987. I came into the world in 1991, and my younger sister Murriel was born in 1993. My baby brother, Ishmael, the only boy in our family and final child, was born in 1996. The real baby of our family was my niece, Neo, Wenny's daughter, who lived with us from the day she was born in 1998. My older sisters would come and go from the village as they searched for opportunities in schooling and work in Johannesburg. I would end up being the eldest in the household and the main caretaker of my younger sister, brother, and niece, while my mother and father worked. I had plenty of extended family in our village—aunts and uncles on both sides with children of their own.

We were not rich people, but we were not poor. Sometimes people say someone is "poor," but they don't know what poverty is. Or I suppose poverty has levels to it depending on where you are. Our family may not have had a lot, but we had plenty of food. I never had to go to bed hungry. For me, being poor is when a family must end the day without eating, when they don't have clothes, and they don't know where their next meal is coming from. "Poor" is when you don't have shelter. Our family had all of this, so we weren't poor.

Our home was large by our standards, with five bedrooms and a living room. We were a big family, and we needed the space. There was no electricity or running water. We fetched enough water from the village well for our needs and used candles and paraffin lamps. When I was four or five years old, my father installed a solar energy system; government-run electricity didn't come to our village until 2001, when I was ten. Our toilet was outdoors, a good walk away from the main house. It was a wooden shack built around a deep hole in the ground. We called it the "long drop." No need for water to flush. You sat and did your business and went on with life.

We had about a third of a hectare of land, and we grew fruits and vegetables on one side and kept our animals on the other. The weather allowed us to farm lemons, oranges, figs, guava, mangoes, peaches, grapes, pomegranates, and even a little sugar cane. We also had tomatoes, potatoes, and spinach. We didn't sell what we grew; we farmed only to feed ourselves. There was an area inside the house that could be called a kitchen, but the actual cooking of meals happened outside in our yard. I loved to run into the bush and collect firewood. We had a pit in the back of our home, and when the wood was glowing red and orange, we'd put our iron pots on it. We owned about thirty domesticated animals—cows and goats and sheep. I loved to take care of them, too.

My mother told me one of our ancestors came to her in a dream while she was pregnant and gave her my full name. Mokgadi Caster Semenya. Mokgadi was my maternal grandmother's name. In Pedi, our native tongue, it means "one who guides" and "one who gives up what they want so that others may have what they need." Caster is an English name, and I learned it means "one who seeks."

I was a big baby, the biggest of all my siblings. I weighed around twelve pounds at birth. I was barrel chested, my mother said, with big lungs that allowed for a deep-throated cry, unlike any of her other daughters. I know that after three girls, my parents probably wanted a boy, but here I was. They were happy. A new healthy soul in the family is always a cause for happiness.

My parents adored me. If they did have a favorite child, it would have been me. I kept going back to that feeling of being adored by the two most important people in my life when later it seemed the rest of the world thought I was some kind of monster.

Chapter 2

A DIFFERENT KIND OF GIRL

THE CIRCUMSTANCES OF MY BIRTH WERE NOT remarkable—except for my size and strength—but, as I would get older, it soon became clear I wasn't interested in the same things other girls were interested in. I'd be given a doll or teddy bear, and I would toss it around a bit and then get rid of it. I never took to dolls the way it is assumed girls should. I also didn't want to play make-believe with the other girls. It seemed to me a waste of time to sit around talking to stones or playing hand-clapping games. My parents say I wasn't soft-acting like baby girls usually were. They'd already raised four of them, so they knew. I wasn't affectionate, and I didn't want to be kissed or held much. What I wanted was to run around, take things apart and figure out how they worked, and I didn't care about getting dirty or hurt.

Journalists swarmed my childhood and later my grandmother's village to find what they call the "smoking gun"—someone, any-one, who would say "Caster is really a boy." I'm sure they were surprised when they interviewed all the people I'd grown up with. Everyone knew I was born and raised as a girl, and no one had a bad word to say about me. They accepted that I was a girl who dressed like a boy, spent most of her time with other boys, and loved sports. I may have *looked* like a boy, which everyone gener-ally agreed with, but that didn't mean I *was* a boy, which was the thing I was being accused of being by the international media.

By the time I became a professional runner, I had already been through years of comments, whether good or bad, about my looks.

The thing was I came from a place where people did not question my gender.

I have one or two baby pictures of myself. I remember one in which I look to be eight or nine months old. I was sitting on a blanket in our yard wearing a cute sleeveless dress and a frilly hat and socks. I have a scowl on my face. Even then, I don't think I liked my outfit. When I was a baby, of course, I had no choice over my clothing. Eventually, though, I learned how to speak. And I was never afraid to speak my mind.

I remember the day my father came home after one of his long stays in Pretoria. He would usually bring us gifts and other household necessities. This time, he was holding up a dress for me. It was red and white and it had ruffles and lace around the bottom with a little belt that tied around the waist.

"Mokgadi, my baby, this is a nice one." My father said with a big smile on his face while turning the dress this way and that.

"Thank you, daddy. It's nice. It's a fine dress. But I don't want to wear it."

"Why not?" Here my father pretended to be surprised but I know he wasn't.

"I will not wear it. I don't like it."

"Maybe you try it on first and then you see what you think," my father pretended to be sad with an exaggerated frown on his face.

"No. You wear it first. You should lead by example, like you say to me. See how it suits you. If you like wearing it, then I'll wear it." It was playful banter between us but it was how I really felt.

Instead of forcing me to wear it, or calling my mother for help, I remember my father just shook his head, laughed, and said, "OK, Mokgadi. As you wish."

That was the day I stopped wearing dresses. More like the day I decided I would wear a dress if, and when, I wanted to. I was maybe five or six years old. When I started preschool soon after, I insisted on wearing track suits, which is what we called the boys' uniform—grey pants and a white button-down shirt. My parents allowed it.

Dresses and skirts didn't suit the life I was leading. I spent my days fetching firewood and pails of water from the village well. I loved going around our yard and tending to our fruits and vegetables. By then, I'd even started heading into the bush with my older cousins to learn how to care for our animals. The bush had all kinds of things that could take a person down. At least wearing pants gave you a fighting chance against something like a sneaky cobra. And I played soccer with the boys in my village. There's a lot of falling and jostling in soccer—I didn't want my teammates to make fun of my underwear. Kids did that a lot. And if they saw a hole or something else in someone's undies you wouldn't hear the end of it for months. Dresses didn't make sense for me. I needed more protection than they offered.

IN MY PART of the world, the issue of gender is simple. If you are born with a vagina, then you are a girl. Hanging around with boys, dressing like a boy, playing sports with boys, having muscles, etc., didn't change your gender. Even if was I occasionally mistaken for a boy when I was growing up.

"Hey, *boy-boy*!" someone would call out to get my attention when I was going around the village helping my mom sell things.

I'd just turn around and reply, firmly, "I am not a boy. I am a girl. What can I do for you?"

That would clear things up right away. I wasn't offended that they mistook me for a boy, and people didn't argue or insult me or insist I was actually a boy. Most of the time they apologized and that was that. People in my village did not meddle in each other's business, especially not the kind of business that occurred below someone's belly button. It is rude and out of order. My parents would say this often to me and my siblings: "Unless invited, you mind your business, let others mind theirs." It is a very good life lesson.

Growing up, I was never made to feel like anything was wrong with my behaving differently from the other girls. It's not that the people didn't make comments about me acting like a boy and wearing boys' clothes. I had some run-ins with bullies, mostly boys, but I learned from a young age how to deal with them. Kids can be cruel. I would find out later in life, once I left my village, that adults, who should know better, are the cruelest of all.

Once I started winning major racing events and the questions about my gender started, I barely spoke about it. I didn't know how to speak about something so intimate. I didn't have the language. I figured the best thing to do was just stay quiet and run. When I was young, though, I had a different way of dealing with things.

"Hey, Mokgadi . . . you look like a boy."

"I know I look like a boy. What are you going to do about it?"

"Why don't you put a dress on and go play with girls?"

"I don't think I'm going to do that. So, like I said, what are you going to do about it?"

By that point, I and this unfortunate kid, whoever he was, would be standing eye to eye, because I was a pretty tall girl. The other kids would have already swarmed around us, anticipating a show.

I didn't like wasting time when it came to these arguments. Time has always felt precious to me, and I had things to do and places to be. I let my fists finish the conversation. Soon the would-be bully would find himself knocked back on his ass. I know that violence is never the answer, and I wouldn't necessarily teach my daughters to throw the first punch. My wife and I plan to teach our daughters to resolve things with words, to walk away from nonsense. That is, unless someone puts their hands on them. Now that's a different story. If you get hit, my philosophy is to hit back as good as you can. Even if you lose, at least you stood up for yourself. I say make the bully work for it. When I was growing up, if you disrespected me, well . . . you were going to feel it one way or the other. That's the law of the bush.

In Ga-Masehlong, I had to be tough, show the boys I wasn't to be made fun of. I never once turned the other cheek as the bible taught us to do; I never walked away from a fight. I'm not particularly proud of the ass beatings I handed out, but I never started a fight with anyone. If someone started with me, I knew how to finish it good. Once I knocked down whatever boy was making fun of me, you could see their brains calculating what to do next— the options were to get up and fight and risk the embarrassment of what could be a severe beating from a girl, or . . . maybe it was wiser to have me on their side. Most of the time they chose wisely.

"Eh, Mokgadi," they'd say while wiping the dust off their pants. "Come on, now. I was just playing with you. No need for all this. Heard you were a good striker. Let's go kick."

The bullies became competitors or teammates, all of us running barefoot on the rock- and bramble-ridden soccer pitches of our village. They learned to respect me because I respected myself. I was fair, I minded my business, and I could play well. I'm still friends with many of those boys today, all now men with families of their own.

What I started realizing even from my young days is that people treat you the way you treat yourself. I never hid or felt ashamed to look and act the way I did. If you gave me something sour to taste, I gave it right back. And no one likes the taste of their own medicine.

I was six years old when I had my first real fight. There was a kid everyone called Biggie because he was fat and reminded us of Biggie Smalls, the American rapper we all loved. Biggie was in my grade. He'd always stare at me and I'd just stare right back at him until he looked away.

He came out of nowhere one day in front of all our classmates and said, "Hey *boy*. You think you're a *boy*, Mokgadi? You're an ugly *boy*," he sneered. "I'm going to beat you like you're a *boy*."

Usually, what happened at this moment is that Biggie would have picked up a stone or a handful of dust and thrown it at me to signal he wanted to get physical. I wasn't one to wait for a pile of dust in my face. If someone says they're going to beat you, might as well get things going. Even at six years old, I wasn't one for talking nonsense. Like I said, I was impatient and didn't like wasting time.

"*You*, the fat ass? *You're* going to beat *me*? OK." Then I just started punching him, and Biggie went down. He tried to hit me back, but I threw myself on top of him and kept punching and kicking. I'm sure we looked like one of those cartoons where the people are twisting around so much you can't tell who's who. I can still hear the sounds—the other kids shouting and the thud every time a hit landed. Mostly mine. Then some teachers came and pulled us apart.

Biggie either told his mom what happened or someone else did because the next day, Biggie and his mom came to our house. I remember it was a Saturday and my mom was out working, and I was home with my younger sister and baby brother. Some of my cousins were also around. Biggie's mom banged on our door. I could hear her even before I opened it. She was upset that a girl had beaten up her son. She was yelling at him about how embarrassing it was and how he'd brought shame on their family.

"You're going to fight this girl right now," she yelled. "She's a girl, for God's sake! You can't let a girl beat you," his mom cried.

Poor Biggie. You could see he wanted to be anywhere but in our yard.

I told my sister to stay inside with our brother, and I came out and shut the door behind me. Biggie's mom stopped yelling at her son, and her gaze settled on me. She was sizing me up, trying to understand what kind of a girl had humiliated her child.

"Are you really going to do this to your child?" I asked.

Then she pushed Biggie toward me. "Fight her."

I guess she was. My cousins just laughed. They knew what was about to happen.

Biggie just took a deep breath and put his hands up in a boxer's stance. I almost felt sorry for him. I walked up and punched him a few times and he went down. He put up less of a fight now than he did at the school. I don't know why I did this but when Biggie went down, I stopped hitting him and instead took off his belt and gave him a few licks with it. I could hear my sister gasp from the window and then she made a sound like she was trying not to laugh. My cousins were bent over howling. A couple were laughing so hard they fell and were rolling around in the dirt.

Biggie didn't even try to grab his belt back from me. He just laid on the ground and covered his head and face. It was done. I threw the belt down and then I looked at his mother, "Your son is not an embarrassment. The embarrassment is you bringing your son to our house for another beating."

Biggie's mother didn't say a word. She helped her son up, dusted him off, and they left our yard. Biggie never stared at or called me a boy again. Whatever issues Biggie and I had should've stayed between us. We were kids. His mother should've never gotten involved except to discipline her son for being a bully. He got what he deserved. I didn't tell my mom about this incident, but she heard about what happened from the neighbors. I didn't get in trouble. Not even for smart-talking Biggie's mom. She shouldn't have encouraged her son to hit a girl or had the nerve to show up at our home. A parent shouldn't force kids to fight.

Biggie eventually moved to a neighboring village. He is a grown man now, still big, and with a wife and children of his own. We crossed paths many years later when I visited that side for an event. We remembered each other instantly and both started laughing.

"Heeeey!! Yoooooo! Mokgadi! You remember? Don't start with me! Don't start with me, girl. We're cool now, you and me."

"This one," Biggie said to his family and friends standing around, "this woman here, she's a cruel one. Took off me own belt and whipped my ass with it." Everyone cracked up. "Mokgadi, the great Olympic champion . . . you did not do me good that time, my friend."

I could see Biggie had enjoyed telling this story, and I reminded him that I'd first whipped his ass at the school, so I'd actually given him *two* beatings.

MY PARENTS COULD SEE I was different than my sisters. All of my sisters took after my mom—they were short, very curvy and pretty, while I was tall, with a wiry muscular frame. They'd wear skirts and dresses and form-hugging clothing, while I preferred my clothes to be loose. I liked that American street style of baggy jeans and shirts. My mom told me she walked by my room one day and saw me organizing my clothes into things I wanted to wear and things I didn't. I didn't know she saw me doing this. I remember I made sure to place the shorts and pants, golf shirts and T-shirts where I could reach them easily, and I put the dresses and skirts in a place where I couldn't.

I wore my sisters' hand-me-downs, but only what suited my tastes. The rest of my things I got from my male cousins and friends. I didn't care about "fashion." I didn't care about being "in style." I also knew my parents couldn't afford these things. If I had to wear used clothes or the same shorts and vests every day for a year, it didn't matter to me—as long as it wasn't a dress. My mother bought our clothes, and clothes were bought only during Christmas. On very special Christmases, we'd have clothes hand-made from a tailor, but those were rare occasions. There weren't any clothing stores in the village. Traders would come to our village and set up street markets. You could find most anything: clothing, food, toys, electronics. It was fun to walk around and look at things. The air vibrated with music and the sounds of adults negotiating prices and children laughing.

I wasn't the only girl who was "boyish" in my village or the surroundings villages. Girls who preferred to wear trousers or who played with boys weren't considered abominations. It really was not a big fucking deal. These girls would grow out of it and get married and have kids with a guy or not. That's life. And it was no one's business but theirs. There are many ways to be a girl.

If there were family members or villagers who tried to discuss my behavior or clothing with my parents, I didn't know about it. Looking back, I'm sure there were comments from nosy adults, but my parents shielded me from those. If anything, as I got older, my mother and father would show appreciation for the things I was willing to do in the household. They'd marvel at how strong and fearless I was and tell me I was a child of God. Once they understood how I expressed myself, I can't say they ever tried to change me. At least not in any real way.

My parents were true believers; they had a deep faith in God and made sure their children had the same. We went to church every Sunday. We attended the special prayer services held in different homes. I loved going to church and prayer services because of the singing and dancing and clapping. Sometimes it got to be too much. The service would last for hours with several pastors delivering hour-long sermons one after the other. By the time it was over, you felt like your brains were messed up.

We had church in the middle of our village. People would gather outdoors and sit on these white plastic chairs. Everyone clean and nicely dressed and ready to hear the word of the Lord. The women wore skirts and dresses. And I did, too. Until I decided I wasn't going to do that anymore. One Sunday, I came out of my room wearing a freshly laundered and ironed pair of pants and button-down shirt I'd gotten from one of my cousins. My mother saw me and didn't say a word. She may have taken an extra-deep breath. It was expected for girls and women to wear dresses and skirts and men to wear pants and button shirts, at least in church. But there weren't actual rules about it. If the pastors and fellow worshippers thought it was inappropriate for a girl to wear trousers at church, no one said anything. The people in my village really did understand the part of Christianity that said, "Do not judge others."

Besides, we may have accepted Christianity, but we still believed in our gods, our ancestors, and our African traditions. We often combined the two. If a pastor said a special blessing or calling must be sought by a particular family, congregations from neighboring villages would come together in someone's yard and it would turn into a huge party. Cows and goats were slaughtered and cooked. There would be morning tea and cakes and fresh bread and candies. I loved these gatherings because after the prayers and singing and drumming I could eat as much as I wanted. Truth be told, people came for the food anyway, not for the prayers. We made sure our African beliefs were mixed in with the White man's religion. Our ancestors didn't make regulations about girls not being able to wear pants when they wanted, so what could a pastor in my village complain about, really?

Our church had a boys' choir and a girls' choir, and they took turns singing to the congregation. They never sang together, always separate. I loved to hear the boys singing. The girls were good, but I preferred the boys' voices. They sounded more like me. This one day, I guess I was filled with the spirit because I jumped up and ran over and started dancing and singing with the boys. No one stopped me. There was no rule that said girls couldn't sing with boys. People seemed to think what I did was funny because they laughed and clapped along to the beat. I knew the song and I had a good voice. I wasn't messing up the boys' performance, so they didn't mind me either.

MY SISTERS GAVE ME a harder time about my behavior than my parents ever did. I loved my siblings. But there were definitely times when we would try each other's nerves.

We only had one television in our house, and when my sisters were home, they always wanted to watch stupid romantic movies.

To me, those things were silly. I wanted to watch things that were exciting—action movies, sports, stuff like that. So, we'd fight over the channel. Each of us would get up and change the channel or stand in front of the TV to prevent the other one from changing it. Of course, during those fights, they'd talk about my clothing.

"Mokgadi, what are you wearing those clothes for? You're really starting to look like a boy now."

And my answer to them was the same throughout the years, "So what?" Eventually, I was the only one who could fix the TV when it broke. I realized all I had to do was make sure it didn't work when my sisters wanted to watch those stupid movies. Then they'd go do something else and I'd get it working again so I could watch what I wanted.

The thing that really pricked my sisters' skin, though, was the household chores.

Where I come from, everyone must contribute to the maintenance of the household, even small children. As I grew bigger and stronger, I made it known that I didn't want to do things like cooking or cleaning. I wanted to do other things, things that challenged me physically.

Our house had a leaky roof, and during the rainy season, we'd have to put buckets all over the house to catch the rainwater. Starting from around eight or nine, I loved to climb up to the roof and patch the holes. It was a one-story house, but that didn't mean it wasn't dangerous to be up on the roof. A fall from up there could've seriously injured me. Still, I enjoyed it because I liked to work with my hands. I liked to put my body in risky situations. I trusted in myself. These kinds of tasks felt natural to me. I was also an amateur mechanic. If one of our machines broke, I would take it apart and fix it. I had a knack for figuring these things out. No one taught me; I learned on my own. If I hadn't found success on the track, sometimes I liked to think maybe I would have tried to find a way to pay for an electrical engineering degree.

I WANTED TO do the gardening and take care of the animals. Of course, it doesn't work that way. As a child, especially a girl child, you are supposed to do what you are told. My sisters would constantly remind me of this.

"Mokgadi. It's your turn to wash the dishes," my older sister Nico would say.

And I'd suck my teeth, "NO. I told you already, *I* don't wash dishes. *You* wash dishes."

One thing I can say about my older sisters is they had no problem whipping my ass. I was much more afraid of them than any bully in the village. When I refused to do as Nico said, she would then have no choice but to give me a few good slaps to keep me in line.

But my sister would have to catch me first. I'd mouth off, and then when I saw she'd had enough and was getting ready to put her hands on me, I'd take off running. Sometimes, I'd make Nico run to the end of the village and back again. People would see me barreling down the road and jump out of the way. They knew what was going on. Nico, like all of my sisters, was short and round, but she was fast and strong; she'd been a good middle-distance runner in her school days, but she could never catch me. At least not until I was ready to be caught. When her legs were gone and she was bent over gasping for air, I'd stop and come back to her.

"Are you done, sister? Are you OK? What was the point of the chase, Nico? You know you'll never catch me," I'd say while patting her back and smiling and waiting for her to get her breath. By this point, we'd run at least 5 kilometers. Then we'd walk or jog back another 5 kilometers to our house, laughing about everything. I was used to running more than that during my soccer games, so Nico never had a chance. We'd just wash the dishes together when we got back to the house.

Chapter 3

I AM NOT AFRAID

O NCE I STARTED SCHOOL, I FOUND A BIG DIFFER-
ence between what was expected of me there and what I
could do at home. Aside from subjects like our letters and basic
math, the girls, and only the girls, had to learn what was called
"handwork," but it wasn't like what I was used to doing with my
hands. It was stuff like sewing and knitting. It didn't make sense
to me. What did I need to learn to sew for? It felt like a waste of
my time. I remember being annoyed and doing just enough in this
class to get by. My guy friends got to do the gardening outdoors,
and they'd occasionally come to the classroom window and point
and laugh at me because they knew how much I hated it. As soon
as the lunch break came, I'd run out to the schoolyard and play
soccer with them.

Our school buildings were simple, square-shaped cement structures. The classrooms were orderly; each had wooden desks for
the students, the teacher's desk, and one large chalkboard at the
front. The students were responsible for keeping the classrooms
clean. We'd all sweep and mop and dust every inch of the rooms
on a schedule. There weren't any sports facilities—no basketball
courts, no gyms, no running track or manicured soccer fields. We
had a large outdoor space, dusty ground strewn with grass and
sharp rocks here and there, surrounded by wire fencing to keep the
kids inside. Once the lunch break was over, the kids would head
back to class, but not me. I'd try to find a way to sneak back home.

School felt like a cage compared to the freedom I enjoyed at
home. My mother got so tired of me skipping out on classes and

getting notices from my teachers that she finally had no choice but to call in the Village Granny. The Village Granny is one of those IYKYK things. She's probably not your blood grandmother, but she feels like everyone's grandmother. More importantly, all the kids respected her. She was that woman in the community who walks around as if she's part police officer and part witch. Fear is the Village Granny's superpower.

Well, our Village Granny had never come across such as me.

My mother would occasionally threaten to get her if I refused to go to school but she never had to because I'd eventually put on my uniform and go. There did come a day, though, when I just didn't care.

"Get her. I'm not afraid of that woman."

I don't remember my mother ever actually leaving my presence, but somehow the Village Granny showed up in our yard. It felt like my mother had summoned her with her mind or something. The old woman was a formidable figure. Tall and strong looking. She was old, yes, but not frail. She could hurt someone if she wanted to. I could see she was a person I should respect, but I did not feel any fear.

And then she spoke.

"Mokgadi. Go to school. *Right now.* Or I will give you a sore ass." Her voice sounded like mine, deep and powerful. I was taller than any other girl in my village, but this Village Granny was even taller than me. Much taller than my mom, too.

I held my ground. This woman was standing in *my* yard, trying to tell me what to do. I placed my hands on either side of my waist.

"No. If you want someone to go to school, take your own grandchildren."

I stared right back at her and lifted my chin defiantly.

I remember that woman looked at me like I was a demon. Nobody talked to her like that. For a second, it seemed like she didn't know what to do, but then she gathered herself. I wasn't sure if she was about to beat me senseless, so I took a few steps backward to give myself some extra room. It was like one of those standoffs in the American Western movies.

"You're wasting your time, Granny. I'm not scared of you." Then I turned toward the bush that surrounded us. I swept my arm around like I was showcasing our landscape, the wild grasses fading off in the horizon toward the mountains. "You better be a good runner . . ."

I knew that no old woman, no matter how strong looking, was going to follow me into that, so I continued, "*I* will go to school when *I* want to."

And right when Granny tried to grab me, I took off running. I could hear her yell at my back, "I'm going to smack your ass when you get back here!"

I wasn't scared of anyone. Not even her. I'm sure my mother was embarrassed and maybe angry, but she knew her child. Years later, when I would come back to Limpopo to visit my parents, I'd see Village Granny. She looked older, but still strong, and I'm sure she was still scaring little kids into going to school.

"Mokgadi!" she'd say, "Are you still crazy, girl? I've never come across such a crazy one as you!" Her gap-toothed smile was wide and free.

"Still crazy, Granny. I'm sorry about that," and we'd have a good laugh about those times.

I was stubborn as hell. I still am. I did what I wanted to do. I would get into trouble with my mom for stupid things like not coming home when I was supposed to, fighting boys who tested me, and constantly skipping classes, but I was not a bad kid. You could say I was mischievous. I'd do silly things like open a school-mate's lunch bag and eat the food inside. It was all in good fun. If your family was rich enough to send you to school with something that smelled delicious, like eggs and bacon, then I'm sure you wouldn't mind if I helped myself. Sharing is caring.

My teachers would complain to my mom. I didn't dedicate myself to my schoolwork the way the other kids did. If there was a shortcut to my studies, I'd find it. I just wanted to get by; I didn't want to take the extra time and excel in schoolwork. My priorities were playing sports and hanging out. Of course, this was upsetting to my parents, who valued education above all else because they grew up during the Struggle, and they'd never gotten the opportunity to study in the way we did.

"She's so fun, really. She's a good kid. Everyone loves being around her. We know she's smart. She's very, very clever, but she just can't follow the rules," my teachers would say.

As I got older, I did start enjoying the lessons. I especially loved geography and history—I enjoyed learning about the world and the important figures who changed it. I started to really understand that the world was much bigger than what was around me. And I knew that somehow, one day, I would get to see it.

With my dad working away from home, and my eldest sisters leaving the village to pursue opportunities in the cities, I eventually took on the role of caretaker. I wanted to help my mom maintain our household, and I was very protective of my family. My siblings knew I would settle their affairs.

One of Olga's favorite stories is when I dealt with a kid who was giving her some trouble. She was in the seventh grade, and I was in the first—maybe seven or eight years old, but I was already a strong figure.

"Hey, what's the matter with you?" I asked her one day. We were in the back of our house, preparing dinner—*pap* with meat and spinach. My sister didn't seem like herself.

"It's nothing, Mokgadi," she sighed, "let's just finish this."

"I know it's something, Olga."

"Eg . . . it will be fine. But, alright . . . there's this kid. He's bothering me. I just don't know what to do about it." She looked away.

"Ahh. . . . Maybe he likes you. Boys can be that way," I said, because I spent a lot of time with boys and I knew their backward ways. I spoke and understood their language. Olga told me that for a month she had endured this kid's insults. Even if he liked her, he wasn't being respectful. He'd started to follow her around and push her and pull on her hair. This kid was torturing her.

I didn't say anything else to Olga. The next morning, we went off to school like any other day.

I had my sister point the boy out. He was talking to his friends. I just went up to him and gave him a few strong slaps to the face. He didn't know what hit him.

"If you bother my sister again, I'm going to beat the hell out of you. I won't be slapping you. Next time, I'll be giving you something you'll really remember." I said and showed him my fist.

He seemed stunned and confused. His eyes popped out of his head and his mouth hung open like a fish who suddenly found itself out of the water. Not one of his friends said a thing. They looked embarrassed for him. Olga and I walked away and they all went back to talking as if nothing had happened. That guy didn't want anything to remember so he never bothered my sister again.

I was a crazy kid. I wasn't afraid of getting physical—I knew I could handle myself. My male cousins were the ones who taught me how to fight like a boy—we'd roughhouse for hours. I could hold my own with any one of them. Sometimes, I'd even fight two boys at a time. And I loved wrestling. The Undertaker, Brock Lesnar, Kevin Nash, Kane, Mark Henry, The Rock, Shoichi Funaki, Rikishi. I watched them all. I thought of myself as a martial artist. I'd seen every Van Damme, Bruce Lee, and Jackie Chan movie. I loved boxing, too. Muhammad Ali and Mike Tyson were my favorite fighters. Then I'd practice everything I watched.

I remember my cousins and I used to make our own punching bags using an old sheet or a cloth bag. We'd fill the bag with sand and concrete and hang it from a tree branch. Then we'd wrap pieces of rags around our knuckles. We'd spend entire afternoons and early evenings training. All I wanted was to get stronger.

When you're young, you feel invincible. I trusted in my body. I was climbing trees, chasing after wild animals. Jumping off cliffs with my cousins into roaring rivers. I wouldn't say we were swimming exactly, but we knew how to survive in the water. We used empty soda bottles with the tops screwed on tightly to stay afloat. The currents were strong, but we were brave. I'd earned my place among those boys. I could do anything they could do.

One day, though, I found out this incredible body of mine had its limitations.

We needed bread, and word was out in the village there was a good batch just baked at a spaza shop a little way from us. My older sister Olga and I went off together and, as often happened, we just started running. It quickly turned into a full-out race. Olga was keeping up with me, but there was a corner coming up. I knew if I took it at full speed, I'd leave her in the dust. Normally people are wary of bends, they naturally slow down, but not me. In soccer, you had to change the trajectory of your body at any given time. I wasn't afraid to run around the corner as fast as my seven-year-old legs could go. I might've even picked up speed as I made the turn. The next thing I remember was a click in my right knee. I kept running but I knew something wasn't right.

Olga and I got the bread and then we walked back home. My leg felt off but I didn't complain, and there wasn't any pain. When we got home, I went to the room I shared with my sister and laid down. Now the leg was hurting. I must've fallen asleep because the next thing I remember is my mother waking me up and asking me what was wrong. She knew it wasn't like me to go to bed during the day. Normally, I'd be out with the boys.

I told my mom I had a headache. She knew I was lying. I finally told her I hurt my leg, and when I showed her, my knee was almost three times its normal size.

"My Lord! Mokgadi." My mother looked horrified. "What happened?"

I told my mom that something clicked in my knee when I was running with Olga to buy the bread, but my mom didn't believe me.

"Climbing a tree. You must've fallen from a tree, tell me the truth!" She was concerned for my leg, but I could hear the change in my mother's tone. She was getting pissed.

Here we go, I thought. She was going to blame my cousins and tell me how I shouldn't be out in the bush.

"You never listen to me. Playing with those boys. You're going to kill yourself one day. Look at you now, Mokgadi. Look at this leg of yours," she shook her head. My mother wanted me to admit I hurt myself doing something stupid, and when I wouldn't, she left my room and came back holding a bicycle gear. She was going to make me talk one way or the other.

"I'm going to smash your knee with this gear if you don't tell me the truth." My mother waved the gear in the air. "I'll cut it off with this thing here, girl. Tell me the truth. Right away!"

If you grew up how I grew up, this doesn't surprise you. Kids would take a fall, and the parents would whip the kid's ass for not being careful. It was hurt on top of a hurt. That's how things were.

"Go ahead and hit me with it, Mom. Destroy my leg if you want to. I'm telling you I wasn't with the boys. I was running with Olga to get the bread." My sister was scared and tried to testify on my behalf, but my mom wouldn't listen.

"Be quiet, Olga. You're covering for her." When my mom got mad, there was no getting through to her. Eventually, it didn't matter how I hurt myself because the following day, the leg was even bigger and I couldn't move it at all. And now I was in serious pain. My mom took me to WF Knobel Hospital, near Kgabo Park, where I'd been born seven years prior. We didn't have a car so we had to wait and secure transport by minibus.

WF Knobel was a public hospital, part of South Africa's public healthcare system and was free of charge for all citizens. The brick building had well-kept grounds; it was modern but sparse. The hospital was clean and orderly, and it had a good reputation. The nurses, who we called "sisters," didn't seem to know what to do at first. I remember how worried my mom looked. She'd been angry before, but now it broke her heart she couldn't do anything more for me.

"You're strong, my girl. You're so strong. You'll be OK," she said and stroked my hair and cheeks. I was in so much pain; I just buried my face in her neck. At some point, they were able to take x-rays and told us it looked like I'd dislocated the patella bone in my right knee. I'd taken the corner so fast, my kneecap had basically popped out of where it lived. They couldn't put it back, so I was admitted to the hospital and given a bed until they figured things out.

I'd taken so many falls prior to this. I could've been paralyzed with the crazy things I did with my cousins in the bush. We'd climb trees and then see who could jump down from the highest branch. We watched so many Jackie Chan's we knew how to roll and tumble safely. I couldn't believe I'd hurt myself so badly just running around a corner with my sister.

Eventually, the doctors decided I needed to have surgery. There was no other way to fix me. My people have some distrust of Western medical practices; we mainly believed in traditional ways of healing with herbs and prayer. This skepticism about surgery is what may have saved my career years later, but at this point, my parents understood the traditional ways weren't going to help, and surgery was the only option for me to ever walk properly again. Unfortunately, our public healthcare system was what it was. I had to wait for a specialist who could do the operation, and I would remain in the hospital for almost seven months before one became available.

Seven months of my life in a hospital room. Looking back, it's almost difficult to believe it. A wild girl like me, used to roaming free in her village and playing in the bush every day, was imprisoned in a hospital for seven months. It reminded me of The Hurricane movie starring Denzel Washington. I missed my family and cousins and friends. I even missed my teachers.

I said I had a happy childhood—this event is the only bad thing

I can remember. Not one for tears, I would cry my eyes out when my parents and siblings would visit me. When they could, they'd bring me fruits and sweets, or buy me ice creams. Things they knew I could only get at home. They would try to cheer me up and tell me about whatever was going on in the village. But all I wanted was to go home. I think the entire hospital could hear me sobbing and begging them to take me with them. There were days I would jump off the bed when their visit was over and hobble after them. I was so desperate to be with my family, I'd have to be physically restrained by the sisters. Eventually, as the time passed, I learned how to exist within the confines of the hospital.

I got along with everyone who worked there, especially the sisters. They quickly figured out I was not a very obedient kid, but I was good-natured and would keep them laughing. I became one of their favorite little patients, and the sisters would sneak me extra food because I was always hungry. If I didn't want to take a medication, I would pretend to be asleep. If one of them tried to force medication into my mouth, I'd act like I'd swallowed it and then spit it out.

I hated the IV drip and figured out how to make it go faster. The sisters used razors for various things, and sometimes they would leave the used razors on a shelf in my room. When I knew they were gone, I'd grab a chair and get the razor and make a tiny slice in the IV bag. I would use an extra sheet or towel to wipe up the liquid.

I spent so much time at the hospital I felt like I owned it. I knew every corner. I studied everyone's movements. When midnight came around, the sisters switched shifts, and they would roll out a trolley with tea and bread. I would wait until they were finished and then sneak into their area and help myself to a cup and all the bread I wanted. I'd put the cup back exactly how I found it so no one noticed anything was missing. And no one ever did.

Finally, my family was told they'd found a surgeon who could operate and I was transferred me to a different hospital near the city of Polokwane. My mother came with me and spent the night. I was back at WF Knobel the next day and then I was finally discharged after about a week. I'd gone into the hospital in early March, and I came home in September. Part of me would miss the constant attention and the kindness of the sisters, but I was happy to be out of my prison. I remember carefully climbing out of the transport in front of our family home, excited to see my siblings, only to find out Nico and Olga had chickenpox. I got infected right away. It meant I had to stay inside for an extra two weeks. No playing with my cousins and friends and definitely no school. But at least I was home.

This injury could've ended any chance I ever had to be a professional athlete. Most people don't know this injury has bothered me my entire career. I dislocated the same kneecap right after the 2012 Olympics where I won the silver medal in the 800-m race and had to call off my season right after. My right leg is weaker than my left leg. Since the day I was released from the hospital to this very day, I have a very distinct hitch when I walk. I wouldn't say I'm limping, exactly, but you can see that there's something unique about my gait. It's not me trying to be cool.

On the rare occasions when I'm out in public trying to do some random thing, like shop for groceries, even if I wear a hoodie and sunglasses, my people recognize me because of my walk. They don't need to see my face. The leg never healed properly. We weren't given any advice about what kinds of exercises would strengthen my leg after the surgery. There was no follow-up physical therapy for this village girl. I went home and resumed my life. I started playing soccer again and running around with my friends. Sometimes, just for fun, I like to think about how much I've accomplished with this injured right leg and how much more I could've won if I'd had two good ones.

Chapter 4

HUNTING WITH BOYS

B Y THE TIME I WAS FOUR YEARS OLD, I HAD started kicking around balls with my male cousins and the other neighborhood kids. There'd be some girls who would play soccer with us, too, but it was mostly boys doing the playing. Our people were obsessed with soccer. We didn't have an actual soccer ball, but we would kick around whatever we had—empty bottles, or we'd make balls out of pieces of cloth and plastic shopping bags.

I remember how happy I was when soon after we had solar panels installed on our roof, my family bought a television. It was shaped like a small box and the images it picked up were black and white. There was always a football game happening somewhere in the world. My dad had been a football player in his youth. My father was fast, and he handled the ball so well he was even invited to try out for the Kaizer Chiefs (they were the Kaizer XI in those days). He told me that right before his big tryout someone cut him off on the pitch during a neighborhood game and gave him a lifetime injury. He never played again. Not that it mattered. My father knew that playing soccer wasn't a stable job, it wasn't something that could have sustained a family. And he was one of those men that knew he wanted a family from young.

My mom was very athletic, too. She may not have been tall, but she was strong and sturdy. In her youth, she loved playing netball, a popular South African game that's kind of like American basketball. You could say sport was in my blood. My siblings enjoyed playing, here and there. A few of my sisters ran competitively at their schools, but they did not have the same intensity or dreams that I did.

When I was around eight years old, whenever I'd see an airplane, I would point up to the sky and tell my sisters, "One day, it'll be me on that plane you see up there. And I'll be passing over this village. Yes . . . I'll be on my way to somewhere big. Everyone will know my name." This girl had big dreams.

My sisters would roll their eyes and say my brains were messed up. They didn't understand where I came up with these things. That I even imagined myself on an airplane or that people would know my name was crazy to them. Only rich people traveled the world. But for me, it was as good as a done deal. Almost like a vision.

"You'll see. I'm telling you. One day, I will be the one who carries this household." My sisters would laugh and shake their heads and keep going about their day.

But I knew it. I knew that somehow, someway, I would leave the village, and I would be something special in this world.

I never thought I'd become a famous runner. No one in my family thought that, either. We all thought I had a chance to make it as a soccer player. Even though I didn't see any girls playing soccer on TV, I was so good I dreamt the men would have to let me play on the national teams.

My father always encouraged my soccer-playing dreams. He loved the way I handled the ball. "Heh! Heh! Did you see my daughter out there? How many goals did she hit this time?" I'd hear him brag to his friends when he was home.

We'd love to sit around and talk about strategy and moves and watch games together when he was around. Sometimes, my dad would help me with my grips and tackles. He knew I was playing with the boys and I had to be careful—I had to earn their respect on the pitch.

BY THE AGE OF SIX, I was responsible for caring for our animals. In the mornings, I would gather our cattle, sheep, and goats and prepare to set out into the bush. I didn't go alone. There were ten to twelve boys and maybe three to four other girls who joined me with their own herd. In the bush, the animals ate as much grass as they wanted and drank from the cool river water. It was important our animals felt freedom since they lived inside the fencing around our yards.

I understood from a young age how essential animals are to our survival. Meat was an important part of our diet, and hunting was one way we provided ourselves with it. We didn't routinely kill our domesticated animals; only during rare occasions or the Christmas holiday would we slaughter one of them. When I told my older male cousins I wanted to learn to hunt, they were happy to let me join. Only the bravest and the fittest would hunt, and I knew I could be one of them.

We would hunt on the weekends, mostly Saturday mornings. There is a lot of running in hunting—we never knew how much of a distance we'd have to cover on any given day. Sometimes it was as little as 3 to 5 kilometers, other times as much as 10 to 15—sometimes we'd run so deep into the bush we'd come to a neighboring village and go through it and into more wilderness. We would set out around six and usually wouldn't come back until after sunset. Time seemed to stop when we ran in a group. We were so busy talking and laughing or just breathing together that our legs didn't feel the work.

I was the youngest in this group and the only girl, so I started off with learning how to set traps for small animals like birds and rabbits. As I got older, I moved on to springboks and warthogs. Warthogs were the most dangerous. If you weren't careful, they would turn on you and gore you with their long tusks. None of us ever got seriously hurt, but I'd heard terrible stories. Warthogs lived underground, so the best way to get them was to figure out where one lived and then kill it while it slept. Warthog meat is delicious: it kind of tastes like a cross between pork and beef.

There are different ways to hunt. A few of my cousins used

spears they carved from tree branches; others used your basic hunting knife, they didn't mind getting up close to an animal. I thought the most skillful hunters were the ones who used bows and arrows because it took years to master those weapons. And then there were the stone-throwers. I tried different weapons, but I preferred stone-throwing. Turns out I have good hand-eye coordination and a strong right arm. If I saw something I wanted to hit, nine times out of ten, it was lights out for that animal. A few years after this, when I was asked what position I wanted to play on the high school baseball team, there was no doubt in my mind I wanted to be the pitcher.

We burned a lot of energy in the bush, so we had to eat well to keep going, and I enjoyed the communal meals during the hunting. Everyone contributed something. We'd bring rice, potatoes, some kind of vegetable. We'd catch something small like a bird or a rabbit and we'd gather wood and make a hole in the ground and barbecue it. For dessert, we'd pick forest fruits, careful to stay away from the ones that could kill us.

There were days the communal meal wasn't enough and, if we were still hungry, one or more of us would run back to the village and help ourselves to whatever was easiest to grab and go. I say we "helped ourselves," others would call it "stealing." I was small and fast so I would volunteer. I knew most of the villagers' routines. When I came across an empty compound, I'd sneak in and grab whatever could fit in my bag. I'd slip into the chicken coop and pick up as many eggs as I could carry. I can still hear those chickens complaining about me.

The more we went out, the more skillful I became. It felt good to come home from a long day in the bush carrying meat for my family. Hunting was about sustenance, yes, but it was also a bonding. An ancestral inheritance that strengthened our ties to each other and to the land. The bush was a dangerous place. The things out there could easily kill us. We took care of each other, and you had to trust the next person with your life. Those of us who hunted together—related by blood or not—feel connected to this day even though time has separated us.

The one person I trusted more than any other was my cousin Jalta. I never really had a best friend growing up, but he would be the closest to it. He's what Americans call a "crazy motherfucker." This guy . . . oh my God. He was out of his mind. I loved him very much. People used to say we were like two dogs no one could separate. There are people whose souls just click, and ours did. Jalta was about eight or nine years older than me. His mother was my father's sister, and they lived walking distance from our home. I hung out with him every day, even spent nights at his home. He treated me like a little sister, which meant he protected and was kind to me, but he also loved to annoy me. I like to think we were like Ghost and Tommy from the Power Book series. Jalta looked like most of the boys in our family. He was tall and thin but he was very strong. Many girls found his pronounced brow and angular face handsome. He had big teeth and my same wide smile and rich dark skin. Jalta always took care of his responsibilities, but he never took life too seriously and always found time to have fun. He was funny as hell. He'd make me laugh so hard I felt like I couldn't breathe.

I remember we'd be sitting somewhere next to each other and Jalta would fart. As soon as the awful smell hit my nose, I'd make a move to get away but he'd grab my arm or put me in a headlock.

"Mokgadi, you must stay here, very close to me, and take in the smell. Don't run away. Don't cover your nose, girl. If you can tolerate my fart, I promise you, you will be rich one day."

I wanted to be known, but I didn't really care about being rich, so I'd get away quickly.

There were these plants in our village that, if you spread open the flowers and rubbed them on your skin, would cause a terrible itch. Resist the scratching, and the itch would go away in a couple of hours, but if you scratched, these welts popped up. The more you scratched the more you'd itch, and the more welts would appear. It was harmless, but the scratching and itching could continue for days.

Jalta would wait until I was relaxed and not paying attention to him, and then he'd quickly scrape that flower all over my arms and chest and my back.

"What the fuck, Jalta! THE FUCK!?" I'd be shouting and trying to swat him off as best as I could. Sometimes I'd get away before he could get too many scrapes in but he always managed to make contact with my skin.

"Don't scratch, Mokgadi. Don't scratch, I tell you. If you scratch, you will have a baby in the seventh grade."

The itch was so terrible that I didn't care about having a baby in the seventh grade. I wanted to have babies one day anyway, so I'd spend days scratching because of this idiot.

I remember the time he pretended to fall into one those boreholes the municipality drilled into the ground in various places on the outskirts of the villages or deeper into the bush. They were supposed to hit water veins for wells, but when they didn't find the water or enough of it, the holes were just abandoned, and no one even bothered to cover them up. One second Jalta and I were standing around, and the next second he just disappeared into the ground. I looked in the hole and couldn't see him. I thought he was dead and started running around in all four directions screaming for help. I loved him so much I thought I would go insane. Jalta let me scream until I just about lost my voice. I was going to fall to my knees and start praying when he climbed out of the hole laughing his ass off. Those boreholes were so deep, you didn't know what the hell was at the bottom. Could've been water or snakes or vampires for all we knew. If a person fell in there, there was no chance of them coming out alive. Jalta had suspended himself inside the metal pipe by holding his body weight up with his hands and legs.

There was a day we went out hunting just the two of us. I think I was nine years old and Jalta was maybe seventeen. The air was still cool in the early morning. It was a perfect day. We started walking toward the bush together, eventually picking up our pace, our steps steady and quiet.

As soon as we crossed into the wildlands, we saw a springbok. It was sleeping. A jackpot right there in front of us. This animal was big enough to feed both of our large families. We could kill this thing quickly and be done early enough to play soccer the rest of the day.

I remember looking up at Jalta, my eyes wide with excitement. I motioned for him to go and get to work with his knife. Jalta just stood there. I don't know what the hell he was thinking. Instead of creeping up and stabbing the animal, Jalta crawled over and lay down next to it.

"Jalta! Jalta! What the hell are you doing, my man?" I whispered. I noticed the springbok open one eye, but it didn't make a move. It closed its eye again. This thing knew we were there. It must have thought it was dealing with some crazy people because who the hell would lie down and start cuddling with a wild animal?

I was standing a few feet away, not believing my eyes.

"*Yooooo*. Jalta. What the fuck? Get your knife and kill it. We don't have time to be chasing this thing," I whispered.

"It's early, *meena*. I'm tired. I'm gonna sleep here for a little bit." And he really did get comfortable.

I didn't know what Jalta was thinking. I sat down and leaned back on the nearest tree and kept a look out for predators. A few minutes passed, I was still looking around, probably chewing on something, humming to myself, occasionally shaking my head at Jalta cuddling with our food.

Then Jalta actually started snoring. The springbok jumped up and took off deeper into the bush. Jalta's head hit the ground and he was startled awake.

When he realized what happened, Jalta started yelling, "SHIT. Mokgadi, RUN! GO, GO, GO! You're fast, you can do it!"

He was nuts if he thought I was going to run after that thing. There were only two of us here—we didn't have a group to surround it or dogs to help us corner it. And what was I supposed to do if I caught it? Grab it and stone it to death? It wasn't just going to stand around and let me kill it.

"Eeeeesh. Jalta. No *fucking* way, my man. You don't actually think I can run faster than a springbok?"

The springbok got away. We could not come back to the village empty-handed, so we had to kill something, but it took us all day to bag a few rabbits. A whole day wasted just because Jalta decided to take a nap with our meal.

I learned a lot from Jalta; I appreciated the way he carried himself. He didn't live for the world, he didn't care much about what people thought of him. Eventually our lives would take us in different directions. Jalta stayed in the village until adulthood, and like most people, he would move to Johannesburg to find work and then have a family of his own. The choices I made in life would carry me away from many familial relationships, but he was an important part of my childhood. I hope he thinks of me as fondly as I do him.

I DON'T REMEMBER my parents ever having a real problem with me hunting with my male cousins. No one told me I couldn't go, even if I'm sure my mother worried about me and maybe wished I didn't. I recognized there were male and female roles in my village when I was growing up, yes. There weren't any other girls hunting when I was growing up. You could say I lived in a conservative, traditional society, but it wasn't like things were strictly enforced—at least they weren't for me. I was a girl but I was allowed to do things more or less as I wanted.

In my household, whoever wanted to do a chore, did it. I wanted to herd and hunt and garden. I wanted to fix the roof and our machines. I could do these things and I did. My skills were valuable and necessary in my home. Why would my parents say, "No, Mokgadi, you are a girl. You are not supposed to be climbing the roof and fixing machines," just because I was born with a vagina? Later, when I became more educated in the ways of the world, I understood that the West had brought many ideas of what being a woman or a man meant to my people. Even though we adopted many of these new, Western ideas, we still maintained our ways. Our ways meant that if a girl was strong enough to hunt, she hunted. If she wanted to be the head of her household, why not?

This is how I approached my soccer playing. Some girls in our village played soccer, but they mostly played with each other. We sometimes had mixed games, but I was playing on all-boy teams because I could handle their heat. The boys were rough and I was rough, too.

By then I played as well as the boys. Actually, I played better than most of the boys my age. I played so well the older boys would ask me to join their teams. I was a multi-use player; I could be a striker or a defender. I knew how to handle the ball, how to open space on the pitch, how to dribble. No one cared I was a girl, they just wanted to win. The kids and adults would all gather to see me play and they'd chant "Mokgadi! Mokgadi! Mokgadi!" I loved to hear my name. I'd love to give those who came to see me a show. You could say I was a performer even from young. I enjoyed being the center of attention.

Eventually it got so people would bet on whatever game I was in. One thing about the village: We may not have had a lot of money, but people could find a few rand for betting. Even kids would practice betting with biscuits and candies.

I wish I had a video of me playing soccer in those days. In the late '90s and early 2000s, we'd barely just gotten an electrical grid in our village. No one owned a mobile. Most of us growing up during that time are lucky to even have pictures of ourselves as babies. The villagers would chant my name, and I could hear people marveling that I was a girl who played with boys. I was different and they thought I was special. This made me happy.

I was obsessed with the great players of the time—Samuel

Eto'o, Didier Drogba. In South Africa, we had Benni McCarthy, Lucas Radebe, Steven Pienaar, Richard Henyekane. These were the South African guys I knew had traveled abroad to play. Our beloved Kaizer Chiefs had "Shoes" Moshoeu, Thabo Mooki, Arthur Zwane, Marc Batchelor. I could name them all. In 1996, our national team went to the World Cup, and I remember how happy we were when we qualified for the World Cup again in 2002. I loved watching the Real Madrid players, David Silva, Xabi Alonso. I loved Ronaldo and Gabrielle Batista, the Brazilians. I wanted to be like just like them.

I would watch the games, completely mesmerized, repeating to myself, "maybe one day, maybe one day, I could play with them. You never know . . . I could do this. I know I can do this." And then I'd practice all their moves on the pitch with my teammates. Such were the dreams of this little girl, and they seemed possible to me. I knew women's soccer existed, too, but it wasn't on television much and no one took it seriously back then. Later, when professional women's soccer became more popular, I loved watching women like Desiree Ellis, Portia Modise, Veronica Phewa, and the American goalkeeper, Hope Solo.

By the time I was ten, I was playing with boys older than me. Imagine a ten-year-old girl on a pitch with fourteen- and fifteen-year-old boys. Soccer is a rough game. Things could get dangerous, but I wasn't afraid. I remember we were playing a practice game on a Saturday afternoon. It was one of those days where everything I tried was going my way. My own teammate didn't like it. I don't know if he was jealous of the way I handled the ball or what. We'd never had any problems before but we weren't friends. He was just a guy on the team. He played well and I didn't really care about him one way or the other.

I was playing barefoot. His family could afford a soccer boot. At some point during the game, he stepped on top of my right foot. It wasn't a mistake, that I knew. My foot immediately swelled and I had to limp off the field. The kid took me out and he did it on purpose. Everyone else could see that, too. I went home, pissed as hell. But there was an unspoken understanding between me and my teammates. I wasn't going to make a big deal of it and mess up the game. I'm sure my cousins would've kicked his ass, but everyone knew I handled my own battles.

My foot was so messed up I couldn't hunt or take out our animals. It took me about a month to get back on the pitch. When I returned to the team, this kid looked scared to death. He was older than me but he knew what kind of person and player I was. If you purposefully tried to hurt me, I was going to make you pay for that. By now, most boys didn't test me—I'd humiliate them verbally or physically. The thing was this—after a month away from the field I had a lot of time to think about the incident. I decide to let it go. I was getting older, less impulsive. On that team I was a defender and he was a striker. If I decided to destroy his leg, he wouldn't have been out for just a month—this kid would never make it back to any soccer pitch. He was a good player; it was in the best interest of the team that he stay on.

"Hey! Mokgadi!" he yelled when he saw me. He ran over before I could walk to the rest of the group.

"Sorry about what happened. It was my fault. Things ran away from me. We missed you out here. Happy you're back," he said and he did look sorry. More like terrified.

"Yo. Whatever. Let's play," I said as I walked away.

Soccer is like that. It can be a cruel game. People got emotional in this game we loved. Especially when there were biscuits and rand involved. The important thing I was starting to learn here was how to stay calm, how to keep my anger under control. I needed to understand that the game itself was more important than just me.

Chapter 5

THE CHANGE

I N THE BEGINNING, THE BOYS AND GIRLS IN MY VIL-
lage within my age-group looked the same. I was a bigger girl
than most, but generally we all looked similar, give or take some
things. Then at a certain age some fundamental bits begin to
change. The boys grew taller, they grew hair on their faces and
other places, and their voices changed. The girls would also sprout
hair in new places, their chests would blossom into breasts and their
hips would widen, and eventually they would begin to menstruate.

Obviously, being that I was a girl, I thought the changes I saw
in these girls and I had seen in my sisters would happen to me,
too. Except, nothing was happening for me. But I wasn't worried
about it. I wasn't in a rush to develop breasts and get my period. I
was playing sports, farming, taking care of our animals, and hunting. I figured having a period would get in the way because I saw
how it got in the way of my sisters' and friends' lives. Sanitary
towels weren't easy to get in Ga-Masehlong or even affordable for
most of us. It wasn't like the spaza shops were selling Tampax
and Kotex. Girls in my village used whatever they could to contain the blood—old socks, rags, even notebook paper. Sometimes
this would bring on problems like infections. I heard my sisters
and friends complaining of pain and bloating. Truth is this thing
sounded horrible. There was also the sense that it was something
to be stressed, maybe even embarrassed, about even though it
was a natural thing that every girl eventually had to go through. I
started noticing girls would just disappear from school for a week

or so rather than deal with having a period in class. It got to where I started to feel like maybe not getting a period would be a gift.

I may not have been developing breasts, but eventually I began changing, too. My already deep voice got a little bit deeper; I grew even taller and more muscular. At this point, it seemed normal. I wasn't built like my sisters to begin with. I looked like a girl who played soccer, boxed, wrestled, and ran and hunted. Anyone who spent every single day—boy or girl—doing these things was going to get powerfully built.

I was deeply aware of and loved my body. My body was strong and sturdy, agile and flexible; I easily learned new moves and tricks. I could ask anything of my body and it would come through for me. I was happy the way I was, but when I'd hear my sisters and friends talk about the budding pains on their chests of soon-to-come breasts, I would wonder about mine. I felt nothing.

I decided to talk to the person I trusted more than anyone.

"Hey mom, I don't think I'm going to get this period thing like the other girls," I said one day while I was helping her prepare the day's food for selling.

"Why do you think this?" My mother turned and looked at me, her eyes wide, her voice serious and almost a whisper.

"I'm not getting these breasts like them. I don't know, maybe it's just not going to happen for me." At the time, it seemed to me that girls would develop breasts and then a period would come soon after. I was completely flat chested and hadn't felt the growing pains my peers described. I figured this meant I wouldn't ever get my period.

My mom reassured me everything would be OK.

"You can't control nature. The only thing you can do is love yourself the way you are. God works in his own time, my child. Be grateful for the life you have been given."

She was right. Whatever this was or would be, it was God's will, and my job was to live my life and thank him every day for the blessing of breath and my family.

Time went on. I was healthy and happy. Every now and then I wondered why my sisters and friends had their boobs and I didn't have mine. Sometimes I'd stand naked in the mirror, turning this way and that, looking at my body from different angles, and I'd imagine what I'd look like if I did have them. Then I would just remind myself, "This is the way things are supposed to be. Don't question God's will."

There were journalists who asked why my parents didn't realize something was wrong, why they didn't take me straight to a hospital when they saw I wasn't developing in the same way other girls were. I hear that in the Western world, a girl like me would have been diagnosed and "treated" from birth or at least as puberty began. This didn't happen to me because no one thought there was anything to treat. We noticed I was different, but different didn't mean wrong. Some girls are what they call late bloomers, anyway.

My body may not have been changing in the way the other girls were, but I felt something was happening to my brain. I was feeling like I had lost control of my mind a little bit. I became aware of feelings I hadn't dealt with before.

I was comfortable being around boys. We played and hunted together. I had no problem fighting them. I could keep up with everything they did. I understood their language and they understood mine. With girls, things were not exactly that way. When I tried hanging out with girls, they'd be talking about boys, which guy they thought was cute and who they wanted to kiss. They'd talk about their periods. I stood around unable to contribute to their conversations. I wasn't interested in kissing any of the guys I was hanging out with, and I didn't have periods. I could've told them which boys were packing big meat and which ones had small meat since I'd swam naked with them, but that wouldn't have been fair. So, when the girls got going on this kind of talk, which was often, I'd just walk away.

I don't want it to seem like I didn't have any friends who were girls because I did, just not too many. I felt a little strange when I was around them, and I didn't know what that meant at the time. Girls could be bullies, too, and I remember more than a few would make fun of me. They'd talk about my secondhand clothes, my unkempt hair, my boyish-looking face. They'd make fun of me for being late to class or when I didn't understand a lesson. I had missed seven months of schooling at a young age because of my leg injury, and it was hard to keep up with my peers. The girls' teasing did bother me, but in a different way than it did when boys did it. For starters, I didn't want to beat them up. I'd seen how most girls settled things when they got physical. They'd pull each other's hair and tear their clothing. Not all girls fought like this, obviously. I was one who threw punches. But if some girl got going with me, I'd just suck my teeth and simply say, "Look, girl, fuck off. If I hit you, you're going to feel like you were hit with a stone. So better to shut your mouth and stay away from me, please."

And most of the time, the girl would mouth off some more, but she'd just go away. Only once did I shove another girl, and only because she shoved me first. Later, it dawned on me that I didn't want to hit girls because I actually just wanted to kiss them.

I was fantasizing about girls the way most of them were fantasizing about boys. And I wanted them to talk about me the way they were talking about the boys. "Ah," I remember thinking to myself, "so, I like girls." I think I first knew when I was about five years old, but at that age you don't really understand that it's a romantic feeling, just more of a curiosity. Once I got older and knew what was going on with me, I had no shame in being clear about it when I needed to be.

I have never been in a "closet." I have never understood the whole Western "coming out of the closet" thing. I never hid who I was or felt I had to. Everyone in my world seemed to know. I didn't go around yelling that I was into girls but, if I had to address it, I would. If some boy tried me, I'd say it straight out, "I'm into girls. Maybe me and your sister can talk. And if you like your dick, let us not speak of this again."

My cousins loved how fearless I was when it came to these kinds of things, and they would use me when they liked a girl and were feeling shy about talking to her. They knew I had no problem going up to a girl and just spitting it out.

"Hey. My cousin is there with you. He's thinking about you in that way. Do you like him?" Then I'd turn around and point to whichever cousin had a crush on the girl. And if there was a girl I liked, I'd tell her.

And there was a girl. The first girl I had a crush on was R. We met in the third grade. I just liked everything about her. She was sweet and very pretty, easy to talk to, and we got along great. She was one of those girls who people just went crazy over. The thing about R was that even though she was a different kind of girl than I was, somehow, we were still the same. She and I became friends, and we'd hang out whenever we could. R was the first girl I ever kissed. We were young and innocent, and it was never anything more than that. Nothing more would happen between us, but I remember the feeling of knowing that kissing girls was what I would be doing for the rest of my life.

Once I knew this, of course, I had to tell the most important people in my life.

One morning, I told my family I had some news to share. It was one of those rare days were everybody was home. Even my dad. They all gathered in the living room. Everyone was waiting to see what I had to say. This way I wouldn't have to deal with so-and-so's parents or relatives wanting to have a talk with my parents about any kind of coupling in the future. And none of my sisters would waste their time coming to gossip or whisper to me about some boy who wanted to be there with me.

"LOOK, don't expect me to come home with a boyfriend because it will never happen. When I grow up, I'm going to marry a woman."

My family shook their heads, and there were some groans and

eye-rolling and definitely some laughter. Just the usual stuff that meant, "Here this crazy girl goes again talking some madness."

I don't know if they took me seriously that day, but there were no comments about it being "evil" or against our religion. Even though the pastors in our village would oftentimes find ways to call people in same-sex relationships "demons" in their sermons. No one in my family started screaming or crying. My parents and siblings did not seem surprised. They knew I was my own kind of person. I said it. I meant it. There was nothing they could do about it except know it.

I was beginning to understand myself. What I wanted from life. I had my family, my friends, and soccer. I could have been a better student, but studying wasn't my focus.

And then, as they say, all good things must come to an end. The life I'd built would change drastically one evening. I had just turned twelve years old.

"MOKGADI. Come here and talk to us," my father said as soon as I walked in the door. Both of my parents were in the living room. It was late. Far later than most kids my age were allowed to stay out. The sun had gone down hours before, but I pretty much came and went as I pleased at this point.

They looked serious, so I sat down and waited.

"Your grandmother in Fairlie is very old now. She is living with your cousins. They are boys. She needs help. We have decided you will live with her. It will be good for you. A new place," my mom said.

I couldn't argue about this. There was no arguing when your elders made such a decision for you. In our culture, it was normal to send one or more of your children to live at another family member's home. My sisters before me had been sent to various relatives' homes to help them with chores or childrearing. I knew my turn would come, but I couldn't help but feel that my parents just wanted to get rid of me.

I was not an easy kid. My parents loved and accepted me, but no parent would be happy about their young daughter hanging out in the bush until late at night. I was wild. I would come home when I was ready to come home. It got so that my mother had taken to locking me out of the house when I didn't come in at sundown. I didn't care. I'd just climb over our fence, and if the front door was locked, I'd sleep in the back of the house, near the fire pit, which would sometimes still have warm embers from cooking. If my mother tried to beat me, I'd just hold her hands until she calmed down and then kiss the top of her head. I was a twelve-year-old giant compared to her. She could no longer threaten me with bicycle gears or any other makeshift weapons. As long as I did my household chores, there was nothing my parents could do. My dad was hundreds of miles away, and my mother was busy working and taking care of my sister, baby brother, and her baby granddaughter. I know I was a valued child in my family; I cared for our animals and garden and I fixed things and helped with my younger siblings. Even though this was part of our custom, I just didn't understand why they would want me to leave.

I sat there and thought back to how frustrated my mom looked when a teacher or a parent complained about my misdoings.

"Mokgadi, what's this now, girl? This person said you beat up their son. Why are you fighting like this?" My mother would say with a tired look on her face.

I'd always answer the same way, "Mom, he deserved that one. That's all I'm going to say." For us village kids, what happened in the bush, stayed in the bush. At least it was supposed to. The boys and I would hurt each other every now and then, and I guess some didn't keep their mouths shut and parents weren't happy about it.

The truth is I was getting into things I probably shouldn't have been. Sometimes the teachers would tell my mom that I was carrying a bunch of money, and they wondered if I was stealing. I wasn't stealing. I was gambling. Like I said, we weren't poor—my father had a solid job in the city and my mother had a spaza shop—but we were a lot of mouths to feed. There were many needs to meet. We also shared what we had with extended family. I couldn't ask my parents for much so I made my own money when I could.

When I played soccer, I was good enough now to bet on myself. I would play dice with the older boys and make money that way. I would play marbles and make money on that, too. I remember these guys from China would visit our village. They ran a type of lotto but with just one number. If you bet half a rand, you could walk away with R12. If you bet R1, you could get R24. I started betting when I was like nine or ten years old. I was good at picking out the number. Other villagers started to notice I was lucky and ask me to tell them which number I was choosing. Eventually, I stopped telling them because I could see they were just using me. I learned how to save my money and make more of it. I was a calculated risk taker. To this day, I'm rather stingy. I don't like to spend money if I don't have to. This has served me well in life.

When I wasn't playing or gambling, I helped my mom at the tuck shop or went around the village with her selling fish, bread, and sweets on the weekends. I wasn't the only kid selling things, so I needed to find a way to connect with people, to make them feel good, to learn how to negotiate so they would buy from me. I was friendly and I made people laugh. And the faster I sold, the faster I could get back to playing with the other kids.

I never wanted to be a burden on my parents. I knew I wasn't a burden to them. I understood they weren't banishing me, even though it felt that way. My heart was sore, but the village of Fairlie wasn't too far from my home. I could walk there in one hour or I could run there in half the time.

I BELIEVE my mother and father felt I was heading toward womanhood and perhaps it was best for me to have a change of environment. I was too comfortable where I was. I ate, slept, played soccer, gambled, went to school only when I felt like it, and that was it. I was in the sixth grade there. They knew I was young enough to adapt, to grow, in a new place.

They were sending me to live with my grandmother because I could help a family member who was struggling more than we were. I instinctively understood she needed a girl child to do traditional girl things. And this is what worried me. I was not a girl who did girl things. Everyone knew that. I knew my life would be completely different in her home. People loved and understood me in Ga-Masehlong. I thought of my friends, the boys I'd known my entire life, the boys who accepted me as I was. I was a free soul. I was a twelve-year-old girl who basically did as she pleased. I would have to leave everything I knew, everything I'd built, and start all over again.

Chapter 6

THABISO

G A-MASEHLONG WAS WHERE MOKGADI WAS BORN.
Fairlie Village was where I became the Caster people
know today.

I look back at the time I was sent to my grandmother's home
with fondness and gratitude. But when my parents had told me
I'd be moving to Fairlie, I'd been overcome with sadness and anx-
iousness. Those feelings would eventually turn into annoyance
and frustration.

The day before I was to leave for Fairlie, my mother packed
my things. I watched as she packed skirts, dresses, and blouses.
My bag was full of my sisters' clothes, not one of the boys' items I
was used to wearing. We didn't talk about it. It was a silent understanding. I could do and dress as I pleased in my birth village,
but this girl was now heading to a new place. My mother knew I
would eventually go back to wearing boy clothes, but I would have
to toe the line as it was drawn when it came to such things and
then find my way again.

I arrived in Fairlie early in January of 2003. I had turned twelve
a day or so prior. My mother and I took a bus that morning. I wore
a plain vest and jean shorts. Just normal clothes a boy or a girl
could wear. It was a short, quiet ride—maybe fifteen or twenty
minutes, but it felt longer as we drove slowly on the rocky path and
paused for the cows and goats that roamed freely and took their
time crossing the road.

My grandmother met us at the door; she greeted me with joy.

"Welcome! Welcome, my grandchild. We are so happy! Happy

to have Mokgadi here with us!" she said as she wrapped me in her thin arms and reached up and kissed my cheeks. I remember her white dress and brightly colored headcovering. She had my father's deep brown skin tone and the same warm eyes and big smile that showed her pink gums. We all had the same smile.

My grandmother's name was Mmaphuti Sekgala. She was what is known as a *Ngaka*, a traditional healer. She was well known and respected for her ability to cure people of ailments using herbs and plants in the old ways of our ancestors. The sick and injured trusted her and came to her, even from neighboring villages. I would find out much later that she was actually my father's aunt and not his mother, not that such things made any difference. Her three grandsons lived with her—Kgabo, an adult who I'd met before, Salvation, who was two years older than me, and Ernest, who was one year younger. This would be my first time meeting my two youngest cousins. I was anxious about Salvation and Ernest and hoped we'd get along. They were my age, so we'd be going to school together and I'd have to rely on them to meet new people.

My grandmother's place looked almost exactly like my family home. It was a rectangular cement house with a living area and three bedrooms. They had a separate structure in the yard where Kgabo lived when he came home from work. Like us, they cooked outside and had no running water or electricity.

My mother sat with my grandmother. I took a look around the place while they talked. It was spacious enough. I knew I would get a bedroom to myself since I was girl. It wasn't dirty, but it was messy and disorganized. There were pots and cooking utensils here and there. Household items and food needed to be put in order. I could see why my elderly grandmother needed the kind of help only a strong girl could provide.

I remember I heard a door open. By then it was mid-morning. Ernest and Salvation came out to the front room. They both looked like they had just woken up. Both were tall and thin, I was the same height or maybe a little taller than Ernest. I could see we were related. Something about their brows and eyes was familiar.

"What's up?" Salvation said and offered his hand.

Ernest did the same, "Hey. Welcome. Happy to have you here."

With that, my mother stood. I said goodbye to my mother. There were no tears from me, although I felt them. A part of me hoped that my mother would change her mind somehow. But I knew that would not happen. This would be my new home until it wasn't. My mother hugged me and cradled my face.

"You are welcome to come home whenever you want. Your home will always be there for you. You will be a good daughter here." She smiled and I could only nod.

Soon after my mother left, Salvation and Ernest asked if I wanted to meet their friends. I was glad they asked. If they thought I looked or acted different from other girls, they didn't say anything about it. I felt like they saw me and thought, "Cool. Let's have fun." It only took one day to understand what kind of boys my two cousins were, and I knew we'd get along just fine. They loved soccer and were just as adventurous as I was. These two did not hunt, so I knew that part of my life was over. There would be lots of other things to fill my time.

I went with my cousins to meet their friends. We were going to chill in the bush, listen to music, maybe take a swim. As we walked around the village, Salvation and Ernest pointed things out—where the shops were, their friends' houses. Fairlie looked almost exactly like Ga-Masehlong, only bigger. Where we had a thousand people, they had maybe twice or three times that. So, there was a little more of everything, more houses, more shops, more kids, more animals roaming around. My birth village was sleepy compared to this. We walked past the houses and into the wild lands and arrived at a river where several boys our age were roughhousing in the water.

I was wearing the same shorts and vest I had arrived in. I looked around, took my top off and jumped into the water, too. The boys were talking about soccer, talking about girls, talking about school. Same old stuff I was used to back home. I fit right in. I was making them laugh. Recreating scenes from the action movies we all seemed to love. Teasing them about this or that. I was talking about my favorite soccer players and their moves. Things would be alright, I thought. That is, until one of the boys asked me my name.

"What's up? I'm Thabiso," I replied.

"Thabiso?"

Thabiso is a boy's name. In Pedi, it means "happy one" or "one who brings joy." I was bringing joy with me that day. I could tell they thought I was a boy so I figured I would go along with it. I mean, I was swimming without a shirt on and I had no boobs. I looked tough like they did. My voice sounded like theirs, too. They would have been ashamed to know they were naked in front of a girl. Neither of my cousins said anything when I said "Thabiso," although they both knew I wasn't a boy and that wasn't my name. In that moment, I knew Ernest and Salvation would let me be me and just have my back as family. It was a good feeling.

Soon after that day, before classes started, my grandmother took me to the school to register me as a student. I'd be entering the seventh grade. I wore a T-shirt and a pair of my sister's jeans, so they were tighter than I liked. There were kids and parents everywhere. I saw a few of the boys I'd swum with out of the corner of my eye. My heart got going a little faster.

"Hey! Thabiso! Thabiso?"

I did not so much as turn around. Then I felt a tap on my back.

"Thabiso? Hey. What's up? You remember you swam with us?" the boy said.

"No. I'm not Thabiso. I'm his twin sister. My name is Mokgadi. I don't know you." I looked at him as if I'd never seen him before in my life.

"You look exactly like Thabiso." This boy looked confused.

"Yeah. Because we're identical twins. Twins look exactly the same. Thabiso went back home." I shrugged my shoulders and turned back around. I don't know how I came up with that. My grandmother was speaking with an administrator, so she didn't witness any of this. The boy walked back to the group and I was close enough to hear him say,

"He says it's not him. This one's a girl. Named Mokgadi. Says she's Thabiso's twin sister. I don't know what the hell is going on, man . . ."

All week I couldn't get this moment out of my mind. I knew I'd have to be myself for school, so I was hoping the boys would let go of "Thabiso." I liked those boys very much and could see them becoming real friends.

By the time the first day of school came, I already had a routine. I'd wake up around 5 a.m. and get the firewood going. As soon as the pot of water was boiling, I'd make a simple breakfast—tea, mealie meal, some sweet bread. I'd washed and ironed clothes for the entire family on the weekend, so our school uniforms were ready. Salvation and Ernest would wear trousers and plain white button shirts, and I would be wearing the tunic—a dress under which girls would also wear plain white shirts. I was in a new place, a new environment. I needed to fit in first and then see where I could go from there.

My new school looked similar to my old one. Basic cement structures bordered a yard, enclosed with wire fencing. Nothing different except the kids were older. I was the tallest girl in my class. I kept to myself. None of the girls introduced themselves, although I know they were looking and whispering about me. In class, I paid more attention to my surroundings than to the teacher, and I couldn't wait for lunch break so I could chill with my cousins and play soccer. When recess came, I grabbed my stuff and walked out into the yard.

"Thabiso?"

This time, I turned around. There he was. The same kid from the river.

"Hey, it's Mokgadi. Thabiso left for the city," I replied.

"I feel like you are Thabiso." His eyes looked around my face and he rubbed his chin. "You were swimming with us naked in the bush. Now you are here wearing a dress." I could tell this boy's brain was turning in circles.

"Look, my man, I don't know you, OK?" I stared straight at him and set my jaw. "Never met you before in my life. I told you I'm Thabiso's twin sister. You were swimming with my brother. How can I swim naked with you if I am a girl?"

He didn't believe me, but he had no other choice. Eventually, he and the other boys accepted I was a girl named Mokgadi and I had a twin brother named Thabiso who had moved to the city. As time went by, the boys accepted me into their circle. By then, I was playing soccer with them and it didn't matter that I was a girl. All that mattered was that I could play on their level.

Every now and then, one of my new friends would say, "Mokgadi. We know you're Thabiso. There's no twin brother. It was you that day in the bush. We don't care. It's doesn't matter to us. Just tell us the truth."

"Nah, man. I have a twin brother; you'll see him again when he comes back to visit. I don't know what you are talking about." Then I'd slap him on the back of the head and we'd go back to kicking the ball around.

Six months went by, and I knew the girl's uniform had to go. I didn't want to wear it anymore. I was tired of having to change out of the uniform every time I had a soccer game. Tired of carrying extra clothes around with me. Changing took time I didn't have. Every minute I spent changing my clothes was time I wasn't playing. And with the numerous responsibilities I had at my grandmother's house, my time for playing soccer was limited.

When I won the world championship and journalists came to my grandmother's village, one of my old friends told them he had no doubts I was a girl because when we played soccer I would walk far away and change my clothes behind a tree.

Getting a boy's uniform wasn't difficult. I told my parents I wanted the trousers and they sent money for me to buy a pair. I was the same size as Salvation, anyway. I didn't ask permission from my grandmother. She accepted me for what I was, a boy-ish girl. I just prepared my clothing and that was that. My grand-mother was like an older version of my mom. Kind, protective. My grandmother was just worried about me and Salvation and Ernest being out late because she knew bad things could happen when the sun went down. I tried to obey all of my grandmother's rules. Given all of my household responsibilities, I couldn't stay out as late as I did at my parents' home. She would lock the doors on me and cousins, too, but for some reason she would get con-fused about the time—she would want us home by 7 p.m. and lock us out at 6 p.m. We'd then climb over the fence, walk into the house through the unlocked kitchen area, and show her the clock so she could see the curfew wasn't up, yet. I learned to manage time while I was living with my grandmother, and I made sure the home was well-kept.

I remember the first day I came to school wearing the boys' uni-form. Some of the girls were laughing and whispering when they saw me. I didn't care. A few of the girls looked at me differently, but they didn't laugh. Those girls had something else in their eyes—looked like appreciation. None of the teachers said a word about it. If they talked amongst themselves about why I wasn't wearing a tunic as most of the girls were, I didn't know about it. I was a popular kid. I got along with everyone. All the teachers loved me.

I didn't know what my guy friends would think, but I also knew they would be fine. Like my cousins, they understood me. We'd been to each other's homes, I knew their parents and sib-lings, we hung out almost every day. They respected me and I respected them.

When recess came, I walked over to my group of friends. They started whooping as soon as they saw me.

"Ha! We knew it!! Thabiso!"

"That's why you didn't take off your shorts that day."

I laughed. Yes, I thought, today is the day I retire this lie. "OK. Yes. I was Thabiso. You guys got a problem with it?"

My friends crowded around me laughing and pushing me around.

"You saw my thing," one of them said. I knew this was going to be their main concern. That a girl saw their dicks. Men can be so predictable.

"I did," and I couldn't help adding, "you got small meat, my man."

"Hey Caster, what do you think about my thing?" the other one asked.

"*Ja.* You got good meat, chief. Whoever's getting that is getting good meat." Our language was crass, but it was all in good fun. We went on like that for a few minutes. Everybody got to hear what I thought about their ding-a-lings. I was relieved it was over. Thabiso never existed. I could put my twin brother to rest. They always knew I was lying anyway.

EVEN THOUGH I had to perform what became "girls' work" in my grandmother's home, my cousins treated me like one of the boys outside of it.

There was a practice soccer game I will never forget. I was around fourteen and my cousin Salvation was maybe sixteen. He was playing for the opposing team. In those days, if the game was going too slow and there were no goals, we incentivized each other with a rule called "shirts." Basically, when a team scored a goal, the opposing players had to take their shirts off. They couldn't put them back on until they scored. My cousin's team scored. This was the first time I was in a game with this rule. All the boys kind of stopped at this point. I was one of them, but I was still a girl. They stood around with these dumb looks on their faces. We weren't small kids anymore. Bodies and interests had already started changing in our world.

"So . . . uh, Caster. . . . You gonna take it off or what?"

They were letting me know I didn't have to take off my shirt but I could if I wanted to. There was nothing to see anyway. I had nothing on top. Zero. I'd already been swimming naked with many of these boys. We'd all seen each other's bits but, like I said, things had changed.

"Ja. I'll take it off. Why not? Those are the rules, right?" I stripped my vest off and gave a "let's go" sign with my hand. I could see a few of the boys sneaking looks around my chest. Maybe they thought I was going to expose a brand-new pair of small breasts, but my torso still looked exactly like theirs. I would say I looked even better than some of them—I was so thin you could see my ribs, but the rest of me was muscle.

The game continued. My team wanted their shirts back, so I hit my cousin with a skill. I drilled him with the ball and caught him off guard and scored. Before I could celebrate and we could get our shirts back on, my cousin knocked me down. Our soccer pitches were never on level ground anyway, and we always had to try and avoid thorns and rocks as we ran around. This piece of flatland was kind of along a hill, and my cousin tackled me so hard I fell over and rolled down the side of it. I've never been hit so hard in my life. This kid took the life out of me. When I stopped rolling, I had rocks and dirt in my hair and in my face and mouth. It took a while to clear my head and catch my breath. I remember I came back up the hill as best as I could, feeling like I had several broken ribs. Salvation must've thought we were playing American football.

"What's this, now? What's this? We're living under the same roof and you do this to me?" I looked at him in complete disbelief. "You play me like that? Same blood you and me." To be honest, Salvation had hurt my body, but he'd bruised my heart a little, too.

"It is what it is, Mokgadi," my cousin said. "Wake up, baba. You're too soft. You needed something to think about. I gave you some medicine." This moment was kind of like when Kobe Bryant told Dwight Howard he was "soft."

"I'm going to get you back, Salvation," I tried to say while spitting out dust and wiping my face. Of course, I let it go. He was my cousin. And he had taught me a valuable lesson. By treating me like everyone else on the pitch, he was forcing me to be tough. I'd need that toughness later on in life.

PART II

THE RISE

Chapter 7

WHERE I BELONG

I HAD BEEN A NATURAL CARETAKER IN MY CHILDHOOD home, but at my grandmother's house, caretaking moved to another level. Here, I did laundry for everyone with my bare hands. I smoothed out our school uniforms with a manual iron I heated up on the wood fire. I did most of the cooking and cleaning, and shopping.

My cousins were pains in the ass because they didn't do much of anything to help around the house. They did stuff here and there, when they felt like it, but for the most part they didn't clean, cook, or care for my grandmother's animals. All they had to do was go to school, have fun with their friends, and play soccer. Occasionally, I'd get pissed about how different our lives were. Sometimes, I'd refuse to make a meal or wash their clothes. I'd run back to my birth village to visit my family instead and leave them to see what it was like to do for themselves. It wouldn't last long, though, because I understood them, they were boys and it wasn't expected of them. They didn't know any better, and it's not like my grandmother told them they had to help me. Sometimes, I wish she had. It didn't matter because I had been sent there to do these things for them. It wasn't fair but, as a girl, it was my duty.

Still, I felt like a slave.

And I felt very alone, even though I knew my grandmother and my cousins loved me, and I had made great friends in Fairlie.

I FELT THAT no one understood me. I felt like I didn't belong in Fairlie. That my place, my true place, was somewhere else. That feeling of want to go, of wanting to be on an airplane to somewhere, grew stronger, until it became constant. I guess you could say my soul was restless.

By my early to mid-teens, I was sure of what I wanted out of life. I wanted to have a wife, to have children, and provide for my family in Ga-Masehlong and for the new family I would one day build. I wanted dignity and respect and happiness. I still dreamt of sports stardom.

I'd tell my cousins and friends that I was going places. I wasn't sure how, but I was going. My friends would laugh and tease me about the dreams I was holding in my heart. They weren't being mean. It came more from a place of just not understanding where I was.

We were at that age where things were "heating up." The conversations turned more and more to romance and who wanted to be with whom. My friends knew which way I went, so they would encourage me to get a girlfriend and tell me how much I'd enjoy certain things they'd already tasted, but I wasn't interested. At the end of the day, I knew I was different. Despite my foul mouth, I was reserved in many ways. I was selfish about myself.

I was determined to make something of my life. I just had the feeling I was meant for a life that was bigger than what the village had to offer. I'd watched enough movies to know there was a big world out there. I spoke English fairly well. It wasn't decent English—the movies I watched were full of foul language—but I knew that I needed to speak English to have a shot at the world outside of my village. Our native tongue was Pedi, and we tried to learn English in school. I would say I learned most of my English by watching American movies and cartoons. I loved movies about gangsters, drug lords, serial killers, and especially about soldiers and war. I loved comedies and anything about martial arts. When I wasn't dreaming of being a famous soccer player, I'd dream of becoming a soldier and fighting for my country. I would practice what I thought was my cool American English. "Yo, man, what's up, homie?" I'd speak about "bitches" and "hoes" and "N words."

Some of the older guys would overhear me and my friends and tell us these were not good words. My earliest interviews were quite colorful until I learned to clean up my language. But I could speak English. And being able to speak English was a way out. English is what we called the "access language," it was the language you needed for entry into any university in South Africa. My family could not pay for me to have any schooling past tertiary, or what is known elsewhere as high school, but I thought if I could speak and understand English well enough, maybe I could get a sports scholarship to a university. Even if I didn't become a professional soccer player, I would have an education, and I could eventually get a good job in a city.

I became more obsessed with sports. I missed my family, I missed my home and my friends, and playing sports provided a distraction from that absence I felt in my heart. I played everything. Whatever the school had available, I played it. I loved baseball. I was a powerful pitcher, but also a good outfielder. When it was my turn to bat, if I got a hit, I'd run like hell. I played basketball with the boys and netball with some of my girl classmates. I took advantage of whatever was offered. Not that the school had much. Nthema Secondary School was the same as my old one in that it didn't have any real sports grounds. The "basketball court" was a rocky field with shoots of grass and a rusted hoop where we also played soccer and baseball.

I had a home language teacher named Mr. Maseko, but we called him Boss. He taught us how to read and write in Pedi. He wasn't a coach, not officially, but he was a sports person. There were no coaches—our school didn't have money for that. Our teachers helped organize the teams and then supervised us when we played. Boss would come watch us play and offer guidance and break up any arguments or fights between the kids.

Boss waved me over one day after a baseball game.

"Mokgadi. You played very well today."

"Appreciate it, Boss."

"There's a new sport starting at the school next year. Athletics."

"Athletics?" I liked the sound of the word.

"Competitive running," Boss said. "You look fast out there when you're playing soccer and baseball."

I'd run before. Never seriously. Just against my sisters and my boys every now and then. As kids we'd drag our fingers across the dusty ground to create a starting line and someone would yell "go." All of my siblings had run in school competitions but it was basically like a physical education requirement. There was no official system that fed talented kids into higher levels. There were no professionals scouting talent in our villages. I knew running as a sport existed, I'd watched the Olympics and world championships before, but it didn't hold much space in my fantasies of making it big. Soccer was the game we were all obsessed with. And I was great at soccer.

When organized athletics started at my new school I, of course, joined. I knew I was fast.

I ran everything from sprints to 4 kilometers, and I was faster than any of the girls in my school. I began competing against girls from other schools, and I was faster than most of them. There was a girl named Dineo who always gave me trouble. She was a sprinter and a long jumper. Taller and more powerful than I was. Later in life, we'd run into each other on the track and field circuits; by then I'd become a solid middle-distance runner and she specialized in the long jump.

Boss would encourage me to race the boys, too. I'd beat the hell out of most of them because most weren't really athletes; they weren't playing sports with the intensity that I was.

I was fifteen years old. I was tall and very lean, nothing but bone and muscle. I was broad-shouldered; the outline of my torso was like the letter V, and from there it just went straight down past my hips. I still hadn't gotten my period or boobs, and I figured if I was ever going to get them, it would've already happened. There was still time for this to change, but somewhere deep inside of me, I understood it never would. People in Fairlie called me a "tough mamma," by which they meant I was a masculine girl. "Looking good, girl," they would say when they saw me running errands or walking my grandmother's animals to pasture.

I still played soccer and baseball, dabbled in netball games, and practiced my martial arts. But now I began to take running more seriously. Boss would always be there at our races. And every now and then, he'd sit and talk to me about sports, about life. Boss was the one who introduced me to the world of competitive running. I already knew the names of the famous runners of the time, but Boss and I would sit and I would learn more about them—Maria Mutola, Marion Jones, and Pamela Jelimo. Jamaica's Shelly-Ann Fraser. In South Africa, we had track and fielders like Christine Kalmer, the Phalula twins, and Janice Josephs.

I REMEMBER I'd just finished a thou-five practice when Boss came over. I was moving well that day, not fast, but strong, centered, and focused.

"Are you really serious about running, Mokgadi?"

"Man, running makes me feel free," I said. "I feel great when I'm running, Boss. I forget about everything in life, just forget about anything that bothers me. I love it. I really do." And it was true that it made me feel free. Here's the thing I realized about myself—I am a human being who likes to be in my own space. I loved team sports, but it's hard to take a loss when you know you're doing your best and your teammate isn't. The worst is when your teammate IS doing their best but it's just not good enough. With running, it's all on you. No one else but you. If I lost, it was my fault. If I won, it was my triumph.

And there was something more that I didn't tell Boss. My mind was never quiet when I was playing team sports. Neither was my mouth. There was constant banter with the other players. You had to deal with their nonsense for the entire game. I was good at talking shit and I knew how to get inside people's brains. In team sports, my mind was turned outward, if that makes sense. Running was different. My mind turned inward, toward itself. I preferred it that way. It quieted down. I felt completely at peace.

"Ah," Boss said and looked at me in a way I hadn't seen before. I think that was the first time he saw me as a real runner. "OK, Mokgadi. I believe you are now ready to hear some things."

I was ready.

Boss told me many things. He said the greatest runners in the world came from Eastern Africa—Kenya, Ethiopia, Somalia. Then he told me that for pure speed the best sprinters in the world were Jamaicans and Americans.

I'd sit with him, completely taken in by his words and the timbre of his voice. I was a girl who'd grown up with a father I idolized but who was away for long periods of time. I was now living away from the comforts of my home. I ached for my birth family. It felt good to be spoken to by an elder man in this way, to be seen as someone worthy of his time.

I loved hearing Boss talk about the Kenyans, especially, because they were the runners to be feared in long and middle distances. The best of the best. I remembered my parents told me that our tribe were descended from the Maasai. The Maasai were Kenyan. Yes, I felt deep in my soul, this running thing was in my blood.

Boss had a way of speaking that made me pay attention. He was quiet. He had a low voice that sounded like rumbling thunder. He gave people the impression that he was kind, but that kindness had a very firm limit. He always told us the truth as a teacher. He didn't like stupidity, laziness, lies. And he only used enough words to get his point across. He wasn't much of a talker, so if he had something to say, it would be said in a very clear and direct manner. The fact that Boss took his time to guide me meant he truly believed in me.

"Mokgadi," Boss said to me at the end of one of our talks. "I believe that one day you will come across the great Kenyans. And what I am trying to say is, you don't know the power you have in you. That is your problem. Focus, child. Because you can be better than them. I see future in you." The corners of his mouth turned up, he gave me a slight bow with his head and walked away.

"You can be better than them" and *"I see future in you"* have stayed with me. I remember jogging back to my grandmother's home repeating his words in my head, "I have a future. I can be better than the Kenyans. He sees this in me. I have a future in this running thing . . ."

I have recounted this story of Boss's encouragement in hundreds of appearances and interviews throughout the years. With these words, Boss changed my life. In that moment, it was exactly what I needed to hear. Soccer was like a great first love. Then you grow up and you discover what real love is. I knew a girl could not get to the level of success I dreamed of playing women's soccer. I couldn't provide for my family playing soccer. By now, I also knew professional men's teams weren't going to let a girl on the team, no matter how well she played. But running was a different matter. There was fortune there for women. There was recognition. Competitive running had real opportunity for a girl like me.

This part of my life leading up to my turning pro feels like a blur to me, except Boss's words. I wonder sometimes if my memory works this way because of what eventually happened.

ONE OF THE THINGS I remember from this period of my life is that as I became a regular in the youth running circuit, my body became more of a thing that was observed and commented on. When people wonder about the source of my mental strength, how

I was able to withstand the public scrutiny that came with winning the 2009 World Championship and go on and win another world championship and two Olympic medals—they can start here.

I'd overhear coaches and other runners say, "That doesn't look like a girl," or "Why is this boy here with us?" I had no problem going right up to them and introducing myself. "Hello. I am Caster. I am a girl. Would you like to see? I can drop my shorts here for you."

I understood humans. How they behaved, what they were probably thinking. This, too, was a gift from God. I had been a girl amongst boys. Even though I was treated like one of them, I wasn't really one of them. Now I was a girl who ran against other girls. And while I was a girl by virtue of nature and law, the girls didn't see me as one of them, either.

I would confront people straight on. It's how I preferred to do things. And that would be enough to shut their silly mouths right up. No one ever took me up on the offer to drop my shorts. Besides, they didn't have to. I wasn't shy. Not only was I direct with my words, but I had no problem walking around naked in the restroom facilities. I was happy to shower with the rest of the girls. I had nothing to hide.

I knew I was being carefully watched by the other girls. After races, as I'd head over to the facilities, many of the other runners would make it their business to walk in at the same time as me. They'd quickly grab their things and follow me. I'd strip and walk to the communal shower area and suddenly I would find myself surrounded by girls who just happened to need to rinse off. They would stare at everything on my body. I was fine with it. They filled their eyes and I filled my eyes, too. I could tell some were disappointed they didn't see what they were sure I was hiding. Others seemed intrigued. They made awkward attempts at conversation during and after the showers. What I now understand as flirting. By this point, I have to say I understood girls found me attractive, or at least they were curious enough to give me some thought.

Even if I was interested, the truth was I didn't have time for it. I was there to run. I wasn't there to make friends or find a girlfriend. I gave respect to everyone as was the manner I was raised, and I made it clear that is what I expected back.

I said earlier that no one ever accused me directly of being anything other than a girl. One day, though, it did actually happen.

I was sitting on a bench in the girls' facility after a regional cross-country race. I was tired and had begun to feel the first pangs of hunger and just wanted to go home. I heard multiple people walking in and I looked up to see a runner surrounded by doping officials. I hadn't seen her before but I knew the drill. They were walking her to the toilets to watch her pee, and then they would test the pee for drugs. I was only fifteen or sixteen years old, but I'd already peed in a few cups myself. The doping officials would have you bring your running shorts down past your knees and roll your shirt up past your breasts. Then some would get up close and personal with your privates because they need to see exactly where the pee is coming from to make sure you are not giving them someone else's.

Me and the runner locked eyes. And that's when she said it.

"What are you doing in here? What's a boy doing in here? This is the lady's facility," she said in Pedi. Her voice sounded like a loud whisper.

The first thing I thought was, "This one thinks she's got balls."

"So? Yes, it's the lady's toilet. You think I'm lost here? Why would they let a boy in the women's facility?" I said. "Why would I be sitting here? For what purpose?"

Maybe it was the way I responded because she suddenly looked embarrassed. I could tell she felt badly about assuming I was a boy and it was an honest mistake. She was wearing a central Gauteng bib, but she replied to me in my dialect.

"I see. . . . My Apologies. I meant no disrespect. What's your name?" She stood there kind of awkwardly. This girl was taller than most, but still several inches shorter than me. She was very thin, the kind of thin you see on the longer-distance runners. She was beautiful; glowing brown skin, high cheekbones, almond-shaped eyes, full lips, but I wasn't thinking of that in that moment.

"What's *your* name?" I said. "Introduce yourself first. You're the one who came in here disturbing *me*." I shot back at her.

And at that, she laughed and so did I. She told me that her name was Violet Raseboya. She was a world-class cross-country runner from Limpopo but running for Gauteng. She was five years older than me, one of the experienced runners who'd already been overseas. She was competing in an 8-km race that day. I was only allowed to run the 4 kilometer because the longer distances were restricted based on age.

"OK, then, Vioooolet." I drew her name out in a teasing manner. "I'll see you out there on the loops."

"What do you mean, little girl? You'll see me on which loops? What loops are you talking about? You think you can beat me?" Violet put her hand on her hip.

This Violet was a sassy girl. I liked that she wasn't intimidated by me.

"Yeah, I do. I'm lethal. Like a cobra." I gave her a half-smile. "I'll come over there on your side and dust you off one day."

The conversation with Violet was brief. I didn't think much of it or her afterward. She was the same as everyone else who'd assumed I was a boy, only she had said it to my face. I couldn't have imagined she would become one of the most important people in my life.

Chapter 8

THEY SAW ME RUN

I HAD DONE SO WELL IN THE DISTRICT RACES THAT I had qualified to compete at a regional-level 800-m race. I knew that if I managed to win at the regional level, then maybe I would be offered membership into an official running club. By now, I'd run enough and talked to enough people that I had a basic idea of how things worked. The running clubs fed athletes to ASA, Athletics South Africa, our country's sports governing body in charge of creating South Africa's national team. Only athletes who were members of ASA could qualify for international competitions, and those races were regulated by the all-mighty IAAF, the International Association of Athletics Federation. ASA was affiliated with SASCOC, the South African Sport Confederation and Olympic Committee, responsible for choosing which athletes went to the Olympics. The Olympics were controlled by the International Olympic Committee and their regulations basically followed the IAAF's.

The 800 meter is about the perfect balance between speed and endurance. You have to run at your almost top speed, ignore the urge to give everything too soon, hold back just enough so you have some energy to explode with near the end. It's about something else, too. Luck. On this particular day, I didn't have it.

In the beginning, I was a back to front runner. I'm a human being who likes their own space, even on the track. I preferred to be in the back, watching and waiting. I knew how to stalk my prey. Then near the end of the race, once I knew who the leaders were, I'd dig deep and do my best to outrun them. In this race, I didn't even get a chance to showcase my devastating kick, because I got spiked by another girl who was wearing track shoes. I was running barefoot.

Collisions happen, especially in the 800-m race, because runners don't have to stay in their lanes after the first turn. Instead, we all come together, everyone fighting for a good position, trying to stay close to the inside, avoid getting boxed in, all while running nearly as fast as humanly possible. People get elbowed, pushed, spiked, kicked—sometimes purposefully. The worst-intentioned would shove you in the back so you lost your rhythm, trip you or knock you in the ribs so they took your breath away. In the men's races, runners sometimes actually throw punches. People would be surprised how aggressive professional running can be; cameras don't capture it all because things are moving so quickly.

This girl had run over my foot, and her spikes had nearly ripped off my pinky toe. I knew it was an honest mistake; she didn't mean to hurt me.

It was over. I came in fifth and limped off the field trailing blood with every footstep.

That loss started a fire in me. I should have won that race. I only lost it because of that incident. I began training like a madwoman. I would miss my beloved soccer games, and I'd pass on just chilling with my boys in the bush. Boss had a friend named Ezekiel Ramahotsoa who worked in the athletics program at a neighboring school called Bakwena about 4 or 5 kilometers away. The school was bigger, and they had a gravel track. When their students would practice, I would join in. I'd run with both girls and boys. I had no coach of my own but I soaked up as much information as I could. I would go there and watch the other runners and imitate their training. Villagers would later recall to journalists that they'd see me training alone, running through the bush, running from village to village.

At this point, I was treating my own injuries. I didn't know anything about nutrition. I knew nothing except what I saw other runners doing and whatever information I could get from people I met in the running world. I had no fancy gym equipment, no nutritional supplements, no state-of-the-art running shoes, no orthopedic doctor and physical therapist at the ready to diagnose, treat, and massage injuries. Not even ice to put on sore muscles. Water was precious in our world. When you have to walk several kilometers to get it, you understand just how precious it is. My feet were constantly blistered, the flesh torn up from being punctured by thorns and other sharp objects. I learned from older runners how and when to drain the blisters and keep going. The goal was to build tough skin.

My grandmother was proud of me. She could see how serious I was about running. She saw my discipline and she loved the little medals and trophies I would bring home from my races. Even with all I had going on in athletics, my grandmother still hadn't distributed the household chores between myself and my cousins. Everything was still on me. I'd wake up in the morning, prepare firewood, boil water, make breakfast, go to school, come home, cook, clean, wash, iron. I was the girl, and that was it. It felt unfair. The boys didn't do shit. I consoled myself by kicking their ass on the soccer pitch. I prayed one day someone would see me run and win and this would get me a scholarship.

When the holiday break was over, I returned to Nthema Secondary School and went straight to my principal, Mr. Modiba. "I'd like to sign up for another year of athletics."

Everyone at our school, students and even teachers, called our principal Mr. Perhaps. Along with being the top school official, he taught us English, and his favorite word was "perhaps." He would say "perhaps" a million times a day. Our principal was a good man. He was one of those people who truly cared. I could already tell by the look on his face that whatever he had to say wasn't good.

Money is scarce in rural villages. Our school did what it could for its students, but the administrators were always juggling the little money they had for us. Things would change every year as funding would come and go.

"MOKGADI, we don't really have any runners here. You're the only one. We don't have any funds this year and we are ending the program. I am sorry."

I couldn't accept it. "Sir, I know I can do this. I just need a chance."

"I know. I'll see what I can do for you, but there are no resources. Perhaps, during your breaks, you can go practice at the other school as long as you keep up with your classes."

Mr. Modiba was as good as his word and would even give me rides when he could. I have always appreciated the way he took the time to help me. Boss and Ezekiel were always there for me, too, encouraging me, and teaching me more and more about runners. To this day, I consider them pillars of my career. These men treated me like a daughter, like one of their own family members. Sometimes even giving me a few rand for food.

I was running in as many races as I could get to and now training at a third school, Bakwena High School, about 5 kilometers away from mine. I'd become popular with everyone in the youth running circuit within a short period of time. The teachers at this school could see I was talented and dedicated. They could also see I didn't have much of anything except my will to get there and run.

I'd just finished my warm-up before a practice race at the school. Occasionally, I'd joke around with the other kids, but I spent my time mostly alone, happy to be in the company of other young athletes. I saw a man walking toward me. I recognized him as one of the schools' administrators.

"Hello, Ms. Semenya. I hear you are a very good runner. It looks like you'll be needing these." He was holding a pair of running spikes. The spikes weren't new, but they were new to me. I'd never owned a pair.

I felt so grateful. I thanked him and he walked away. I don't know how he knew my size, but they fit perfectly. The moment I put those spikes on, I felt like I had turned professional. To be allowed to use such a big resource like a pair of running shoes meant others believed I was going places. I put those shoes on and did a few run-ups. It was a relief to know that I didn't have to think about rocks or thorns. My feet would be protected, even from other runners.

That day, I felt like I floated to the finish line. I won my 800-m race, and then I sat and immediately took off the spikes. I remember I held the shoes, touched the metal bits on the bottom, and marveled at this piece of equipment. I carefully wiped them with what was left of my drinking water and my sweat rag. I made sure they were completely clean and then I found the school administrator.

"Thank you so much for letting me use them. I appreciate this very much," I said as I handed the shoes back to him.

The administrator looked at me and smiled. "Ms. Semenya, no need. Please." He held his hands up. "They are yours. They are a gift from us to you."

I heard him, but I was overcome with emotion. I don't know if he could see it on my face. I stood there holding the shoes without saying anything for what felt like forever. Finally, all I could say was, "Are you sure?" The man just smiled and put his hand on my shoulder and assured me they were mine to keep. I asked if he was sure several more times. I remember my spirit felt lifted. I was being seen.

That moment has never left me. That little girl who stood there astonished at the gift of a pair of secondhand shoes is still the person I am today. Grateful for everything I have.

From that day on, I used those spikes for every training run, for every race. All athletes are a little superstitious. They were my lucky spikes. They made me feel like I was going to take over the world. I know I could have continued running and winning barefoot, too, but I didn't have to anymore.

I eventually qualified to run in a national youth race. I would be representing the Limpopo province against the best youth from all over the country. I ended up with a silver medal in the 800 meters. It was the first time anyone from my province had won a medal at a national event. The girl who beat me came from a province called Mpumalanga, which is not far from Limpopo. She was a very experienced runner, and her win was expected. I was proud of my performance.

After this, it seemed like everyone started talking about me, the girl who was running on another level. People would call my name in the stands or crowd around me after a race. If a girl like me, who did not even have a real coach, could win a silver medal at a national, I could do more. I made it my business to go up to running officials and sports coordinators in Limpopo before and after races to introduce myself and ask questions. I'd ask everything from how the running system worked, how fast I needed to run to qualify for higher level events, and where the next race would take place. I didn't have the internet in those days. There was no Facebook or social media to rely on for information. I knew these were the people who could see me run and help me one day get a scholarship. Like my father used to say to me, "If you don't ask, you won't know and you won't get."

I understood now that if I was going to make it in the running world, I had to give up everything else. Professional runners are professional runners. You had to focus on it to the exclusion of all else. So, I decided to give up all other sports, including my beloved soccer. On the soccer pitch, I was a defender, a striker, a prized penalty kicker. My teammates were pissed and disappointed, and they had no problem letting me know. They were about to lose a big piece of their game.

"What do you mean, you are now only a runner?" my friend Tumelo asked.

"Running for what?" my other friend Ewe asked with a puzzled look on his face. "What is the purpose of this running? You're not even chasing anything . . ." Then he acted like he was running and out of breath and bent over laughing.

Even my cousins piled on. "Caster's going to be a famous runner now," Salvation yelled to the other kids in the yard during our lunch break. There would be more laughing, and my friends would come and jostle me. They'd go on and on about how athletics was a waste of my time.

They were all good soccer players, but they knew they weren't great. And most of them were playing for fun, they weren't dreaming of getting on airplanes and being a professional athlete like I was. "Doesn't matter what you say. You can't understand," I'd say to them. "I can see light with my running. All of you are here just chasing a ball around a field. Where's that going to take you?"

I had to be as harsh with them as they were being with me. I wanted to live in a proper city, travel the world, be known and appreciated for my talents. And I was doing something toward these goals each and every day.

I qualified to represent South Africa at a racing event in the neighboring country of Botswana. I called my mom; she was surprised at the news. It wasn't that my family didn't know I was running, but they didn't think that it was a very serious thing. This would be my first trip out of the country, about a seven-hour bus drive. Aside from my father, who had visited several countries in Africa as part of our church's congregation, no one in my family had ever left South Africa.

I didn't do well in the event. I came in fourth and to this day, I don't know what happened except to say I couldn't find the zone. I didn't yet understand that racing wasn't just about being fast, it was also about strategizing and quieting the mind. I was used to running alone, my only company at times just cows and sheep and goats. I was used to running in South Africa. I couldn't yet control my nerves. I resolved to learn and never lose again.

Right after Botswana, I won a silver medal at the 2007 Confederation of School Sport Associations of Southern Africa championships, and I was approached by the Moletjie Athletics Club. I was sixteen years old. The club was run by two men, Jeremiah Mokaba and Phineas Sako. They said they'd been hearing about me and had seen me run. They believed they could help me run better and put me in front of good people who could help me with schooling and supplies in the future. It was a big deal to be asked to join an organized professional running club like Moletjie—only the runners with true potential were asked. Most importantly, they were affiliated with Athletics South Africa. The only problem was that since I would no longer be running as a student, I wouldn't have access to free bus rides, so the traveling expenses and member dues would have to be covered by my grandmother.

When I was racing against kids from other schools, transportation to these competitions was free, so I didn't need money from my family to participate. We'd just get on a bus the school secured for the students. I had no money for snacks when the bus would make a stop at a petrol station. Some of the other kids did. They'd buy chips, soda, juice, or kota bread with all the fillings. If they offered to share, I'd take something, but I was usually anxious and rarely felt hunger before races. I was usually starving after the races, but it was fine. I knew I was going straight back to my grandmother's home to cook for all of us.

I told my grandmother about this, but she didn't immediately agree.

She knew I was running and winning medals, but this was different. This required us to put money out, and we had very little of that. Given my history of mischievousness, I think my grandmother may have assumed I was being a sneaky teenager and lying about the opportunity to join a running club just to get a few extra rand out of her.

My grandmother was a pensioner; she had stopped working long ago. Salvation and Ernest were just kids, and Kgabo had his own family and situation to deal with. We had enough to eat but nothing more. This was a big decision for her. My parents gave me what they could when I visited home, but they too had just enough to maintain the household. I'd taken to saving the few rand my mother would give me so that I could buy supplies, but it was not enough to pay my way to these high-level races. Transportation would cost around R50 per trip, almost 2 dollars at that time.

Mokaba and Sako offered to come see my grandmother in person and explain things to her. I remember she told me she was surprised when these two men showed up. They sat in our living room and talked over tea. I was visiting my family that day, so I wasn't there.

"If she tries her best, and we have seen that she does that every time, there will be men with big bellies who can help her get a scholarship to a university," Sako told my grandmother. "She will be getting an education while running. And then she can begin to win good money to help the family."

The meeting worked. My grandmother understood that if these men were willing to visit her home and sit with her, then this was a real opportunity. Granny would later tell journalists that she oftentimes borrowed money from friends and relatives to give me for transportation.

Now, for the first time I would have people who were only focused on running and could help me develop and get me to the races that mattered. I ran everything, even the longer distances in the cross-country season. The first year, I qualified for the nationals in the 4-km distance but I didn't do well—I was ranked thirty-four in the country. It did not matter; I didn't let it get me down. I knew what kind of runner I was—I was a pure middle-distance runner.

The 800 and 1500 meters, specifically. At these distances, several things matter at the same time—speed, endurance, strength, and power. I'd been a hunter so I knew about patience, I could endure the many kilometers it took to stalk your prey; my baseball, soccer, and basketball playing had developed my explosive speed and strength and power. I had big lungs and could control my breathing. Longer distances I could use for training.

"YOU NEED TO OPEN a bank account, Mokgadi," my grandmother said one day after I'd won another race.

"What am I going to put in it, grandmother? The medals?" I wasn't winning any money as a youth, and the medals themselves meant everything to me but they weren't things we could sell, not that I ever would have sold them.

"These medals, they symbolize your future wealth. I am telling you, Mokgadi, one day, they will turn into money that you can put it in the bank," she said.

One day, I thought, but actual money in a bank still seemed a long way off. What was important was that my grandmother believed in me. Granny never made my cousins help me with the cooking and cleaning, but she saw a future where I would no longer have to do those chores. I can still see her face, her big smile, every time she handed me the rand I needed for transport to a race. "I know you will win, Mokgadi," she'd always say, her eyes full of hope.

Chapter 9

ON THE WAY UP

M Y WINNING BROUGHT MORE SCRUTINY AND
questions about my body and gender. Sako and Mokaba
would later tell journalists that other coaches would approach
them and ask if I was really a girl. They would confirm that I was.
Most people let it go, but the discussions always continued. Other
runners would whisper about me. Some took issue with my running style; that I seemed too powerful, too masculine. Even if I
wasn't the fastest. Like I said, I knew how to shut down rumors—
all I had to do was confront it straight on. Confront and shower.

There was another major issue that I would soon encounter.
Race. I knew something about "the Struggle," as South Africans refer to the apartheid period. My father would sometimes
talk about when they couldn't go into certain towns or cities, the
humiliation of not being able to use public toilets or eat in certain
restaurants. I was born in 1991, the year that the IAAF allowed
South African athletes to rejoin international competitions after
the fall of apartheid. I was born what is called free. Racism, the
actual act of it, is something I hadn't directly experienced. There
were no White people in my village or in Fairlie. I would see them
from time to time, they'd come with equipment to dig boreholes in
the bush or set up electrical grids. Sometimes, they'd be roaming
around our village buying cattle and sheep. But I'd never lived with
a White person or had a real conversation with one. I rarely had
the opportunity to come into direct contact with them. I understood that White people lived in the cities. But once you are traveling around the running circuits, everyone is there.

When I arrived at the facilities for the cross-country 4-km junior nationals, I went to look at the room list to see who I'd be sharing a room with. I saw the name of an Afrikaner girl. We weren't friends, but I knew who she was. I looked around for her. She was standing with her mother, also reading the room list. She looked at her mother and mouthed some words and then she motioned toward me with her head. I remember how her mother looked at me. I could tell, instantly, there was a problem. I watched as her mother went over to the registrant. They ended up paying for a separate room, and I had the room to myself for the event.

Was it because I was a Black girl? Was it that I looked like a boy? Either way, it did not hurt my feelings. They had the money to pay for a separate room so the White girl did not have to share one with me. What did it matter? I liked having my own space anyway.

My father would always tell me, "Mokgadi, a White man will always be a White man." As I got older and came into contact with more people from around the world, I would tell him that the world had changed. That there were plenty of good White people, that Mandela had helped change our world and that things were moving forward. And my father would just repeat himself, "Maybe so, my child. But you must never forget. A White man will always be a White man."

White man or woman or whatever, I won the race. And with the national cross-country 4-km title, I now qualified to attend the World Junior Championships, which would be held in Poland that July of 2008.

The only way I could get to Poland was on an airplane. This was it. The dream I had, the dream I held so close to my heart, was within my grasp.

Attlee Maponyane, who was the president of Limpopo Athletics and also a vice president at ASA, drove me and a few other runners to an athletic store near a mall in Polokwane. I made sure to ask lots of questions in the car with him.

"Sir, so if I win this one, how soon do I get to the Olympics?"

Some of the other kids laughed. I was only half joking, but I could see the way he looked at me in the car's rear-view mirror. He was impressed.

"Well see, Mokgadi. If you win this one, there are a few more before you get to the Olympics, but I like the way you are thinking. You have the fire in you."

I could tell Maponyane liked me.

This was the first time I'd ever been to a shopping mall, the first time I'd even seen or been in an athletics-wear store. The store manager was sponsoring the athletes who were heading to the World Junior Championships. I'd never owned anything close to brand-new sports attire. They gave us a pair of sneakers, a pair of new track spikes, and a white and blue track suit. I was on top of the world.

The Moletjie Athletics Club was too far for me to train with them on a consistent basis. The majority of the time I was alone, training alone, implementing whatever I learned on my own. We would get in contact only when we were approaching a specific competition they thought I should run in. Then I'd find a way to meet them and I'd train with the other runners in the club.

One of our training sessions to prepare for my trip to Poland was held at the University of Pretoria, about 400 kilometers away from my grandmother's village. It was a four-hour bus ride. Pretoria was a proper city, one that people like me dreamed of living in. My father worked in the city as a municipal gardener, but I'd never visited before. This would also be my first time seeing what a university looked like.

The University of Pretoria's grounds were beautiful. Bigger than I'd imagined—well-kept trees were spread around the manicured lawns. They had a stadium, cricket field, soccer field, rugby field, tennis courts, and even swimming pools. Student housing surrounded the university, and there was a place inside the grounds called the HPC—the High Performance Centre—which housed athletes visiting from all over the world. The University of Pretoria had been a segregated institution, with an exclusively White student body. From 1982 to 2008, as South Africa charged into democracy after the fall of apartheid, the university transformed itself into a multiracial, multilingual, fully integrated institution.

We were stretching and moving around on the grass surrounded by the track when I noticed an older Black man with a stopwatch in hand standing next to an orange plastic chair placed just inside the track's inner edge. He barely moved from his spot. He just stood there, clicking the stopwatch, blowing the whistle hanging around his neck, occasionally saying a word or two to his athletes. He'd look over at me every now and then. He never raised his voice.

I knew who he was. I'd seen him once the year before at a cross-country competition, and people talked about him. His name was Michael Seme. He was a Zulu man from Soweto, well known for helping runners achieve their maximum potential. He was kind of like the Mr. Miyagi of running, and he had a long list of accomplished athletes, including Stephen Mokoka, already an international long-distance champion.

I was lying on the grass when I heard his voice.

"Hello, there! Semenya, yes?" I turned my head and saw Seme wave and smile as he walked toward me. "I'm Michael Seme. I hear you are preparing for the World Junior Championships in Europe. I see you are a good runner. I can help make you great. Would you like to work with me?"

I looked at him. Part of me expected this, part of me couldn't believe it. "I know who you are, sir. I need a coach. And I have no doubts about myself being great. I would like to join you." Not one to waste time, I said what was on my mind. "If I join you, that means I would be a student at this university, yes? Then I would need a scholarship. I will run for you."

He asked me what school year I was in, and when I told him I was in my last year of high school, Seme said all I needed to do was graduate and he would do his best to get me in the school on a scholarship.

And that was the problem.

I had become a better student after I moved to my grand-mother's village. I went to school every day. It was better for me to be in school than to be in the house doing chores. I was enjoying the lessons, but as I took running more seriously, I couldn't keep my grades up. Where I'd previously been an average student with average grades, now I was barely passing. More like failing.

My principal had tried to talk some sense into me when they saw my grades slipping. "Perhaps less training and racing and more studying, Caster," he said. But I didn't want to listen.

"Look, none of you can give me an opportunity to travel the world. None of you can buy me a ticket to Europe or Asia. Just let me be me. If the running doesn't work, it doesn't work."

"Your education has to be priority, Mokgadi. It doesn't matter how well you run anyway, you cannot get a scholarship to a university and bigger opportunities if you don't matriculate," my principal said.

And he was right. I could spend all the time I wanted training and racing, but if I didn't have the marks to graduate from high school, a real university with a sports bursary and a proper system would never be a reality. I could never attend the University of Pretoria and train with Michael Seme without getting through high school.

I knew I had to dedicate myself to my studies, but first, I had to go to the World Junior Championships in Poland and win.

This would be my first time on an airplane. My family couldn't believe it. They didn't understand how it was possible their young daughter was now heading overseas. They were happy, of course, but probably more surprised that my running had progressed to this point. It wasn't like I was telling my parents or siblings everything I was doing. Life was busy for everybody.

I don't remember much about the flight to Poland that July. It felt like just getting on a giant bus to me. The plane had a layover in France. When the team went through customs to board the next flight to Poland, the customs officer opened my bag and confiscated my cologne, toothpaste, and lotion. I had dipped into my meager savings to pay for them, and that bottle of cologne was the most expensive purchase I'd ever made. I asked the officer what they were going to do with my things, and they said they were going to throw them away.

"Ok. Give me my things. I'll break them and throw them away myself." The officer looked at me like I was crazy as did everyone else on the line. But if my things were going to be thrown away, then my adolescent mind felt it should be done by their owner. I stood there and broke the bottle of cologne, emptied the lotion and squeezed the toothpaste out of the tube, and put them in the dustbin.

I arrived in Poland completely focused on winning. I was not going to repeat the same mistake I'd made in Botswana. Normally, I don't care to think about any other runners. To me, they didn't exist. The only person who mattered was me. I was fearless when it came to competition, but the truth is there was a runner who scared me, one runner out there who could ruin any chance I had. Phineas and Sako would mention her from time to time.

Her name was Pamela Jelimo and she was from Kenya.

This girl had already clocked a 1:54 in an official 800-m race that same year and had set various records in the 400 meter. Everyone thought she was going to break the 800-m world record of 1:53:28, set by the Czech Republic's Jarmila Kratochvilová, unbroken since 1983. Jelimo was the entire game at that point in middle-distance athletics.

"How in the hell?" I remember thinking. I could not even imagine what it was like to run a 1:54. My fastest time at that point was like 2:08. If we were to run together, the time gap would look like she would cross the finish line when I was only halfway through the race. Just the thought of lining up with Jelimo made me sweat.

Thankfully, I needn't have worried about Jelimo. By the time, I got to Poland, Jelimo no longer needed to play with kids. She was nineteen years old, and given her speed and age, her people had decided she would go pro. Her time was better spent preparing for the August 2008 Beijing Olympics, where she would go on to win gold in the 800 meter.

This was my first IAAF-sponsored World Junior Championships. I was coming in at a disadvantage. My injuries weren't properly treated. I couldn't afford any outside professional care. I was taping myself, bursting my own blisters, trying to figure out the best way to stretch pained muscles. I had never had the benefits of regular healthcare. Here, I got a taste of what professional athletes were offered in terms of meals and medical treatments in the Western world. Physiotherapy was available free of charge to all the participants and I, of course, wanted some of this modern treatment. I told the therapist I was suffering with shin splints, and they went to work on me.

Unfortunately, I was in more pain after the therapy than before it. When I got to the track to run in the first heats, the pain was almost unbearable. I lined up with the rest of the girls, and I felt like a baby. Even though we were all juniors, everyone there was taller and looked much older than me. These girls had already been running in the junior international circuits, and it showed. Halfway through the race, I tripped on the track's inner border lip and almost fell. I came in seventh and ran a 2:11:00. Not bad for a seventeen-year-old at her first international event, but nowhere near what I needed to move on to the final for a chance to win a medal. The runners here were two years older than me and running 2:06 and 2:08s just in the heat, and they could go faster than that.

I knew I was as good as or even better than the rest of the field. I just needed the right conditions. I got another chance when I qualified for the 2008 Commonwealth Youth Games in India that October. These games were held every four years, almost like the equivalent of the Olympics for youths, except you could only go there once or twice since the age range was only fourteen to eighteen years old. I had three months to prepare, and I knew I would perform better because I was now training with other experienced athletes, and I had Sako and Phineas to show me the way.

When I got back to South Africa, I remember telling my cousins and friends, "See? You said I was running for nothing. I have already boarded a plane. I went all the way to Poland. I touched down in Europe. Now I am going on another plane soon. I am going to the Commonwealth Youth Games in India. This is how I will be signing my name in the future . . ." and I started signing my name in my notebook for them.

"Yeah, well, you didn't win, Caster," my friend Commy said. But I could see how happy he was for me.

"That's OK. I'll win in India." I grabbed his notebook and signed my name on a blank page. "Keep this in a safe place, my man. That's going to be worth a lot of money one day."

"Sign your name on my paper, too," my friend Lethabo said, "I don't want to take any chances and miss out on some money in the future."

My friends laughed but I knew they were proud of me.

I WENT TO THE Commonwealth Youth Games in India and I won the gold medal. My time was 2:04.23. Just like Boss had foretold, I beat the great Kenyans and I also beat a girl who, many years later, had much to say about me. Her name was Lynsey Sharp, a British runner. I didn't really pay any attention to her. She came in third at these games with a time of 2:06. She wasn't my target. I was preoccupied with the Kenyans, of course. But I think this Commonwealth Youth Games is where Lynsey Sharp began to have an issue with me.

At the 2016 Olympics, Lynsey came under criticism for her poor sportsmanship when she ignored my attempt to acknowledge and congratulate her after we ran the 800 meters. I won gold and Lynsey came in sixth place. The way she behaved was disgraceful. Lynsey had beaten me several times after India and before the Olympics.

After she was criticized for her behavior, Lynsey tried to clean it up by saying she had tremendous respect for me and that we talked regularly on the circuit. Neither of this is true. She always looked at me as if I was less than human. And we never did any regular talking on the circuit. Lynsey's a good runner; she would have been even better if she had just bit her tongue and trained.

WE HAD BEEN GIVEN around 800 American dollars as pocket money when we went to India. I returned to South Africa with every single dollar. I never spent a cent of it. I ate what was offered, trained, and otherwise stayed in my room the entire time. As soon as I got back to school, I pulled out the entire stack of cash and was showing it off to my boys.

"Hey, my friends, what do you call this? These here are Benjamins. These are not rand. This is what I get when I run. Now who is chasing nothing? Who is chasing dreams?" I made sure to spread it out like a fan in my hand so they could see each crisp $100 dollar bill. I felt like Rick Ross making it rain.

I had some plans with that cash, some things I wanted to buy. But instead, I helped my mom pay off some debts. It felt right to do that. After all, I did say I would be the one carrying the household one day. I was happy this was already happening.

Now, all I had left to do was pass my final exams and get into the University of Pretoria on a scholarship. My teachers had allowed me to delay my exams until after I returned from India. They all knew about Michael Seme's offer. I had neglected my studies so much my teachers and the principal were worried I wasn't going to make it.

I wasn't worried at all. My view was that if I didn't graduate, I would just repeat my grade. I would take a break from running in official races, continue to train, focus on my studies, and come back to Michael with grades that would get me a scholarship. I would not be the first or the last student to have to repeat a grade.

Unlike many others, though, I had a good reason—I had won a gold medal at an international competition. The Commonwealth Youth Games, like the World Championships in Poland, were IAAF-sanctioned events. These were the big leagues. People knew my name now. I was officially in the record books. In my mind, I was well on my way to being a professional runner.

Chapter 10

A HIGHER EDUCATION

PASSED. MY GRADES WEREN'T GREAT, BUT I CALLED Seme at the university and told him.

"Ah! Mokgadi. Congratulations. You will need to fax me your school transcripts. I will apply for you here and let you know what happens."

A few weeks later, it was official. I was accepted to the University of Pretoria with a scholarship. If things went as planned, I'd be graduating with a one-year diploma in sports science. I would get to study so that one day, when running was over, I would have the credentials to get a good job. The scholarship covered school fees and accommodations. Seme would help me enroll in an additional program that paid for the things athletes needed, like food and health insurance. Student athletes in South Africa were allowed to make money while studying, so I could run in any race I was invited to or qualified for and keep my prize money.

I would have a real coach, someone I would see every day who cared about my progress, in a professional running system. I would learn about the kind of nutrition that was best for athletes, and my injuries would be treated by experts. I would have access to a state-of-the-art gym. And I didn't have to worry about that thing that had burned me for so long—watching my cousins Salvation and Ernest just live their lives while I slaved over the household. I would now live at the university; I didn't have to balance training with my obligations at home. No more being the first to wake up to fetch water and firewood and cook and clean and launder and iron clothes.

Before I left for the city of Pretoria, I went back to my birth village of Ga-Masehlong, back to my parents' house. I knew this would be the last time I'd see my family in a long time. It was early 2009. Both of my parents and my siblings and nieces were there to see me off. They knew I was on the path I had seen for myself.

I was eighteen years old and full of the blind hopefulness, bravery, and certainty about the future only a young person can have. There were no tears from me. I don't cry. I do a lot of things to show how I'm feeling. Crying is not one of them. As I write this, I am thirty-two years old, and I can count on one hand how many times I've cried. I cry at death, because when someone dies, that is something we cannot know.

My mother hugged me for a long time. She looked at me like she always did, with the deep knowing only a mother has.

"Take care of yourself. Don't worry about anything or anyone. Your home will always be here. You will always be loved here. Don't stay away for too long."

I wondered, years later, if my mother knew what would happen, in the way that only mothers know about their children. I don't mean that she knew what would happen, exactly. My parents, such as they were, what knowledge they had about the world, could never imagine it. How the world would consume me, how perfect strangers would treat my body like a science experiment. They had no idea that whatever was going on with me was a "medical issue" to the outside world, or that what should have been my private business would be used to continue a public conversation about gender and biological sex that the world had been having for thousands of years.

I wondered if maybe my mom and dad felt that my being a different kind of girl would make me a target outside of Limpopo. I showed myself to be a fearless kid in the villages, but my parents knew a little more about the world than I did. When you are older, you have more knowledge, about the past, about the way people had been and the way people can be. They remembered the times our people, Black people, weren't free.

I WALKED OUT of my first home and sat with our animals for a while. It had been almost six years since I'd really taken care of them. Some had died, some had been born while I was living in Fairlie. I took in the sight of everything—our home that always felt like it was falling apart and yet still stood strong. Our small patch of land where we grew just enough fruits and vegetables to sustain us. I closed my eyes and listened to the kwaito music that was always playing from somewhere, and I saw myself once again as a toddler running and falling and flying. I saw myself being chased by my sisters.

Before leaving, I spent some time with my childhood cousins and friends—the first boys I'd loved, the ones who taught me to hunt and swim and who accepted me as one of them. Some of those loves would stay in our village for the rest of their lives and others would, like me, go out and try to find something else. I'm not judging those who stayed or those who could not leave. I try never to judge. That's what our Christian religion says and yet so many people forget that basic rule—do not judge others.

"Have time for a game, Mokgadi?" one of my cousins said.

"Why not? I could kick your ass again."

A small crowd of villagers gathered around us. They shouted "Mokgadi! Mokgadi! Mokgadi!" like they had done when I was a kid. Maybe a few placed bets. They knew I was a sure thing. Even though I'd stopped playing organized soccer games a couple of years before, there was still no one who could handle this girl.

I traveled the next morning to my see my maternal grandmother. This is the grandmother I am named after. It is our custom that when we are to embark on a long journey, we must seek the blessing of our living elders as well as our ancestors. My grandmother and I prayed together. I could feel the joy, anticipation, anxiety, and hopes of my family. I was carrying the dreams of our people.

I ARRIVED AT the University of Pretoria at the beginning of February 2009. I had turned eighteen in January. The school didn't have a dorm room ready for me, so I moved in with Michael Seme, my new coach. There was another girl—Miriam, a runner from Malawi—living with Seme when I arrived. She was also waiting for her dorm room. We ate whatever Seme had available and cooked together and talked about running and life. It felt good. I was comfortable.

At this point in my life, the fastest I'd ever run an 800-m distance was 2:04. In order to be considered a top prospect and qualify or be invited to senior-level events, I would have to run much faster than that. Michael and I got started on my technique right away.

And here is what made Seme an excellent coach. He knew I had been coaching myself. He first wanted to understand what I had been doing, mostly on my own, to bring me to the point where he would notice me. And I told him. I was doing the things I'd seen athletes at bigger schools with actual tracks do. I told him I would run by myself when I wasn't taking care of my family home. I remember Seme nodded and then just added to the foundation I'd laid for myself. He found my running form to be too loose, he felt I swung my arms too much and held my head too far back. He would eventually help me get to the form that made me a winner— arms locked in close to my body, chest high, head centered.

Seme was a coach who understood where you were. This is why, despite everything that came between us in the future, I will always say he is the best coach I've ever had. He became like a father to me. Seme knew when to push and when we needed to rest. To be with him was to know he believed you were gifted and could make your talent shine. His gift as a coach was making his athletes feel seen and understood. When you were with Seme, you were the only person who mattered, and he could make an entire group of athletes feel like this.

And we were truly a talented group of runners. My main training partner was a runner named Stephen Mokoka, an accomplished long-distance runner who has represented South Africa in World Championships and the Olympics. There was Shinle Ziqe, also from South Africa, who eventually became my roommate; Miriam, the young girl from Malawi and her fellow countryman Mike Tebulo; and a Ugandan runner named Daniel. Coach Seme knew how to put together runners who would both challenge and strengthen each other's weaknesses. We had incredible chemistry.

In the running world, elite women runners often run with men. That's normal. I've never been faster than an actual male athlete, not even close, but the idea is to run with someone who will give you a hard time. Seme paired me with Mokoka because together we were what the other needed. I was a middle-distance runner who needed endurance, and Mokoka was a long-distance runner who needed speed. Seme knew I had speed, but I just couldn't maintain it. I would run the first 400 meters well, and then lose steam in the second 400 meters, and the girls at the school would constantly beat me. Seme had us start a training session every morning at 5 a.m., and then we'd go to classes and have a second training session at 4 p.m. I was getting frustrated about my constantly losing to the other girls at the school, so Coach had me go up and down this steep hill that surrounded the track. Up and down, up and down I went until my legs burned past the point of pain and I couldn't breathe at all. As I got stronger, going up and down the hill became easier until it felt effortless. It would eventually come to be called Caster's Hill.

SEME CARED ABOUT his athletes, but he also liked money. Every race that had money attached to it meant our coaches also made money. A coach would take a percentage of what an athlete earned at the end of the year. When there was money available, Seme looked like one of those cartoon characters where the eyes would roll with dollar signs or his face turned into one of those casino slots machines. CHA-CHING $$$$. If there was a race that paid, Seme would make sure we were there.

The money was in the Yellow Pages race series, and the most important thing about the Yellow Pages series was that ASA used the qualifying times at these races to create South Africa's national team. The first Yellow Pages I ran as an official University of Pretoria student was in Stellenbosch on February 23, about three weeks after arriving at the school. I won the race in 2:03. It was good, not anything stellar, but it was a solid run.

I spent my days training and getting acclimated to living in a bustling metropolis, a world that was very far from the small village surrounded by wilderness I'd come from. I remember one of the first things the university did was to have the new students take a tour of the city. Our guide was a senior student who showed us the places where just a few years before Blacks would not be welcomed. I looked at the public parks and bathrooms, the stores, the museums, and marveled that I had made it all the way there.

I began to see more of the runner I'd met a few years prior. Violet: the senior runner who'd mistaken me for a boy in the women's facility at a cross-country race back in 2006. I'd seen her once in 2007 and then I saw her at a couple of regional races in 2008. Each time, we'd say hello and move on. But now Violet had begun coming to Pretoria on the weekends to train with Seme and became part of our group. We'd spend time together and began a real friendship. Violet had been nursing an injury, but at only twenty-three years old, she was still young and considered a top-five prospect in the 8- and 10-km cross-country circuit. She'd already represented South Africa at the World Athletics Cross Country Championships in 2005, 2006, and 2007. She was living and working in Soweto and was in a relationship with a guy who lived there.

Because she was from Limpopo, being able to spend time with her made me feel less homesick.

I was also friendly with the other students—not friends, just friendly. My focus was not on making friends—it was on running. I had been warned about how people changed when they got to the cities. And they often changed for the worse.

Pretoria provided plenty of distractions—there was access to everything at any time. Boss had warned me about this. My parents, too. You could easily fall in with the wrong crowd. There were too many stories of promising athletes who ended up in a bad way—drugs, alcohol, partying too much. I only wanted to run and win. As far as these things went, I was innocent. There was nothing worse than alcohol and weed where I came from, and both of those were bad enough to end an athlete's career.

I knew from what happened to my father and what I'd seen on television that a career in sports didn't last forever. Athletes have a small window of time to work with their body. And injuries don't care whether you are young or old. The important thing was that if running didn't work out for me, I would at least have a diploma from a respected university that would help me get a job. That would be my future, I decided, but for now, I had to get faster.

Everyone wanted to get faster. And that could become a problem. I remembered how Boss would tell me about great runners that sometimes turned to dangerous things.

"Mokgadi, as other people smell your success, they will come to you. Offer you things to eat and drink. These things are not right." He would tell me stories of athletes like the sprinter Ben Johnson and his fall from grace. The way Boss put it, being a clean athlete was everything. He told me not to trust people. To stay humble.

So, I was prepared when an older man approached me one day outside of the university. I was walking back to my quarters. He was standing in front of a nice car; he was dressed well.

"Hello! Hello! Hello! Ms. Semenya. . . . Hello! I hear you are a new student. A very good runner, yes? Maybe I can interest you in some vitamins. Some very special vitamins . . ."

"Vitamins, eh?" I replied. I had no idea who this man was but he already knew my name. And I already knew exactly what kind of vitamins he was offering me. The kind that would make me fail a piss test.

"Yeeeessss." He sounded like he was hissing. "These vitamins are very good for the body. I also have nutritional supplements you can put in your water or milk. Also, good for the body. They will help you be your best."

"I see. . . ." I remember I furrowed my brow and bit my lip like I was really thinking about it. "Well, I don't have any money to pay for vitamins and supplements. They are giving me free food at the cafeteria so I'll get my vitamins from there, chief. Have a good day." And I walked away. He'd just have to try elsewhere. I was a clean athlete.

The weekend after I ran in Stellenbosch, I entered another Yellow Pages series race, this one in Germiston. I won the 800-m event in 2 minutes flat. I knew that one day I would run faster than my personal best (PB) of 2:04, but I didn't think I would hit the 2-minute mark so quickly after I began working with Seme. With just one officially certified 2-minute run on the books, my life began to change.

The day after my win, Michael said he needed to talk to me about something important. And that something important was money.

"Caster. I am your coach. My job is to condition your body and help make you great. You see how you ran the 2 minutes. You will get even faster. So now you need someone to take care of your business. To bring you more opportunities. Things I cannot do for you."

"OK," I said. I knew what he meant. I knew the best athletes had sponsors, companies that paid them, and this could lead to many more opportunities like being the face of sports drink, shoe, and clothing brands.

"There's a man here who wants to meet you and make you an offer." Seme had that look in his eyes that I knew so well.

"Alright, if you say, I will meet him, Coach." Michael walked out of the room and came in a few minutes later with an older White man. He was a sports manager named David Oliver. He immediately pulled out an agent contract and made a big deal of gifting me a cellphone. It was one of those flip phones. I'd never had one before.

"Caster, we must sign this one, yes? And he will find opportunities out there for you. Big races are coming, you need someone to be ready," Seme said.

The truth is my heart wasn't into signing with this David Oliver, but Michael knew more about these things than I did. I signed, and now I had an agent and a cheap cellphone just in time for my next race. With the 2-minute run in Germiston, I had qualified to run in the South African Athletics Championships held in March at the Coetzenburg Stadium in Stellenbosch. This annual competition was organized by ASA, and it would be my first senior-level event.

At eighteen, I was still considered a junior runner, but I would finally get to see what it was like to run against more mature athletes and even meet the runners who would eventually make it on to the senior-level international stages where the real fame and fortune were.

I won the 800 meters with a time of 2:02. Seme had traveled with me, and he was so happy because I was getting faster. With this victory in a senior-level event, I was officially a professional runner. I was satisfied. I knew I was on my way. I had already earned a place in the African Junior Athletics Championship that would be held in July on the island of Mauritius, but now that I'd run with the older athletes, I knew I could hang with the big guys.

On our way back to Pretoria, Seme got a call from my new agent, David Oliver.

Seme had been smiling when he first answered, but he slowly stopped smiling as he listened to whatever David was saying on the other end.

"What's going on, Coach?"

When Seme got off the phone, he took a deep breath and then told me that David thought I ran the race "like shit" and that he couldn't get me any significant deals if I didn't get faster.

I knew exactly what I had to do. I told Seme to call David and tell him I was terminating our contract with immediate effect. I knew the paper I signed said I had thirty days to change my mind. It hadn't been thirty days yet. I had never tolerated disrespect. I wasn't going to start tolerating it now that I was a working athlete.

Seme asked me if I was sure.

"Coach, I want nothing to do with this man. I can tell he doesn't think I'm human. He thinks I'm a horse. Just an animal he can use to make money. Everything isn't about money. He's finished. Get him out of my life."

A few days after the incident with David Oliver, I was speaking with a middle-distance runner I greatly admired named Mbulaeni Mulaudzi. He'd also been a student at the University of Pretoria, and we had met a few times over the last couple of years while I was running in provincial and regional races. He'd taken a liking to me, and we understood each other because he, too, came from a rural village in the province of Limpopo.

By the time I arrived at the university in 2009, Mbulaeni Mulaudzi was a highly decorated athlete, already a world champion several times over and an Olympic silver medalist. He was quiet and incredibly focused, character traits I admired and aspired to. He listened to my story about David Oliver and told me that he would send his agent my way. He said this person would never hurt me or do anything to destroy my future. Mulaudzi said I needed a manager who was interested in building me as a human being and that this person was a man they called Madala. To us, "Madala" is an affectional term that means elder. His actual name was Jukka Harkonen, and he was a well-established Finnish sports manager. He had plenty of Olympic and world champions on his client list.

A few days later, we had a training camp at the university's

High Performance Centre. Jukka was there, and we officially met in person. I trusted my instincts about people—later I would learn I wasn't always right—but Jukka made me feel safe. He said he'd heard great things about me and that he would like to see how he could help me. He did not take out a contract and try to pressure me into hiring him as my representative. He said that he first wanted me to think about what I wanted in my life, what I wanted to achieve as an athlete, where I saw myself in the future, and that we would speak again soon. I knew I wanted to sign with him. Here was a man who never once mentioned money. To me, that was a real businessman. It wasn't that I didn't need money, because I did. But to this day, money doesn't drive me. Money isn't what pushes me to do this or that. It's always been about something deeper. For me, it was about dignity, about pride, about the respect I freely gave to others and expected back in return. I may have been a young girl from a rural area, but my parents taught me to value myself, to never think of myself as less than anyone else, regardless of my background or circumstances. And I feel like Jukka saw this in me and understood it. Jukka said he was going back to Finland, but he would be back at the university in about a month.

While Jukka was gone, Michael said there was another person he wanted me to meet, a man named Mr. Newton, a former sprinter. I told Michael that my heart was with Jukka and that I wanted to wait for him to return.

"There is no reason why not to meet with this person, Caster. You must see all of your options."

I remember on the day of the meeting, this Mr. Newton walked into the room dragging a fancy briefcase on wheels behind him. He was wearing a really nice suit, an expensive watch. Very clean cut. Everything about this man screamed money.

"Hello, Ms. Semenya. I hear you are a future star," he said while he put the briefcase on the table. Then all I heard was CLICK, CLICK . . . he opened the briefcase and gestured to it. I leaned forward a little from my chair and looked inside. There were a bunch of American dollars in there. I know how to count money. I've always been good with numbers. It looked to be anywhere between $10,000 and $20,000.

I was young and innocent of the world, but I wasn't naïve. Some man hanging around a university with a briefcase full of American dollars didn't seem right to me. Reminded me of the vitamin guy.

Seme was beaming, he was doing a little dance in his chair. "Caster! This is the one. This is the one right here! Look at that! US currency!! Yes!! Oh, yes!!"

Everybody went crazy for US currency. But not me.

"Look, sir. What are these American dollars for exactly? And when I spend these dollars here, you're going to give me more every month?"

Mr. Newton seemed disappointed I didn't immediately jump out of my chair and grab the money. It was as if he expected me to just faint or start crying and get down on my knees to thank him. When he started to speak, I said, "Better for us to speak again another time. Thank you for coming."

I left the room, and Michael came with me.

"Caster! What are you doing? You are walking away from all that money?"

"This man here is trying to buy me. That's not my money. That's his money he came in here with. The money I earn, with my work, belongs to me. I take that briefcase and then what, Seme? What do you think he's going to expect? You can tell Mr. Newton to take his dollars and shove them in his ass. That's not what I want."

Looking back on these moments in my life, I see that Seme just didn't know any better. He wasn't trying to hurt me; he just wanted me to take whatever was being offered. He knew where I came from, and he also knew these careers could be short. That briefcase full of dollars was real. In his mind, what if I never got the chance again?

Still, I did not care. I had this idea of what professionalism was.

And it wasn't being shown a briefcase full of money without even a proper introduction. I was offended. I was no drug dealer. I may not have had much, but I wasn't desperate. And I wasn't stupid. I knew my worth. If I could run 2 minutes, I could run faster, and be worth a lot more than what was in that briefcase.

A month later, just as he'd promised, Jukka returned to the university. I met with him, and he was holding two packets of paper, one in each hand.

"Caster, I hope you have thought about the things we discussed. I have two offers for you from two companies. Adidas is in my left hand and Nike is in my right hand. Take a look and let me know what you think."

Before Jukka could hand over the papers, I said, "I don't care what's inside those contracts. I'm going with Nike."

Nike. The only other South African athlete at the time who was signed to Nike was Oscar Pistorius. All the other athletes I knew had signed with Adidas.

"Nike. Are you sure? Look through them and see first."

"Nike," I said. "That's the one for me."

Today, I am still a Nike athlete. It was one of the best decisions I ever made.

It would just be me and Oscar Pistorius with Nike. And that felt good. I first met Oscar in 2008 when I was training for the World Junior Championships in Poland with the Moletjie Athletic Club. They had set up a training camp at the University of Pretoria.

I was stretching, running, and dreaming of winning when I saw him. At first, I couldn't believe it was actually the Blade Runner. South Africans loved Oscar. He was a hero. He had already won gold and silver medals at two Paralympics in 2004 and 2008 in the 100-m, 200-m, and 400-m events, and he was fighting the IAAF to allow him to run in the Beijing 2008 Olympics with able-bodied runners. The IAAF had banned people like Oscar from running with sports prosthetics because they considered it an unfair advantage. They set out to prove it by commissioning a study on Oscar in which he willingly participated. The IAAF then banned him from running based on the findings of the study they had paid for. Oscar appealed to the Court of Arbitration for Sport, which found the study was faulty and ruled in his favor.

I looked at the "maybe Oscar" and thought I had nothing to lose by going over and at least seeing if it was really him. If it was really him, I could just tell him how much I admired him.

When I got close enough, I waved and said hello. He looked at me, smiled, and said hello back. He seemed friendly enough, so I asked him if he was Oscar Pistorius.

"Yes. It's really me," he said laughing. I asked him where the blades were I saw him run with on television. He told me he only used those blades for racing and training. Not for regular walking. I talked to him about the races I'd seen him in. I could tell he was impressed that I knew so much.

"What's your name, little one?" Oscar asked.

I told him my name was Caster Semenya and that I was an athlete, too.

"I look up to you. And you must watch out for me because I have a great future. You will hear my name and, one day, I will be running in the Olympics with you," I said. I can still remember the look on Oscar's face. He liked my courage.

"Then it shall be so, little one. I will see you again one day." He shook my hand again and walked away. I stood there and watched him walk to the parking lot, get in his jeep and drive away.

I didn't own a cellphone then so I couldn't take a picture. It didn't matter to me. Just having a conversation with Oscar and being able to shake his hand meant more to me at the time than any picture of the moment ever could.

I ran into Oscar again on the same field the following year in 2009. This time, I was an official student. Even though I was still considered a junior runner, I had been given a spot on the national team that would soon take me to the World Championships in

Berlin. Oscar actually remembered me. This time, he walked up to me.

"Hey there, little one."

I smiled at him, I was what is called starstruck.

"So, it looks like you were right. I would be hearing your name. Caster Semenya." He smiled and held out his hand. I took his hand, and with that simple gesture we began an easy friendship that would last several years.

Oscar and I began to train together, we pushed each other, and gave each other advice. Not that long ago, Oscar and I could not even eat at the same restaurant, much less speak or train as equals on a running track. Here we were from completely different backgrounds. He was a middle-class Afrikaner boy from Johannesburg, and I was a Black girl from the most impoverished province in the country. Oscar was twenty-two years old when we met—barely an adult himself. We were linked by something that went beyond running. We were drawn to each other and found comfort in each other's presence. Maybe it was because of the way the world looked at us—our difference written on our bodies. Our conversations will stay with me and me alone. No one could foretell how our lives would eventually play out. Each of us would come to be seen as both heroes and villains, admired and scorned by the world.

Chapter 11

THE TROUBLES BEGIN

AUGUST 14, 2009. IT'S THE DAY BEFORE I AM TO leave for my first major international competition. The world championships. I am laying on my back, naked except for a hospital gown, my legs are in a pair of these metal things and splayed open. A doctor is looking at my private parts. I can't tell what he is thinking. His face is neutral.

I am fucking pissed, but not at him specifically. He is doing his job. And he is going about it in a professional way.

"Did you finish filling your eyes?" I asked him. "I told you; you will not find what you are looking for."

"I am sorry, Ms. Semenya. I truly am. It's just part of the process and I will soon be done," the doctor replied.

He was a nice man. Very respectful. I had never been to a gynecologist before. The only time I'd even seen the inside of a hospital was when I injured my leg as a seven-year-old. It was surreal to find myself in this position. I came from a deeply conservative community. I knew that people could be together, in the physical sense, before they were married, but we also believed the only person who should be looking at you down there was the one you chose to spend your life with.

I wasn't having a medical emergency. I was sent here for what I'd been told was a routine doping test. But I knew doping tests were done with syringes and plastic cups. This . . . this was clearly not a doping test.

So how did I get here?

EVERYTHING HAD BEEN going well for me. After a few months at the university, I'd started to make good on my promise of helping my family financially. Every cent I'd earned so far had been put away in a bank account I opened when I first arrived in Pretoria. I remember my parents asking me if I needed any money right before I left. I knew my family's situation—they had none to spare. Whatever money they gave me would mean they would go without a basic necessity. I thanked my parents and told them I would be sorted out as soon as I got to school. I have never wanted to be a burden on others; I have only wanted to make my own way in the world.

The last thing I said to my parents before I left was, "The next time you see your daughter, I will be a champion and I will help carry this home." I was sure of it. I believed in myself that much.

Since my housing and meals were covered by the university, I was able to use the money I'd earned from racing to help my family. My mother had purchased a refrigerator. We'd never owned one before. She couldn't pay for it outright so she put it on what we call "lay-by," where the store holds the appliance while the buyer makes small payments. I called my mom to tell her I'd started making a little money and would send what I could so they'd get the refrigerator sooner.

When the school break began in late June, I traveled back to Ga-Masehlong for a few days. I couldn't stay long because I had a Yellow Pages coming up and then the African Junior Championships were a few weeks after that. I would be heading to Mauritius in July to run both the 800 and 1500 meter. There, I would compete with the best young athletes from all over Africa.

I never told my family I'd also been given a spot on South Africa's national team and that I was going to Berlin soon after Mauritius. To me, Berlin was an animal to be dealt with at a later time. The African Juniors were for athletes aged nineteen and under; Berlin was the major leagues. I've always been the kind of person who likes to deal with what's right in front of me. I try not to worry about the future, about things I cannot control. This way of being is what I believe prepared me for what was to come.

I won gold in both races at the African Junior Champs. I ran the 1500-m race in 4:08:01—a personal best and a championship record. But it was what I accomplished in my favored distance, the 800 meters, that would eventually land me in a gynecologist's office at a private hospital in Pretoria and change my life. I won in 1:56:72. I'd never run so fast in my life. It was a personal best, a championship record, a national record, and a world-leading time that year in both the junior and senior levels. I remember I called Seme from my room, and he couldn't believe it. I told him I ran a 1:56 and he yelled, "A WHAT? A 2:06?" I repeated a 1:56, but his mind couldn't process it. "Ah! OK. Did you say a 1:58 or 1:59?" And I said, "No! A ONE. FIVE. SIX. Coach." Seme was quiet for a second and then started hooting.

What I remember clearly of this moment in my life was a feeling of inevitability. That everything I had worked hard for was about to come true. People in the South African athletic world were really talking about me now. I was the new kid on the block. I had thrown down a 1:56 at the age of eighteen. That was Pamela Jelimo level of speed. Even the seniors at the university would find the time to give me a word or two of encouragement when they saw me training or in the cafeteria.

The Berlin World Championships would take place two weeks after the African Champs. This was it. I was going to compete on the international stage. This would be the biggest race of my career. The gold medal came with a $60,000 cash prize. I don't know if I thought I was going to win so much as I believed I had earned my right to be there. But if I won that gold medal, or got anywhere near it, it would be the beginning of so much more in my career. I would get invited to even more lucrative races. I could be offered more sponsorships. And I knew my Nike contract came with incentives and performance bonuses. I could see my life as a famous athlete right in front of me.

The world championships are the premier IAAF event—more than two hundred countries send their best athletes. It is held every two years, and the lucky host country usually sells hundreds of thousands of in-person stadium tickets for the multiday event. Millions upon millions of people around the world watch the televised event. There's a lot of money and a lot of politics. I can't say I understood the magnitude of it at the time. I felt the same way in Berlin as I did when I competed in the Nationals and the African champs. For me, the biggest thing was having a spot on the national team. This eighteen-year-old girl would be among the best South African athletes, people I'd come to admire, like Mbulaemi Malaudzi, Godfrey Khotso Mokoena, Janice Joseph, Johan Cronje. For that short period of time, I would be one of them, sharing meals and asking them questions about their careers and how things worked at this level.

I wasn't nervous about performing or being seen by millions of people. The truth was I didn't even know who my competitors would be—except the Kenyans, Pamela Jelimo and her countrywoman Janeth Jepkosgei, of course. Those were the only two I thought about. As for the other runners, I never thought to study their running styles or anything like that. Seme and I had created a plan for how I was going to tackle the heats and the final. I was there to run fast, stay out of the pack, try to grab the gold medal and bring it back to South Africa.

I even started to think about what kind of signature move I would make if I won. My favorite wrestlers like Lex Luther, Hulk Hogan, and The Rock, had a move they made when they won. Running wasn't wrestling, but it was still a show, and I wanted to give the audience something special.

It took a while but I finally came up with something. I'd spent most of my childhood in the bush. I was a hunter and a herder. I grew up respecting nature. Out there in the wilderness, you had to understand the ways of the animals in order to survive. One of the animals that commanded the most respect and fear was the cobra, one of the deadliest, most venomous snakes in the world.

"Yes," I thought, "I'm lethal . . . like a cobra—that is my running style." Once I decided to strike, to make a move on the track, no athlete could keep up with my pace. So, I would bring my arms up and flex my biceps. I'd hold that pose for a second or two, then I'd flip my wrists out and open my fists so that each of my hands looked like the striking head of a cobra. And, since I'd killed off and buried my competitors, I would then cross my arms over my chest and use my open palms to "brush the dirt off" my shoulders, like it says in the Jay-Z song. I also loved eagles. Eagles were strong and defiant. If they had a carcass and you tried to take it away, the eagle would come after you. You can't take something away from an eagle easily. When I held my arms out, they also looked like wings. Eagle wings. "OK," I thought, looking at myself in the mirror, "I've got something going here." The series of moves looked cool, they looked good. It was perfect for me.

I was like a kid playing make-believe in front of the mirror, only it wasn't make-believe. I was a Nike athlete, I had a sports manager, I had a national *and* African junior world title. I had a sub-2-minute 800-m run on the books and had already started to earn money from my work. I was a professional athlete headed to the world championships. The only thing bigger than the world championships were the Olympics. I practiced until the signature move felt natural and smooth. Each pose flowed seamlessly into the next. And now I was ready to show it off to my best friend.

Violet's job had transferred her to Pretoria from Soweto, so she was now living near the university and still training with Seme. It was great because we hung out all the time. I was very focused on my career, and Violet never got in the way of that. We'd chill a little bit, talk, cook together, watch some TV, listen to music, and crack jokes. I wasn't a drinker or a smoker, so I never participated in any of those kinds of gatherings. I also never went out—no bars or clubs. I was at university for two reasons—to win and to study.

My usual thing was to hang with people occasionally for a couple of hours and then head back to my room. I always preferred to be in my own space. And I rarely had visitors. The only one who was welcomed to hang with me anytime was Violet. She'd broken up with the guy she was seeing before she moved. It didn't have anything to do with me; we were just friends. I knew I had feelings for her, but I wasn't sure if she had feelings for me. Didn't matter. Neither of us were ready to take our friendship to a different level. The friendship meant more to me than anything else.

She came over one night after I was done with classes and training. Berlin was a few days away.

"I have something to show you," I said.

Violet had that look on her face when she knew I was getting ready to say or do something crazy—which was often. We'd been sitting cross legged on the floor eating takeout. I stood up. "OK, so I was thinking I needed a signature move for when I win the championship."

Violet started laughing and almost choked on her food. "OK, Caster. Let's see it." She got over her coughing fit and put her fork down. Then she stared at me wide-eyed like a kid about to see a magic trick. I had her undivided attention.

I took a few steps in place like I had just crossed the finish line. I made the whooshing sound of the crowd applauding me. I went through my Cobra-Eagle hybrid moves and ended it with the shoulder dust. I may have even added a kiss and a peace sign for extra dramatic effect.

Violet just sat there and continued to stare at me. And then, like my sisters had many years ago, she shook her head and said, "Caster. You really are crazy." But I could tell she liked it. Then Violet got up and went over to her bag.

"I brought you something," she said while looking through her things. She handed me a folded piece of cloth. I thought it would be a T-shirt or a blanket for the plane. It was the South African flag.

"For when you cross the finish line first," she said.

I took the flag and held it up behind my head and ran around my small room. I was already in Berlin; I was already on the winner's podium.

THE DAY BEFORE I was to leave on August 7, I got an early morning phone call. Seme told me ASA had reached out. They were sending someone to meet with me about "some tests." He didn't say what tests, and I assumed it was the usual kind.

When Athletics South Africa requests a meeting, the only answer is yes.

An hour or so later, I heard a knock on my door. Michael was there with an older White woman. They walked into my room, and I closed the door and sat on my bed. Both Michael and the woman stood.

"Hello, Ms. Semenya. My name is Dr. Laraine Lane. I am a psychologist with Athletics South Africa."

I wasn't expecting a psychologist. Michael's face didn't look one way or the other, so I couldn't get anything from him. Dr. Lane seemed nervous. She kept rubbing her hands together as if she was washing them. I kept thinking things didn't feel right.

"You should be very proud of yourself, Ms. Semenya. Everything you've accomplished up to now. Your family is proud. Your country is proud. But, you know, people talk. That's what they do. They will always talk. We don't know what the results of the test will be, but you should be proud of yourself."

"OK. But what is it that they're talking about? I will be taking the test and the result will be that I don't do drugs, so we can just go ahead and move on from this. I'm packing. I'm leaving for Berlin tomorrow."

Dr. Lane took a deep breath.

"Well, the thing is that you may not run in Berlin, Caster. Maybe, your career has to end sooner than you thought. It happens sometimes this way. Over things we can't control."

"Well, since I'm not doing drugs, and I can control taking drugs, I don't see why anything has to end," I said to her.

At this point in my life, I'm just a young village girl. But I'm also stubborn. I don't know what she's talking about, and I really don't care. I'd been running competitively for several years and had already won a few major races. All I wanted was for her to leave so I could keep packing.

"Caster, they are going to run tests on you at the Medforum hospital in Pretoria. Today. You can't get on the plane to Berlin without taking the tests."

"That's fine. I'll go to the hospital. Because I am getting on that plane." I was thinking that they'd take my blood, take my urine, see I am a clean athlete, and this will be done and over with.

Near the end of our conversation, which was mostly Dr. Lane talking about how special I was and repeating how I had already brought great pride to my family and country, she took off her necklace and gave it to me.

I liked it very, very much. I'd never owned a piece of jewelry before. It was a gold necklace with a gold running figure pendant. I thanked her and put it on immediately. In my mind, it was a gift, just like the rest of the gifts I'd received because I was a professional athlete.

Masilo, the executive at Nike who was handling my contract, had sent me a pair of white and gold Mamba spikes I would run with in Berlin. I had a year's worth of Nike training attire as part of my contract. I'd be given things here and there as an athlete. So, Dr. Lane's parting gift seemed very much the same.

After the psychologist left, Seme told me that Toby had arranged a transport to take me to the hospital and that I should meet the car outside of the HPC.

I went to the hospital alone.

A nurse met me in the waiting area and escorted me to a patient room. There were two chairs and an examining table with what I now know are stirrups. I had never seen those before. She directed me to the chair. Soon, an older Black man entered and introduced himself as a Dr. Oscar Shimange, a gynecologist.

"Yes. . . . Hello. What's this?" I pointed to the table. "I'm here for a doping test, Doctor."

Dr. Shimange sat in the chair across from me. He looked at me and brought his thumb and forefinger up to the bridge of his nose. "No, Ms. Semenya. Did these people not tell you what you are here for? You are not here for a doping test."

Looking back, I can't say this is the moment I knew what was happening or about to happen. I knew something didn't feel right when the psychologist came to see me, but I didn't imagine it would be this.

When Dr. Lane realized no one had told me about the tests, she talked to me in circles. I believe Michael knew, too, but in our culture, it would have been inappropriate for an elder man to speak to a young girl about such things.

Years later, Dr. Lane told an investigative committee she didn't tell me it would be a gender test because she realized I hadn't consented to being gender tested prior to her arrival.

Dr. Shimange, unlike Dr. Lane, didn't talk around the truth. He came straight out and leveled with me.

"Look, I'm going to be honest with you. It is my duty as a doctor to do no harm. I have been asked to perform a gender test on you. It is your right to refuse to take this test."

I knew what the word *gender* meant and so I wasn't bothered. I felt something more like annoyance.

"Ah. This thing again. OK, then. What's the problem? Do the gender test, doctor. Let's not waste time. I have a plane to catch. A gold medal to win."

"Ms. Semenya, this isn't as easy as you think. I'm required to do a full examination."

"OK. Then, do it," I said. "What do you want from me? You need to see my things?" I sat further back in the chair and crossed my arms.

Dr. Shimange took off his glasses. "Ms. Semenya . . . are you a boy?"

I laughed. I'd been accused of this before. "I have nothing to hide, doc. I'm a girl. I have only girl parts. Do you have a wife? You know what a vagina looks like? If you know what a vagina looks like, that's what you're going to see here."

Then I undressed, put on a hospital gown, laid on the examining table and spread my legs for the first time in my life to another human being.

Dr. Shimange looked at my privates, he never touched or asked me any questions during the exam. I couldn't tell from the expression on his face what he was thinking. At some point, I felt the need to say something.

"And don't try anything funny with me, doc. I may be a girl, but I will beat you down like a man."

Doctor Shimange chuckled. He brought out a sonogram wand and placed it on my lower belly. He drew blood and then the exam was over. Once he was finished, I got dressed and we spoke as two humans, not as doctor and patient. I could tell that he was a good man.

"Caster . . . I am going to tell you the truth here. You are not built like most other women. I know you already know that. But these people are looking for a specific issue . . . a hormone in your blood called testosterone. Both men and women have this hormone, but you may have a higher level of it than the sports people allow for your gender. I am sorry . . . I think the results will show this is the situation with you, Caster. As a fellow African, I have to tell you . . . I think the chances of you running in the world championships are very low."

I just sat there and listened. He went on to mention "chromo-somes" and "Xs" and "Ys" and how sometimes there are certain functions that are blocked in the body when there is a hormonal imbalance. The words and science were beyond me at the time. I'd never heard these terms before, and I didn't hold them in my mind. Still, I understood he was saying that even if I was born a girl, I was different because of this hormone.

He was right. I didn't have the curves African women are famous for and I still hadn't gotten a period, but those things didn't matter to me. I dealt in practicalities. There were plenty of female athletes whose bodies resembled mine, and who, like me, had not once had a period. They were there with me at the university and in the running circuits. I'd sometimes overhear their conversations. If I had a "condition," then I had it. It didn't change the fact that I sat down to pee like every other girl.

Once he was finished, I spoke.

"It is God's will, Doc. It's a part of life, this thing you say I may have. If I have it, God gave it to me. I've been able to live my life and be successful with it. I don't see why this would be a problem now. I've been running in the system this whole time. All I know is I am a girl. I don't have a penis. You saw that with your own eyes. That's all I know. You can finish your tests. If they say I can't run, then I can't run. But they haven't stopped me yet. Thank you for your time."

I called Violet when I was standing outside the hospital wait-ing for the HPC transport. I asked her to meet me in my room. I needed my friend. I don't even remember the ride back to the university, only that I arrived on the tree-lined block. Violet was already in my room.

We had made plans for her to come over that night and help me finish packing. But she knew something was wrong when I called her early in the day. Whereas before I was confused about the psy-chologist and then annoyed at the doctor's office, now I was just angry about what happened. Not just angry, I was furious. I told her everything.

"These people lied to me, Violet. They should have just told me they didn't want me to run. Just straight up, like that. Just say it. Wasting my time, my whole day on this shit. Invading my privacy. Looking at me down there. Talking to me as if I am something less than human." I was walking around my small room in circles. "They are here trying to say I'm not a girl. Maybe I just won't go. If this is what is going to happen, I rather just stop now than force myself into an environment where I am not welcome." Then I sucked my teeth. "That's one part of me. The other part of me says, FUCK THEM. FUCK THEM AND THEIR MOTHERS. I'm going to the championships, I run this thing. I trained hard. FUCK THEM ALL." And with that I was done. I felt like my fury had died down a little bit. I sat on the bed and just held my head in my hands.

Violet, my soft-spoken, soft-hearted friend, was listening like only she did—intently and without interrupting me. Once she sensed a pause in my venting, she suddenly burst into tears and began sobbing.

"What is this? Why are you crying? I am not crying. I am pissed the fuck off. There's no need for you to cry. Please, Violet, don't cry." Despite what some think is my harsh demeanor, I don't like causing others to cry. I don't like making other people emotional. I remember I put my arms around her.

Five years older than me, Violet understood—more than I did, I think—what the implications were. After all, she was the first competitor who ever told me to my face that she thought I was a boy. Her running career was on hold because of her injury, and she needed to work to provide for herself and her family. I knew it meant the world to her to see me succeed.

Violet gathered herself. "Caster . . . please, listen to me. You are young. Too young to deal with such things. I am sorry this is happening to you. But remember you are an incredible person. I've never met anyone like you. Go to Berlin and enjoy yourself. You worked hard to get here, and you deserve the chance. Win or lose, you earned the chance to be there. Focus on yourself. Everything will be fine."

Violet spent the night with me. We talked late into the night. The next morning, we said our goodbyes.

Whatever doubts I had the day before were gone. I was on my way to Berlin.

Chapter 12

BERLIN

O N THE FLIGHT TO BERLIN, I TRIED TO RELAX AND not think about the gender test the day before. The doctor had told me there was a chance I wouldn't be able to run based on the results of the test. I didn't know when those results would come out. Still, I was determined to make the most of the opportunity that had been given to me. I couldn't or didn't want to believe that I would be disqualified because of the body I'd been born into.

There are things I know about what happened in Berlin because I experienced them directly, and things I came to learn much later. From what I understand, sometime after I arrived in Germany, during the week or so we were to train and acclimate to the new environment, ASA officials had been told by Dr. Harold Adams, ASA's team doctor, that he'd communicated with Dr. Shimange in South Africa. He told them that the results of my test either were, or would be, "not good." Dr. Harold Adams was supposedly the first to receive news that the IAAF wanted me tested since he was also on their payroll as an IAAF medical counsel. What bothered me was that Dr. Adams, a South African man, never came to me, never discussed anything with me. I had no idea I was walking into a gender test that day in Pretoria. There were internal discussions about withdrawing me from the race. I would never hear back from Dr. Shimange about my test results, and not one ASA official who traveled with us to Berlin mentioned anything to me. I did not discuss my medical consultation with anyone but Violet. It was something I just wanted to put away. Almost something I didn't want to believe had happened.

The night before the heats, ASA's national team coach, Wilfred Daniels, who I'd known for a few years and who I'd always speak to as I traveled around the runners' circuit in South Africa, gave me a printout of the stats. All of my competitors' times at their last major race were in front of me. I didn't spend time studying the forms or strategies of the other runners. I believed in the potential for my own greatness; the person I spent time studying was myself. That's the thing about running: At the end of the day, it's the person you are right now, against the person you were on your last run. You are racing yourself. What mattered to me was just how fast I needed to be in Berlin.

I remember looking at the printout and immediately understanding what needed to be done. Like I said, I'm good with numbers. I understood the heat was probably going to be 2.1 or 2.2. If I hit that, I would move on to the semifinal. I'd need to dip under 2 in the semi to make it to the medals. If I made it to the final, my God, if I made it to the final . . . "whip their ass," I thought. In my young mind, that was all. Simple.

The 800-m heats were held on August 16. I just needed to keep up with the Kenyans. One was Pamela Jelimo, the 2008 Olympic gold medalist and 2008 Golden League jackpot winner of one million American dollars. This was still the only woman who scared us. Jelimo had that 1:54 on her legs; the fastest I'd run was 1:56, and I'd only done it once and only two weeks ago. That's a two-second gap. The other Kenyan was Janeth Jepkosgei, the reigning 2007 World Champion. That woman had run 1:56 several times over.

My Berlin experience could well have ended the day of the heats. Two hundred meters from the finish line, Jepkosgei was leading and I was right behind her, on her right shoulder. I wanted to pass her, so I made a move to the outside. Jepkosgei moved at the same time. I don't know if she realized what I was trying to do and didn't want to let me go by. I accidentally clipped her heel, and she fell. It was an accident borne of my inexperience; I was staring straight ahead, unaware of my surroundings, and I wanted to come in first. I ended up winning the heat in 2:02.51. Jepkosgei recovered but came in last.

I am not one of those runners who intentionally inflicts harm on others. If the officials believe an athlete purposefully hurt a competitor, that athlete is disqualified. Thankfully, they could see it was an accident, and I was not disqualified. Jepkosgei's people appealed and she was reinstated for the semifinal.

I had never run in a senior event like this before. I'd never tasted a Diamond League; I'd never had any real races in Europe or the States. I was in Berlin now because of my 1:56 run in the African Junior Championships the previous month. Prior to the first heat, I don't think journalists or my competitors thought of me as a real contender. I was a baby to them, taking up space. For all they knew, my 1:56 in Mauritius had been a lucky break—maybe there had been a strong wind that day. Once they saw me run and win the heat, I became more real to them.

And something else became real to me—I had a problem with my right leg again. I twisted my ankle when I tried to jump over Jepkosgei's falling body on the way to the finish line. The same ankle I'd hurt playing baseball years ago. It hurt like hell, and I limped my way back to the locker room. I remember a few reporters asking me about the accident, and I'd responded that I'd hurt my ankle and might not be able to continue running. Again, that was my inexperience talking. Experienced runners don't discuss injuries so openly. Years later, people speculated I pretended I was hurt in case I had to withdraw if or when the gender issue was exposed. Not true. I hurt myself and I really didn't know if I would be able to run.

After the heats, I went back to my hotel room. My mind was on my ankle when I heard a knock on my door. It was the vice president of Athletics South Africa, Attlee Maponyane. Such a high-level representative would usually not be visiting an athlete's room, but in my case, we were close because Maponyane was from

Limpopo. He'd been the president of Limpopo Athletics when I was running in the districts, and he'd taken a liking to the kid who was never afraid to follow him around after events and bother him with all kinds of questions. He liked that I had guts and I wasn't ashamed to put myself out there. We had a good relationship. I was the youngest runner at the world championships, and I had the feeling ASA officials felt like they had to take extra care of me, even if I acted like I didn't need it. I wasn't surprised he came to my room.

"CASTER, how are you feeling?"

"My ankle hurts. Maybe I need the physios. But I'm feeling good. I ran well. I didn't see Jepkosgei there. That could have been bad." I was sitting on the floor, icing my ankle.

"Caster, now . . . look, this is not easy for me to say but these people don't want you to run anymore."

"Who doesn't want me to run anymore? I'm fine. I can still run with this." I expected he was going to say something like, there was no need to blow my leg off at my first-ever world championships. That I was still young enough to continue in the junior circuit and come back to the majors.

"People are talking. The IAAF is concerned you may have some kind of issue in your body. They want you to withdraw. Maybe they won't let you run. I think it's best you take yourself out. You can just be done with it now."

Maponyane looked at me the way a parent looks at a sick child—with affection and concern. It was clear to me by the way he was talking he knew about the gender test in Pretoria.

I shook my head and continued icing my ankle.

"You made it all the way here and you won the heat, Caster. You proved yourself. Now your ankle is hurt. You are young. You will have more opportunities."

But what more opportunities could he be talking about to a girl like me? A girl who had made it all the way from a village in South Africa to the World Championships in Germany and had just won her first heat? What better opportunity than this one, right here, right now? A gold medal and cash prize for my family?

I had to run. That was the only answer.

"NO. I'm going to run. If the IAAF wants me out, they will have to come drag me off the track. I came here to win. I didn't come here to run a heat. I came here to get that gold medal. And I qualified for the semis. I'm tired of this gender stuff. Just a waste of everyone's time. I don't take drugs and I am a girl. You all know I'm a girl. The doctor in Pretoria saw it. I'm not going anywhere. This thing is in God's hands."

"Caster, these things are complicated. We are hearing the results of the test will not be good. I don't know what it means for you . . . we don't know what will happen if you continue. What we can do is bandage your ankle. Tell these people you are too injured to run. This is a good solution. The talk has already started and this way, you . . ."

I've said before that I don't cry. I can count the few times in my life that I have. To me, tears are useless. I know how to swallow them. This was one of those moments when I couldn't hold them back, and I didn't want to.

What I felt in that moment was that if I did not run, my life was over. Not over in the way a teenager feels like their life is over because they couldn't go to a party or they wanted something their parents couldn't afford. I felt like my life would be over in the sense that whoever I was and whoever I was meant to be would cease to exist. I was sure of it. I knew it then, like I know it, still, to this day. My eyes burned, the tears fell slowly.

Attlee knew I wasn't an emotional person. I could see in his face that seeing me this way moved him.

"You see these tears? I don't cry for shit, sir. I haven't cried for anything in my life. I didn't beg to be here. I worked to be here. I earned the spot you people gave me on this team. I am going to run in the semis. If the IAAF wants me out, let them come and take me out." I looked back down and kept working on my ankle.

"Caster . . . things are in such a state we believe this is for the best. Your ankle is hurt anyway. You can go now and we sort this out at home," he pleaded.

"Who would it be best for? Why should I withdraw? Because of what? Where are the results? What have I done wrong?" I asked him.

Maponyane seemed like someone who was trying to handle something but did not know how to. He explained there were no results from the test but that even if I ran in the semi, these people could disqualify me.

"I see my name is still there," I pointed to the television. "They could have disqualified me after the heat and they didn't. I worked hard to get here, sir. I don't do drugs. I don't know what this thing is about and I don't care. My business is to run. Let *them* disqualify me. But not you. Not my own people. Your job is to support me." And here, I stood and leaned against the desk in my room.

After a few seconds of silence, Maponyane brought his hands behind his head.

"Caster, what happened in South Africa, the test . . . the IAAF wanted it done there and they will do it again here. Even if you go through the semis, Caster, you will have to do their test to run in the final. Do you understand? Do you know what's coming? Are you prepared to deal with that?"

"I am prepared for anything, Attlee. Whatever's coming, I'm ready for it. What I know right now is I'm going to run this shit. I'm going to reach for that gold medal. I will go home after that. The rest will follow."

Maponyane came over, put his hands on my shoulders, nodded, and left my room.

Go home or run. The choice was a simple one. If the IAAF was going to disqualify me after the final, I was fine with that. All I wanted was a real chance. I heard later that Leonard Chuene, the president of ASA, was going to remove me from the race. Of course, as the president of the federation, it was in his jurisdiction to do so. I knew they had sent Maponyane because of our close relationship in the hopes he would convince me to withdraw on my own. But after Maponyane told him about our conversation, Chuene changed his mind. "She will run," he had said, "we will stand by her."

Later that day, I had another knock on my door. This time it was an IAAF doping official doing a routine, surprise blood draw. I held my arm out. Whatever was going to happen would happen, but I had to run.

AUGUST 17, 2009. I woke up, put on my gear, got on the team bus, and headed to the Olympic stadium. None of ASA's officials said a word about me not running. I stayed quiet. I stayed in my own mind. I didn't eat. I still don't eat before races. Maybe I adjusted because of the years ignoring hunger pangs on my way to races around Limpopo. I didn't strategize with a coach. I knew the plan for the semi—stay in the front, avoid a collision, dip below 2:00.

I remember walking out to the track, warming up. I could feel the heat of the other runners' eyes. They were watching me closely. Whispering amongst themselves. Most of the runners were at ease with each other, probably from the time spent together competing at this level. I was the stranger here. Occasionally I'd look back at them to let them know I was aware they were watching me. Nothing more. It didn't matter to me. Whatever they were thinking was their business.

If the gender issue came up in my mind, it appeared as something completely ridiculous. The whole thing made no sense. Whatever these people said was in my blood did not take away the fact that I was a girl. My ankle still hurt but it felt better and

I could run. One thing at a time—right now, the track was there, the finish line in front of me. Just get through this, I thought, one step closer to the gold.

I won the semi—1:58.66.

Jelimo, the 1:54 runner I was most wary of, had been nursing an injury and jumped out halfway through the race. She would not be in the final. Jepkosgei came in second. I'd beaten the great Kenyan to the line for the second time.

Now the young girl from Limpopo was getting all the attention. I remember being surrounded by reporters and cameras. Now they were interested in my life story—where I came from, how many siblings I had, what my parents did for a living. I was answering as best as I could. My English was rusty, and there were things I obviously couldn't understand. They asked about my leg, why I seemed so relaxed on the track even though I was so young and had never been in a high-level international race before.

I was nervous, not used to being asked so many questions, not used to having cameras so close to my face. If you look back on these videos, you can see me there . . . apprehensive, sometimes smiling because they've asked me about soccer or life at home, other times furrowing my brow as I tried to understand the English words and phrases coming at me too quickly. While I was answering these questions, I was thinking about how my family had no idea I was in Berlin. For all they knew, I was in my room in Pretoria.

The reporters asked me about the 800-m world record. Surely, they said, I'm running so fast it's within my grasp. The thought excited me, but I answered the way I'd seen other seniors do. "We're going to work hard and hopefully get there someday." There were more questions about my leg and how I planned to run in the finals. All I wanted was to take a shower and eat with my teammates. I wanted to go back to my room and chill, listen to music. I couldn't wait to call Violet and tell her I had won. That we were one step closer to the gold.

And I almost made it. I'd just walked past the barrier that

stopped the media from walking into the locker room when a reporter called out to me. I stopped.

He was a middle-aged White man.

"You have improved tremendously in your times. With that comes rumors . . . there is one that you were born a man. What do you have to say about stuff like that?"

I don't remember his face, but there is footage of this moment available on the internet. I took a breath. Even knowing what I knew, I was thrown by the question.

"I have no idea about that thing . . . I haven't heard about that thing. Who said it? I don't give a damn about it," and I walked away.

I was fucking angry. What kind of person asks something like this of another? Here I was, a kid, and some adult man questioned my womanhood while holding a microphone. "This mother-fucker," I thought, "asking me some shit like this." This is what I mean about the indecency and cruelty of people.

Obviously, it wasn't true I hadn't heard about "that thing." To some extent, I had always heard about it. I'd heard I looked like a boy my whole life. I'd had a gender test in South Africa. Mapon-yane told me there was a problem. I might be disqualified over this bullshit. But now a foreign reporter was asking me about rumors that I was "born a boy?" And then what? I had cut my dick off just so I could run with women? We didn't have running water or electricity in my village. Where would people like us get the money to change genders?

What I wanted to do in that moment, more than anything else, was smash this motherfucker's face. I wanted to beat him like I'd beat the bullies from my village. Let him get a taste. I thought he was lucky he asked me this question after I knew I had qualified for the finals. He was lucky I'd stopped settling things with my fists years ago. I wanted to make a scene right there, but I understood where I was. What could I have gained from physically attacking a White man at the world championships? Especially in my situation? So, I shot those words at him and walked away.

I told no one about what had happened. If any of the team heard about it, no one mentioned it. I remember getting back to my room. I talked to Violet, but only about good things, positive things—I told her how I was going to win now that I had a spot in the final.

I had started to loosen up in my room when an IAAF doping official came to take more blood from me. Maybe they were taking multiple samples from all the athletes, but to me it felt personal. I knew the plan was to disqualify me, so maybe they were purposefully trying to annoy me, to get me to withdraw, and avoid some scandal at such a high-profile event. It didn't matter. Until someone from the IAAF came to me and said, "You can't run," I was going to ignore them.

I went to bed dreaming of gold medals.

AUGUST 18 WAS supposed to be a rest day. I remember my phone rang early that morning. It was our team coach, Wilfred Daniels. He told me that the IAAF needed me to take some tests at a nearby hospital and that he would come with me.

Wilfred Daniels had been a great middle-distance runner in his day, but he'd never had a chance to fulfill true his potential because South Africa's athletes had not been allowed to compete internationally during the apartheid. By the time they could, Daniels was well past his prime. Like Maponyane, Daniels was fond of me, and he would always find the time to answer my questions and encourage me when I was starting out.

I met Daniels outside of our hotel. We normally traveled to and from the stadium and hotel on regular buses, but this time the IAAF did not want me to take a bus to the hospital. They had sent a black car with tinted windows. You could barely see who was driving it. "I see . . ." I thought, "They need to keep this thing quiet." It seemed clear to me the IAAF did not want anyone to know what was happening.

On our way to the hospital, Daniels and I talked about running.

Our conversation was light and good-humored. Sometimes, when we were silent, I'd look out the car's tinted window. I knew these people were taking me to a gender test. It wasn't easy to sit in that car knowing where I was going. I saw it as an attempt to break my spirit. The blood draws and now this were meant to drain me as a human. To force me out. Well, they were going to find out what I was made of. I don't quit.

I don't know if Wilfred knew about my conversation with Maponyane or even if he knew everything that had happened prior to the car ride. When we arrived, a woman met us in the waiting area. She introduced herself as a German-to-English translator.

"What the hell is she translating?" I thought. I had a better than basic understanding of English, and I could barely understand what the hell she was saying. I was to follow her, and she motioned that Wilfred should stay in the waiting area.

I remember we took an elevator ride that seemed to go on forever, and when we walked into the patient room, there was an almost identical examining table and the fucking stirrups. There were several medical personnel in there—I don't remember how many or what each of their titles were. None of them spoke English, or maybe they pretended not to.

"What am I here for?" I asked. I knew what I was there for.

The translator turned to me, "Ah. Yes. They need to value you, Ms. Semenya."

"Is this a gender test?" I asked. I knew it was.

I don't remember the reply. It didn't matter. What did any of it matter at that point? I had to go through with whatever the hell this was because I was going to run in the final.

"OK, you want to see my vagina? Do what the fuck you need to do. Let's get on with this shit, then. You are wasting my goddam time."

I don't know if they knew my words were rude, but they understood my tone. No nonsense. What was happening here wasn't respectful, anyway.

I have never discussed what happened in that room. I put it away for a long time. I'm good at putting things away. I think now it's better to just get it out.

I TOOK OFF MY CLOTHES and put on a hospital gown. At least in South Africa I was surrounded by the sights and sounds and smells of my people, at least the doctor was someone who felt familiar, even if I'd never met him before. How different these people seemed with their cold eyes and even colder demeanors. The room was chilly and smelled like it had just been disinfected. I lay on the table and placed my legs in the stirrups. Unlike the doctor in Pretoria, who never touched me, one of these doctors came right over and began to pat around my vagina with a gloved hand. I assumed he was looking for the dick they thought I was hiding.

"You won't find what you are looking for. You won't find it because it isn't there."

The doctors spoke to each other in German. The translator didn't say much of anything, and I don't think she was translating for me anyway. I think she was there for legal reasons.

"Look around as much as you want. Only a vagina here," I said, and then took a breath, "being that I'm a girl. And that's what girls have. We have vaginas."

I was taunting them with my words. I wanted to irritate these people in the way they were irritating me. I remember I cradled my head with one hand and tapped my fingers across my stomach with the other.

Then one of the doctors brought out what I now understand to be an internal sonogram wand and handed it to the one that was doing the examination. To me, at that time, it looked like a big fake dick. And I knew what dicks were used for. The doctor made a sort of motion with it that meant to communicate to me that he was going to insert it.

"NO. FUCK. NO. You're not putting that shit inside of me."

I waved my hand and shook my head "no" in case my words weren't clear.

There was more talking, and the translator turned to me.

"Very sorry. Must for procedure. Check inside."

What I knew in that moment was that if I didn't let them look inside my body, I wasn't going to be allowed to run in the final. This wasn't about me having a vagina. They'd just seen it with their own eyes and touched it. And this also wasn't about something in my blood because they had plenty of my blood already. So why did they need to look inside my vagina? It's one thing to spread my legs and let them look and touch me, but this, *this* was a whole other level.

Maybe there was another option.

"Look," I said to the translator, "I will not allow that. If they have to stick that shit in me . . . they're going to have to find another way . . . they can go in my ass."

It was like one of those moments in a movie or a TV show where you hear a record scratch and time stops. All the people in the room where like, *"HUH? . . . WHAT DID SHE SAY?"*

"Uh, no, not understand . . ." said the translator. I think they understood because their eyes were wide.

I said it again, more slowly and loudly, "ASS-HOLE. GO. IN. THE. BACK."

Then I made the universal sign for a hole with one hand, held the index and middle fingers of my other hand together, mimed a penetration, and then pointed down past my vagina.

"Tell them they can stick it in my ass . . . that's it. Don't cross that line with me. You don't know me. I will break every fucking machine in this room if you try anything other than that." I pointed to their machines.

They knew what I was saying because some of the people in the room started moving the equipment away from the examining table.

I was eighteen years old and still what we call an "innocent." I wasn't going to let these people penetrate me. They talked some more amongst themselves. I could see some thought going "in the back" could work for their purposes and others didn't.

I lay on the table, legs wide open, watching these crazy fuckers discuss how they were going to get inside my body.

"I'm an African," I told them. "I'm a hunter. I will slaughter you with your own instruments."

And I meant it. Come what may, they weren't going to get that part of me.

If this was the moment it was all over, then this was the moment. I keep saying I'm not a quitter. But I would have given up the gold medal final over this. Allowing this to happen to me would have been a complete violation. I wasn't going to let them hurt me in that way. In my adolescent mind, I thought the ass was OK. Whatever, it was just an ass. Everyone has one. Shit comes out of it, anyway. I don't know. Maybe it was my religious upbringing, the way I looked at the idea of being intimate with a person. I could not let this happen to me.

Finally, the doctor walks back over with the wand. He seemed uncomfortable and irritated, but it was clear to me they'd decided to do as I said. I can't lie—I enjoyed seeing his discomfort. It satisfied me to know he was frustrated because they were not going to get what they wanted.

He put a lubricating gel on the wand and then inserted it. He moved it around. He kept studying a screen with a stupid look on his face. He shifted the wand to the right. Then to the left. Back, again.

"Yeah, motherfucker. Keep turning it . . .," I said. "Keep turning it. Are you finding something? Do you see anything?" The doctor was really annoyed now.

I didn't care which way he went. I just laid there looking directly at him. I didn't feel any pain. My mind wasn't on pain, it was completely focused on them.

It seemed he couldn't see whatever it was he wanted to see or thought was there.

"Are you finished, yet? Done filling your eyes, doc? Stop wasting my time. I have a race to run tomorrow."

Finally, he took the wand out of my asshole. I remember I wished I'd taken a shit right then so the doctor would be even more irritated, but I hadn't eaten so my stomach was empty, anyway.

Then he got a different wand, with a flattened top. This one I recognized from the South African doctor's office.

He placed it on my lower belly. It tickled. When he was finished, they took more blood and urine.

More blood. I remember wondering if I had any blood left in me to run the final. They took my blood after the heats, more blood after the semis. Now, again, blood. For now, though, it was over. I put on my clothes. The translator silently accompanied me to meet Wilfred in the waiting area. She had me sign some paperwork. I don't remember reading it. It didn't matter. I didn't care. We took the car back to the hotel.

I know people wonder about how I felt afterward. I understood the test was part of the process that would allow me to run in the final. It was a fucked-up thing to have go through. I was angry, yes, frustrated, definitely. I didn't understand how I'd gotten caught up in this whole thing. This was the price I had to pay to run because someone had called the IAAF before I went to Berlin and told them I wasn't a girl. I had to go through this bullshit because I didn't look how they thought girls should look.

I knew the world could be fucked up, that people could be cruel, but I was mostly pissed at the timing. I had already been through this shit in South Africa. It should have been put to rest there. Why did I have to go through it again in Berlin? On my one rest day before the biggest race of my life?

I told Wilfred soon after we got in the car. I told him because I trusted him. Even though discussing something like that with a man who wasn't even part of my blood family was inappropriate. In that moment, I just had to tell someone.

"I thought this whole thing was about doping, but these people really think I'm a boy. Same shit here that happened back home. They had to look at my privates again."

I didn't tell him exactly what they did, but he looked pained and stunned. I remember he made a sound, a sound like we do when we feel shame but also helplessness. We didn't speak any more about it.

The other athletes were eating, laughing, calling their families and friends. Rest days are for unwinding our minds and bodies. I went to my room and slept. I didn't call Violet that day.

AUGUST 19, 2009—the day of the finals. The test made me all the more determined to win. All I cared about was winning now. That was my primary focus.

Somehow, the media got a hold of the fact that I'd been taken for gender testing the day before. Someone at the IAAF "accidentally" sent a fax about my gender test to a journalist.

Instead of saying "no comment," the IAAF confirmed, three hours before the final race, that there had been questions about my improvement over the last year. Initially, they said, it had to do with doping, but the concerns had moved on to whether I required gender verification. They refused to say where the "concerns" originated from. Nick Davies, the IAAF spokesperson, told the media I would not be withdrawn from the race because they did not have any conclusive evidence yet.

"OK," I thought. The most important thing is I wasn't going to be withdrawn from the race. They were going to let me run. But now it was out in the world. And I wasn't stupid—this was part of whatever "was coming" Maponyane had warned me about. I know the IAAF didn't "accidentally" send a fax to a journalist. The plan was to use whatever they thought was wrong with my body to shame me out of the final. They miscalculated with me; I wasn't ashamed about my body or the way I looked.

I remember sitting in my room watching people talk about me on television. Journalists were casually saying things like:

"South African women's 800-meter runner may be a man . . . IAAF is investigating . . ."

"Quick, look at this picture, is she a girl or is he a boy?"

"There is now a sex change controversy at the world championships . . ."

"Has South Africa knowingly placed a teenaged boy on their girls' team?"

"A scandal is brewing in the women's 800-meter final, where there may be an African boy . . ."

It was chaos. I willed myself to not care. I had an opportunity to do something great. This was my chance, and no one was going to take it from me.

About an hour before the final, I got to the warm-up area. I could feel something had shifted in the air. Everyone had heard about the gender test.

Normally, I don't care who looks at me. I was used to being looked at; I was used to being whispered about. The other runners had ignored me when I first arrived and then seemed more interested after the heats and semis. They were experienced runners, champions, world-class athletes. To them, I had come out of a jungle a month before to qualify for the championships. No one had given me the time of day, or a chance, until they saw me run the heat and the semi. But today, there was something else in their eyes. When I occasionally caught the other runners looking at me, what I saw in their eyes was fear. The only thing they saw in me was *fearlessness*.

I sized them up quickly. Defending champion, Janeth Jepkosgei was ready to go. Britain's Jenny Meadows looked good and determined, and so did her fellow countrywoman, Marilyn Okoro. The Ukrainian, Yuliya Krevsun, looked like she didn't want to be there. Russia's Mariya Savinova looked fucking tired as hell—that woman wasn't going anywhere, I could see her legs were gone. I thought nothing of the rest of the field. None of these women spoke to me in Berlin; there had been no words of encouragement or attempts to make small talk. I remember when I first tried to greet Pamela Jelimo, even before the heats, before the gender test had been leaked, the one runner I was excited and nervous to meet, she looked away from me and made a face. I would have told her how much I'd admired her, how much she'd inspired me. "OK," I thought, "Rude. She doesn't care about me. Then I don't care about her."

The other athletes wanted me to feel like I didn't belong. Bad sportsmanship is what it was. The only runner who acknowledged me and wished me luck the day of the final was Marilyn Okoro, a British woman of Nigerian descent. I remember she'd been really nice to me.

The annoying gender tests, the IAAF's confirmation to the press, the possibility that I would be disqualified after the final . . . I put all of this somewhere in the back of my mind. I was going to win. That was the IAAF's mistake—thinking the shaming would destroy me. The other mistake was not having me removed before or after the first heat.

I could see the women following me around while I was doing my warm-ups, drills, run-ups. I don't play "mind games" on the field, but I will say this, if you're staring at me, you've already taken yourself out of the race.

I was the entire game in the 800-m final. I realized at an early age, if people are watching me, that means I'm valuable. I train hard, I work my ass off, 365 days a year. I looked good as hell at the Berlin championships. My body was in peak form, and I was only eighteen years old. If these girls wanted to stare at me, well, then I was going to give them something to look at.

I did ten 100-m-dash run-ups and made sure I hit every bend around the track so each country's athlete and their coaches and officials could see me. Instead of focusing on their business, they were distracted. Fine by me; this meant I won the race before I even ran it.

My plan for the final remained the same. Give it all I had. Fuck everyone else.

The call room is the final place where all athletes gather prior to taking the field and lining up. This is where IAAF officials come up and check your outfit, make sure you're wearing legal spikes, make sure you are not bringing anything you shouldn't onto the field. The athletes are in very close quarters here, usually loosening up, stretching. You can hear everything. What they said specifically doesn't matter. I knew they were talking about me, laughing at me. It probably made them feel better to make fun of me when the reality was, they looked like they wanted to shit their pants.

I felt relaxed, totally chill. I didn't need to stretch. I was ready. I crossed my arms and sat back in my chair with half-closed eyes. Someone came, checked our outfits, bibs, shoes. Then they moved us to the tunnel that leads to the stadium. Still, more talking, more whispering about me. My upbringing, my very nature, had conditioned me to take in these kinds of situations and pass through them. "I don't give a fuck about any of you, bitches. I don't care, I don't care," I said to myself.

The truth is I came to Berlin hoping I would be in the top five. Maybe even top three. I would get some experience, go back home, work on getting faster. But now, I knew I was going to win. The last person I spoke to before the final was my coach. Seme was in Pretoria because there was no money for him to travel with me. I have no idea if he knew the things that had happened to me in Berlin but it didn't matter.

"Hey Caster! OK, I saw the heats. Now you know what you can do. No one on that field today is better than you. That gold medal is yours. Go, kill them and bring it home."

FINALLY, we were let out onto the track. We were introduced to the spectators. I knew the rumors about me being a boy were going around; I knew what some people were thinking when they called my name. Here is where the feeling of shame and embarrassment would have caused most people to crumble, to cry, to walk off the track, even. But not me. I just took whatever this was and let it pass through me. I lifted both hands and waved to the crowd.

Like all other athletes, I shook off the nerves at the line; I release them as soon as I take my stance, settle into my lunge, bent at the waist, left leg forward, waiting to go.

Just the year prior to this one, I hadn't yet learned to quiet my mind. I would sometimes talk to myself at the line, trying to bring myself under control. But I felt myself in a different space after being and learning with Seme. By the time the gun went off, my mind was totally blank. I was not thinking of anything at all. I didn't hear any sounds at first.

I was in lane four, three from the inside. The first 200 meters felt too slow, so I jumped out. Jepkosgei came with me, and we were side by side for a few steps. She tried to take over, but it seemed like she changed her mind and hung back. I think she remembered I was eighteen and had a 1:56 on my legs, and she needed to conserve her energy. Approaching the bell, at 400 meters, I made my move.

Now I was flying.

When I heard the final bell, I made sure I was out in front of the pack. Then I took over. I could see the finish line. I remember I turned my head slightly to make sure there was no one near me, then I started to pull away. The sounds of breathing and the pounding of the other athletes' feet faded away. I could hear the roar of the crowd around me.

No one could follow me in those last 200 meters. I did what I had been training to do.

The little girl from a tiny village in Africa had won the gold medal in 1:55:45.

Jepkosgei came through to win silver almost two seconds behind

Me at six months old in Ga-Masehlong. I would start walking the following month.

School outing to South Beach, Durban, 2007. I took our teacher's wig and posed as Tito Jackson. She still has no idea who took her wig. She'll know now when she reads this book.

I'm fifteen years old.
Class trip to a beach
in Durban, 2007.

"Spring lessons"
at camp, wearing
provincial colors, 2008.

Running in an
interprovincial
cross-country race,
2008.

Me with all
my medals, 2008.

Fans welcome me back to South Africa after I'd won gold in the 800-m distance at the Berlin World Championships, 2009. (Photo by Gallo Images/Foto24/Felix Dlangamandla)

At OR Tambo International Airport in Johannesburg with Winnie Madikizela-Mandela, 2009. (Photo by Gallo Images/Foto24/Felix Dlangamandla)

Crowds of people gathered at OR Tambo International Airport to welcome me and the South African national team, 2009. (PHOTO BY GALLO IMAGES/FOTO24/FELIX DLANGAMANDLA)

Celebration in Ga-Masehlong after I returned from the Berlin World Championships, 2009.

Violet and me outside of the University of Pretoria's campus where Violet was living, 2011.

My father's mother, Mmaphuti Semenya, in her home in Ga-Masehlong.

Me getting ready for the 12th IAAF World Championships that started in Berlin on August 16, 2009.
(Photo by Gallo Images/ City Press/ Khaya Ngwenya)

With my parents on my twenty-first birthday, 2012. (Photo by Gallo Images/ Daily Sun/ Rebecca Nemakonde)

Greg and me in Switzerland after the Court of Arbitration case in 2019.

Masilo from Nike and me
on our way to Cape Town,
October 30, 2019.

My manager
Becky and me at
her wedding in
Johannesburg on
April 9, 2019.

me. That was the huge gap between me and the other runners on the field that people remember. I didn't know the other runners were that far behind me. People still talk about that gap. The conditions for that gap were set because the rest of the field had been racing all over the world that year. They had a lot of mileage on their legs. While they were traveling and racing, I had mostly been training. My legs were young and fresh. Theirs weren't. Simple. It was a spectacular win for me.

Right after I crossed the finish line, I remembered to do my winning move. I hit the Cobra. I knew Violet was watching back home. I knew my family would soon know. I was given a South African flag and I did a victory lap around the stadium. Whatever came after this didn't matter. If I was disqualified, it wouldn't change the reality of what had just happened. No one could take this feeling, this moment away from me. I would always be there, my win had been captured on video, seen by millions of people. "I'll go home happy, now," I thought.

This is where my story as an athlete truly began.

Soon, the best day of my young life would turn into an international scandal.

And despite what I have endured after winning the gold medal, I want everyone to know that I would do it all over again.

PART III

THE AWAKENING

Chapter 13

NOT WOMAN ENOUGH

"JUST LOOK AT HER," SAID RUSSIA'S MARIYA SAVI-nova with a mocking look on her face. Right after I'd won the gold medal, journalists asked her what it was like to run with me. The implication, of course, was that by "just looking" at me, anyone could see I shouldn't have been allowed to run with them.

Italy's Elisa Cusma at least had the balls to come right out and say it. "These kinds of people should not run with us . . . I am not taking her win into consideration. For me, she's not a woman. She's a man."

Jelimo murmured, "Well, if they allowed her to be there, then they allowed . . ."

Not one of my competitors came to the defense of a fellow woman and runner, a teenager. Instead, they came with their knives. I would experience this again and again throughout my career. I'd run with and shake hands and hug women that had no issue walking over to the cameras and casually saying I wasn't one of them.

After my victory lap in the stadium, I went back to the hotel with the team. Someone pulled out a bottle of champagne, but I only had water and juice. There was a party with great music and plenty of food. Everything was beautiful. I had accomplished my mission—I had come up against the world's best that year, and I had beaten them. Soon, I'd come home and celebrate with my family, is what I was thinking.

At some point, though, things started to look a little different. I did not attend the winner's press conference with the silver and bronze medalists right after the race. I had no idea there even was a press conference to attend. Pierre Weiss, the IAAF general secretary, had sat in my place and proceeded to discuss my gender and what may or may not be happening with my body. To this day, I have never watched this press conference. I've heard about it, but I don't care to see it.

"There is a question of whether this person is, in fact, a lady," Weiss had said. He followed that up by saying the tests they'd done so far showed I was "clearly a woman, but maybe not 100 percent."

There were questions from the media on whether I would be allowed to receive the gold medal at the ceremony the following day since the results from the gender test could take weeks. Since I hadn't been immediately disqualified after the race, I didn't know there was ever any question about my receiving the medal. I was busy enjoying the fact that I had won.

I spoke with Violet and never once mentioned anything about the test. I told her about the excitement of the competition, how ready I'd been. Looking back, it's hard to believe, but aside from what I considered the stupid gender test and the conversation about withdrawing and the possibility of being disqualified, nothing seemed out of place to me. Those had been the only discomforts.

The next day, August 20, I went back to the Olympic stadium to receive my medal. I felt proud. Accomplished. For me, it was the culmination of my hard work. Like any other race I'd won. I remember they called my name and put the gold medal around my neck. The crowd roared their appreciation of my performance. It was an amazing feeling to stand on the highest podium and see them raise South Africa's flag and hear our national anthem.

Immediately after the medal ceremony, we were taken right outside the Olympic stadium to plant trees. I didn't know the significance of this event at the time—it turned out to be some environmental initiative. Each of the forty-seven world champions would plant a tree to create an "Avenue of Champions." This is where the state of things started to make themselves clear to me. Something was wrong.

There was media there, but my people refused to let them talk to me or take my picture.

"No. No, please. Back. Stay back. Respect, please. Respect," I remember one of our ASA people said to the throng of photographers who were aiming their cameras at me. She put her hands out in front of their lenses and wouldn't let them get a clear shot. Still, I did what I was asked to do. I planted my tree, took a group picture with the rest of the winners, and went back to the hotel. All I wanted now was to go home and celebrate with my family and see Violet.

We were in Berlin for a few more days. I cheered on my teammates and mostly stayed in my room. I sometimes watched myself being discussed on television. I would sit in my bed just staring at the screen. I didn't have social media back then, so my interaction with the world was limited. I heard the way the television people from all over the world were talking about me, but to me they weren't real. I just didn't understand what the fuss was all about. Everyone was weighing in pretty much saying the same thing: "Boy or girl? We think this person may be a boy. Could be an actual cheater or maybe someone with male and female attributes" is how the conversations would go. Everywhere I looked in Berlin, there were plenty of female athletes that were even more muscular than me and acted like boys. Truth be told, there were a bunch of men athletes in Berlin that looked the way women are supposed to look and act like, I guess. To my young mind, this was all just a stupid mistake that was going to get cleared up in a day or two. I was irritated, but it was not something worth bothering myself with. I had a gold medal. I was a world champion.

We left Berlin on August 24. What I did not know was that from the moment the IAAF confirmed that I'd been gender tested, media from all over the world had already reached out to my parents, siblings, aunts, uncles, grandparents, cousins, childhood friends, teachers, old coaches, training partners, running officials, anyone at the University of Pretoria. Journalists were contacting anyone they even suspected of having ever been within two inches of my person. Newspapers were already filled with quotes from people in my life, including my parents, who brought out my birth certificate and a copy of my passport to prove I had been female since birth.

People at the Berlin airport recognized me. Some yelled congratulations or pointed at me and whispered to each other. The South African national team had been successful at these championships: we came back with three medals. Both Mbulaeni Malaudzi and I had won gold medals in our respective 800-m races, and our teammate Godfrey Khotso Mokoena had won silver in the long jump. People hardly talked about the other South African winners that year; their accomplishments were eclipsed by the controversy surrounding me.

By now, my teammates knew what was going on. The whole world knew. They did their best to protect me on the way back home. I was the baby in the group. I remember how they tried to keep me from seeing the newspapers in the hotel and in the airport. That was an impossible task. The world championships were watched by millions of people in almost every country, and a half million tickets had been sold just for the stadium. So many amazing performances that year and Caster Semenya's genitals seemed to be the main story. The headlines were crazy:

"PROVE THIS IS NOT A BOY"

"HERMAPHRODITE CONTROVERSY"

"SOUTH AFRICA'S GOLDEN GIRL MAY BE BOY"

"MAYBE NOT 100% A SHE"

"GENDER ROW RUNNER!"

At the airport, it felt like I was on every television channel, in every language. I never did imagine that things would get this big.

This was no longer about sports. People were dying of hunger, people needed housing, people were being killed . . . and I was the main story.

I just shook my head and told my teammates, "Look, this is a piece of shit, man. I don't have time for this thing. You guys, come on, if you think I'm about that life of reading newspapers . . . I don't give a shit what these people are saying about me."

I was insulted. In the immediate aftermath of this thing, I was not hurt in the sense that I was going to sit around crying or get myself down about it, but I was offended. I had been through enough in my childhood, had been raised to be strong, so no, I can't say that I was feeling hurt, but I did feel disrespected as a person. I came from a place where people minded their own yards, where gossip was seen as the devil's work. It was just incomprehensible to me how people could discuss such intimate matters in public in this way. It felt like I came from a different world, one that operated with different rules than what I was seeing. And the thing that pissed me the hell off was that it felt like I was being called a cheater. I hadn't done anything wrong.

By the time we arrived at the airport in Johannesburg, South Africa, on August 25, IAAF had leaked the initial results of my blood tests to the international press. When I landed, the newspapers had even more fuel for the fire—they reported that tests showed I had three times the testosterone level of a typical woman. The speculation was that I was either a boy or a hermaphrodite.

If the newspapers were to be believed, they had indeed found the issue in my blood that the South African doctor had mentioned to me, but I wouldn't know what it meant until much later. There is footage of the South African national team arriving at OR Tambo International Airport, and sometimes it's hard for me to relive this moment.

I never expected what I walked into when we got past customs. It didn't feel like an airport at all. The place had been transformed into a concert. Thousands of people were jammed inside the arrivals area. It seemed like every media outlet in the country was there, along with every major politician. I was in shock. You can see it on my face. Music was blaring from everywhere. People were singing, shouting, dancing, waving the South African flag and holding up printed and handwritten signs that said, **"OUR GOLDEN GIRL," "CASTER YOU ARE A BEAUTY," "CASTER, YOU GO GIRL," "OUR FIRST LADY OF SPORT."** Others were holding up newspapers with my birth certificate plastered on the cover and a headline that read, **"YES! SHE'S A GIRL!!"**

I had seen things like this happen on television to the Maradonas and Pelés of the world—big sports stars who came home from winning championships. Now here it was happening to me. Everyone was calling my name. I didn't know how to react. Airport security and policemen surrounded me and my teammates, they tried to get us through the crowd, but they were no match for the people who swarmed around us. They pushed their phones in my face, trying to touch me, hug me, kiss me. I remember people grabbing and yanking on my track suit. I was being swept this way and that by the mass of people.

I knew this was a celebration but nothing seemed right to me. I'd won gold, but the celebration seemed about something other than my actual win.

The national team finally made it onto the double-decker bus. It was one of those open-top buses, and it circled the airport so we could wave to the crowd. I kept being reminded by others to smile and wave. And I would occasionally do so and hold up my medal for everyone to see. But then I would suddenly go blank and the smile would just slip off my face. Part of me wanted to celebrate with my people, to just be joyful. The other part kept asking, "What is it that I've done wrong? The only thing I've done is be an athlete and win. Now all these people are saying there is something wrong with me, they are saying I'm a cheater. That I don't deserve the medal."

The bus ended up at the airport's parking lot. A stage had been set up there. So many people were there, including my entire family. That was a beautiful surprise. My family had come. The people I loved most in the world, who had no idea I was even going to Berlin—my mother, my father, all of my siblings. They were standing shoulder to shoulder with famous politicians I'd only ever seen on television. There was Winnie Mandela, our beloved Nelson Mandela's former wife. She was a member of parliament as the MP of the African National Congress, and a much-loved figure in her own right. There was Julius Malema, the head of the African National Congress Youth League. I always loved to hear him speak on freedom and revolution on television. I remember thinking that all of these big people, who I'd never met in my life, seemed to love me as if I had been born in their household.

"OK," I thought, "This means I matter the most. Let me carry on, enjoy this moment." Even if the truth is that, for me, it was not enjoyable. I was there with everyone, but it felt like I wasn't there at the same time.

We got off the bus and onto the stage. I'm singing. I'm dancing. There's a singer who prompts me to do my signature winning move. The Cobra. So, I do it. There, you can see I am truly happy. The Cobra is all mine.

"Be happy," I remind myself. "Look at what you've done for your people."

Smile. Dance. Wave. "The outside world thinks I'm a cheater, they are saying something is wrong with me, but here, my people are celebrating me. So . . . it's OK," I reminded myself, "I don't care what other people think. Stay here, be present, with your people. You are famous now. This is what fame must feel like . . ."

Then there was a press conference where politicians each took turns to speak about how my human dignity had been violated. I just sat at the table. Thinking of nothing. This thing was beyond me. Thinking of just getting some sleep.

We were then taken to the presidential guest house in Pretoria. The national team was to meet the president of South Africa,

Jacob Zuma. The president made a short speech on how proud he was of the South African athletes and the five medals we had brought back. But my teammates' accomplishments were once again overshadowed by my plight. The media only wanted to hear about me. President Zuma addressed what he called my public humiliation and said that I and my family had the country's full support. I remember staring at my hands while he spoke, playing with my nails. Wishing I was somewhere else, even though to be there was such a great honor.

I was asked to speak, and it was the first time I was able to address the media directly. I remember saying it was good to win the gold medal and bring it home. I talked about taking the lead at the 400-m mark in the race and how I celebrated in my mind at the 200-m mark because I knew none of the other runners could follow me. This is what I imagined speaking to the media in Berlin would have been like had I been given a chance to attend the winner's press conference. No one asked me directly about the gender test, but it was more than clear that this is what they all came to talk and report about.

A journalist asked President Zuma if the IAAF was going to take the medal away from me.

"They are not going to remove the gold medal. She won it. So the question does not arise. There's no worse that's going to come," President Zuma confidently said.

He was wrong about that. There was, indeed, plenty worse to come.

But before the worse was to come, there was one more person I got to meet because of my win. An icon of freedom and perseverance—Nelson Mandela. I grew up loving him and what he represented. I never dreamt I would one day meet him face to face. By then, he was ninety-one years old. He told me I was special, to not allow this discrimination to stop me from accomplishing my dreams. He said I was a great athlete and that I'd made him and the country proud.

"You are strong, Caster. I believe in you. You must believe in yourself."

In the moments of darkness that were to come, I remembered his words. If someone like him could survive and overcome twenty-seven years in prison and become a symbol of love and freedom to our people—why couldn't I endure this? What I was going through seemed like a small thing compared to what he had survived. Compared to all those who had died during South Africa's struggle for independence and democracy.

A few days later, on August 30, I traveled back home to Limpopo to celebrate with the people I'd grown up with. It was the same story. I was there, but I was not there. The village was full of people—many familiar faces and many faces I'd never seen before. There were more visits from politicians; even our village king paid a visit to our family. My parents greeted and fed visitors day and night at their home. I did everything I was supposed to do. I posed for pictures and showed off my medal. I caught up with my childhood friends who I'd missed so much after I moved to my grandmother's village. And I ate and ate and ate. I'd missed my mother's cooking.

My family was so proud of me. My sisters were in the front yard of our home showing reporters the medals I'd won before becoming world champion. My mother and father were freely talking to journalists because there was nothing to hide—they gave birth to and raised a girl. They were humble, rural people and couldn't understand how it was possible for anyone to question their child's gender. Their view of the whole thing was that the White people had gone crazy and that we were not going to listen to anything they were saying. That was it.

The journalists were looking for someone who would say they had seen a penis on me, or maybe even find a picture of my privates. Either way, the journalists never got what they wanted. What could they possibly get? The story never changed—I'm a girl. "A different kind of girl," everyone would say, by which they meant that I was boyish acting, but "Caster's a girl."

Gender is a simple thing in my part of the world. Mostly, people are born boys, or they are born girls. There is also what in our Pedi language we call *lahara matana*—a person born with two genders, meaning they are born with both a penis and a vagina. In my culture, these people are not assigned a gender. They are allowed to live their lives and decide which gender is dominant in their soul. They go about their business, and everyone is supposed to mind theirs. I have heard that in rich countries doctors can "fix" a child born like this. But how do you "fix" something if you don't know what the child will want to be? We didn't believe in surgical intervention on infants for such a thing.

No one ever told me specifically about *lahara matanas*. I just knew there were people like this when I was growing up. And I wasn't one of them. I was born a girl, and I have never felt confused by that because there's nothing confusing about having a vagina, even if my mannerisms and interests were considered boyish. If some idiot in my village or grandmother's village called me a "he/she," which is basically the same thing as a hermaphrodite, I'd just say "your mother" and then wait to see if he needed to discuss things further with my fists.

I knew growing up there were other girls like me, meaning girls who didn't sprout breasts, who had deep voices, or girls who were just not into girl things. I grew up with some of them, played soccer with them. They were around just like I was around. It wasn't something we ever talked about directly. There was no conversation, like, "Hey, I see you are one of those girls who likes to do boy things." It was something acknowledged without words.

My mother told me they found out I won the gold in Berlin when my baby brother, who was thirteen years old at the time, started screaming for my mom to come to the living room because "Mokgadi" was on the television. He told her they were calling me "Caster" but that he knew it was me.

My mother said she couldn't believe what she was seeing on the television screen, but almost immediately our home phone began to ring. Some of the calls were congratulations from family and friends, but many of the calls were from journalists and other media personalities. They all wanted to know if I was really born a girl. I can only imagine what my mother's heart was feeling in those moments. This woman who had given birth to me and changed my nappies and taught me so much about kindness, and humility, and strength.

My family accepted me the way I was, but it didn't mean they didn't deal with comments about my looks and behavior. But my actual gender had never been a thing to be questioned, much less tested. That's the thing people didn't seem to understand—it was one thing to talk about how I behaved, how I looked on the outside—my clothes, my voice, my musculature—but questioning someone's gender, discussing it in public . . . that is just unheard of in my culture. The idea that their child had been subjected to gender tests was a horror to my family, something deeply offensive on many levels. I was a little Black girl in a foreign land; to them, the White people had taken their child and violated her based on nothing but "rumors."

The gender issue became a difficult one for the politicians in my country. Everyone seemed to support me and my right to run. They saw in me an innocent Black child caught in a terrible situation. For us, it became about more than gender—it became about race. It became about White people coming and telling us Africans what we were and what we were not based on our looks— the same categorizations and violations of human rights that were happening during apartheid. I became a symbol of how Black people have been violated and exploited throughout history. Would this be happening to a White European teenage girl? When did "rumors" become an official accusation that had to be investigated? My blood and urine had been tested dozens of times by ASA and the IAAF at official races prior to Berlin. When did the issue move from doping, as they said, to actually questioning whether I was even a woman? To actually testing my femaleness? To this day, no one knows exactly what happened. Me, I didn't give a fuck about it. It happened. And now I was dealing with it.

Our politicians were having press conferences day and night. Some asserted this was an agenda by a White international racist media to discredit an African girl's win. They said they rejected the colonizers' language of "hermaphrodite" because such didn't exist in our society. Still others said there was nothing wrong with being a hermaphrodite, if that was what I was, because I was God's creation. Everyone was trying their best to support me and protect me. And I understood this, even if the reality is I wanted everyone to just stop talking about me.

I had promised my family I would make something of myself, that I would bring honor and provide for the Semenya clan. In the immediate aftermath of the win, I became South Africa's Golden Girl, but I didn't imagine that my tremendous victory would also come with whatever this was.

Chapter 14

YOU MAGAZINE

A FTER THE CELEBRATIONS IN MY VILLAGE WERE over, I returned to the University of Pretoria. All I wanted was to go back to my room and see Violet. I missed my family, but Pretoria had become my home, my own space. I was done with celebrations.

Toby Sutcliffe, the acting director of sport and CEO of the university's High Performance Centre, met me as soon as I arrived at school. I'd become very close with him. I still call him "dad" to this day. He always talked to me in the way I preferred—directly. No beating around the bush. No pushing around the corner. He had a gentle but firm demeanor, someone you knew you could depend on.

"Caster, we've decided you'll have to move out of the regular residential sports houses and into the HPC. It's the only way to keep the media away from you. They are everywhere and there's not much we can do to stop them," he said.

And he was right. Journalists and cameras were everywhere. Large groups of them at the gate of the school, others hanging off the fence that enclosed the school's track. Some even tried posing as students and faculty. Every one of them hoping to get a look at me and hopefully get me to talk. I wouldn't be able to rest if I stayed outside the school grounds. I'd be safer at the High Performance Centre, which was located inside the grounds with its own restaurant, offices, and workout facility. This was the place elite athletes from all over the world stayed when they trained in Pretoria. For anyone to get in there, they'd have to go through at least three different reception and security stations. I have many reasons to be grateful to Toby, and his instinct to protect me was one of those. He knew I needed to be in a quiet place, that I needed to be inside of my own mind to process what was happening.

Toby introduced me to a guy named David who worked in guest relations at the university. David was assigned to bring me whatever I needed and to keep everyone away from me. He was to stay by my side from the moment I woke up to the moment I went to sleep. I felt like I could trust him almost immediately.

While I was getting settled into my room at the HPC, the media storm continued to rage. Leonard Chuene, president of ASA, had stepped down as a council member on the IAAF while we were in Berlin, in protest of the IAAF's initial leak to the media. It hadn't yet come out I had been gender tested in South Africa first, with his approval. That all would come out soon enough. It didn't matter to me. What mattered was that I was able to run in Berlin and win the gold medal. And now, all I wanted to do was go back and run. I wanted to show the world I did not become a champion by mistake.

Occasionally, I'd speak to Violet on the phone. I wasn't able to see her immediately when I returned, and it was for the best. Toby said no one but my family should be around me. Violet had been working for Transnet in Soweto, and she would visit me every weekend when I first came to Pretoria. After I came back from Berlin, Violet received a work transfer, and she rented a room in a building that was close to the school. Violet was still running competitively and training with Seme on the University of Pretoria's grounds, still trying to get past the injury that would eventually end her career. I was going to tell her how I felt when I got back from Berlin, but I didn't expect to come back to this. She didn't know what to say to me except to stay strong and that this would pass.

A few days after getting back to the University of Pretoria, Athletics South Africa approached me about a media opportunity.

You magazine, a well-known South African glossy, wanted me on their cover. The shoot would be the first time I'd be photographed for a mass audience and the first time I'd be formally interviewed.

I didn't know what the shoot was going to look like, but I knew *You* was the biggest English-language magazine in South Africa. Violet came with me. With all the craziness, I was still waiting for the right moment to tell her I loved her and that I wanted us to be in a relationship.

When we arrived at the magazine's offices, I was told the theme for the shoot was "Glamour Girl." The room was full of outfits, everything was sparkly and shiny. There were several different kinds of high-heeled shoes. I'd never seen so much jewelry in one place. I'd never seen any of this kind of stuff in real life, only on television. These were the kinds of things only the rich and famous people wore.

My first thought was, "OK, yes. Let's have some fun."

I had left my village only six months before winning the world championship. I was a teenager, and I wanted to experiment. I'd always wondered what I'd look like, what it felt like to wear clothes like these.

The magazine people were happy to let Violet try things on, too, and we both got a full beauty treatment—manicure, pedicure, facials—and we had our makeup and hair done, too. I thought I looked cool and different from my usual self—the self who ran around in sportswear and spikes. As I grew older, I started understanding myself better. Sequined dresses and high heels are not my style. I prefer pantsuits. I don't mind wearing makeup, just as long as it looks natural.

But on this day, Violet and I were like two schoolgirls in a movie, laughing and changing into different outfits. Violet even jumped in during the shoot, and we took some pictures together that ended up being printed in the magazine. We enjoyed ourselves. That's what I remember clearly from this experience, all the fun I had that day with my best friend who I was also in love with. I remember telling the interviewer, "God made me the way I am and I accept myself."

The shoot became another scandal. Politicians, journalists, gender academics, people on the street—everyone had something to say when the magazine came out:

> *"Semenya is being taken advantage of. What cruel treat-*
> *ment of this young girl."*
> *"They made Caster look like a drag queen just to make the*
> *White people happy."*
> *"They forced Semenya into a dress and threw a wig on*
> *her when even her own parents said she doesn't like*
> *dresses."*
> *"Caster Semenya forced to change herself to run."*

This magazine shoot is still discussed in women's and gender studies classes. People have written entire dissertations about how my naturally masculine gender expression was made to conform to feminine gender stereotypes. I'm fully aware of all that. And I'm not saying it isn't worth studying. I just want to tell the world what actually happened from my perspective as an eighteen-year-old.

Money talks in this world, and I was a kid who loved business. I grew up without money, so I knew how important it was, what it meant, what kind of life I wanted for myself and my family. I'd been that way since I was a little girl betting whatever rand I could scrape together and helping my mom pick numbers in the Chinese lotto.

I don't do shit I don't want to do. Never have. I considered myself the master of my own destiny. My goal was financial security—I understood it to be a type of freedom for a village girl like me.

You was offering me money, and I had already been told I wasn't going to make any from racing until the test results were figured out. I wasn't going to get any sponsorships until companies were sure I would be running and winning again. I didn't have a local

manager, meaning someone who could get me opportunities outside of sports. All I had was my sports manager Jukka and Athletics South Africa. The IAAF was still holding my prize money. Even
though I'd brought the gold medal back with me from Berlin, the
IAAF had requested I not wear it in public after the initial celebrations. The medal was in a safe in Toby's office at the HPC.

I had nothing. So I did the shoot.

You wanted to pay me to take some pictures. Why not? If someone had offered me money to run an exhibition marathon which,
as a middle-distance runner, would have taken me 24 hours finish,
I would've done it. For me, this photo shoot was part of my work,
part of getting into the industry, building myself, building my
name. I'd always been a performer anyway. No one said, "Caster,
we need you to look more like a girl so you can keep your medal."
It wasn't about that, at least not to me. Maybe it was about that
to others, maybe ASA felt that the world needed reminding that I
could, in fact, be a certain kind of girl, but it wasn't about that to
me. Moolah. Benjamins. Rand. That was it.

If some ASA official or politician thought doing the shoot would
help my case with the IAAF, then it was their business and they
were doing their job.

The same day *You* came out, Wilfred Daniels, ASA team coach
I'd been very close to, the person who accompanied me to the second gender test in Berlin, quit his position with ASA. He talked to
the media, said he felt terribly about the magazine shoot and felt
sorry for whatever part he played in the Berlin situation. He called
for the resignation of anyone who had something to do with my
appearance in Berlin, especially ASA President Leonard Chuene.
Daniels believed I should not have been allowed to run. I cared
about him and respected his decision. That was his and his alone.
I don't blame him for anything. But the decision to run was mine
alone. The decision to appear in the magazine was also mine.

Here's the thing. I don't care what people say about me. Or I
should say, I learned not to care what people said about my looks.

People are going to say whatever they're going to say. I don't control their mouths. Some people thought I looked like a man, and now they said I looked like a drag queen. Other people thought I looked good as hell in the magazine; I was one of them. The point is, neither the magazine spread nor the comments about it was going to change my reality. Nothing was going to change the fact I couldn't run until the test results came down. Nothing was going to change the fact the whole world was talking about me because the IAAF had deliberately leaked news of my situation to the media. The IAAF wasn't going to change its mind about me running because I took pictures with a dress and heels on. They were going to go through whatever process they'd been going through with women like me.

On September 8, the day after the magazine came out, the IAAF announced they'd have the results of the gender test in two weeks. They confirmed there was no doping issue and I would get to keep my medal, although they still hadn't released my prize money. I was relieved about the medal, of course, but I still had to wait for the results.

I already knew I was a different kind of woman. I had always wanted to know what was going on with my body. I never thought anything was wrong, I loved the way I looked, but I was curious. Growing up, I understood I didn't have the resources or access to the kind of medical facilities that would help me get answers. But now it had been done for me. What I did not know, what I wanted to know, I would find out soon enough.

Chapter 15

THE NOTHINGNESS

THE NEWSPAPERS HAD LEAKED THE REPORT OF the elevated testosterone in my blood tests the day I returned home from the championships. And now, an Australian newspaper had gotten ahold of the IAAF's gender test results. There it was. The things I did not know about my body.

I found out, along with the rest of the world, that I did not have a uterus or fallopian tubes. The newspaper reported I had undescended testicles that were the source of my higher-than-normal levels of testosterone. They went on to call me a hermaphrodite. In my culture, this term does not apply to people like me, but the world media forced that label on me and that is what I am called to this day. Sometime later, the term would change, and some people would refer to me as "intersex" and as having a DSD—a disorder or a difference of sexual development.

I had only been home a few days. I'd hoped that things would begin to quiet down and normalize themselves, and then suddenly with the release of that news article, it was as if some kind of bomb had exploded . . . and the fallout just kept getting bigger and bigger.

I couldn't escape it. I was on the cover of every newspaper, on every single television station, and radio show in South Africa. And the explosion wasn't just in my country; my face and story was plastered across televisions screens and newspapers all over the world. It was as if the entirety of humanity had discovered some kind of alien that looked like them but wasn't them had been living amongst them. That's what this felt like.

I remember thinking, "Now what? What does this all mean? What are the implications of it? Am I going to run again? Am I going to get my medal and my money?" My mind raced through these questions and more—

"OK. . . so this explains why I haven't gotten a period. . . . Now I know it will never come."

"This is why my hips aren't rounded."

"This is why I can gain muscle quickly when I work out."

"Alright . . . if these people are saying I don't have a womb, then this means I will never be able to carry a child. I want a family. I can still raise a child because I have many nieces and nephews."

"Well, thank GOD . . . I don't have to endure the pain of childbirth . . ."

"God made me. If he allowed me to live when I was born, he made me this way for a reason . . ."

These are the things that went through my mind at the time. I have always been a practical girl. I thought only in practical ways.

A part of me had always known, even if I didn't know the specifics. Even if I didn't have the language and the knowledge. I had sisters and female friends. I was a girl just like they were, but their bodies worked in a different way than mine did.

Reports said I was immediately placed on suicide watch because I was ashamed and afraid of myself and afraid of what would happen to me now that my "secret" was out. That wasn't true. Maybe the people who were handling me thought this. But those were their thoughts, not mine. I wasn't suicidal at all. I wasn't afraid of myself. I was angry because there was no need for the world to know my business. That is what I found unfair. It wasn't the world's business what I was carrying around inside of me—they didn't have a right to that.

Looking at it the other way, whoever leaked the results did me a big favor. I now knew what was going on with my body. I had top-level medical information, free of charge. I thought of all the people in the world who were like me and would never have access to this kind of knowledge. At least I knew. And now everybody else knew, too. And if everybody knew, that meant I never had to talk about it if I didn't want to. And I didn't want to. I was done talking. All I wanted now was to switch off my mind. Just stop time.

This was who I was. Whether it was leaked or not, I was going to find out one day anyway. My parents were deeply hurt by all of it. They were offended people had taken their child and done these tests without their knowledge or permission. They couldn't understand how something like that could happen.

My family didn't have media handlers, so they hadn't been given talking points or advised to not speak to the media. Whenever journalists came around, they would show them pictures of me as a baby, pictures of me with my siblings, my classmates, talk about how I grew up, show them my birth certificate, my passport. They would have neighbors come over and validate it all. They wanted the truth to be known—whatever the science said, I had been born and raised as a girl, and that had never changed. They would never accept that I was anything other than a girl.

I didn't like seeing and hearing the desperation in my parents' eyes and voices when I happened to catch one of their interviews on television or the radio. Over and over, I would hear them or someone from my village talk about how they changed my nappies and they knew what I had between my legs.

The South African government tried to do what they could for me. Politicians came together and approved a grant so I could build a house next to my parents in our village. They knew I and my family didn't have much money and didn't know if I would ever run again. I was happy about this. I would have my own home, and it meant that family members and people from my village could be hired to build it.

The government also announced they would file a human rights violation petition with the United Nations. Politicians and government officials were outraged at this new leak. Winnie Mandela and Julius Malema were saying this all felt like a racist European system trying to deny a Black girl child her win and suppress her talent.

All I cared about was running. All I cared about was the dream—the joy of being successful, of helping my family, helping others, being an asset to my country.

I didn't worry about things I didn't have. If they're saying I didn't have a uterus, that I didn't have fallopian tubes, why worry about something that wasn't there? If I don't have it, I don't have it. So what? What I wanted was to keep running. And whether I was going to keep running hadn't been sorted out yet.

The South African navy reached out to me during this time. They wanted to offer me a place in their ranks. Their representative said they were looking for tough ladies to join the service and they'd be happy to train me. It would be a stable job with benefits. I had dreamt of being a soldier when I was a kid. It was a good opportunity, but I would have to leave the university and move to Cape Town. Once I signed with the navy, I knew I would never run again. And despite it all, I wanted to run. I told them I was grateful for the offer but that I needed to see my athletics career through.

Life at school was totally different now. As the days passed, the lush grounds and state-of-the art facilities at the HPC seemed more like a prison. Before, being here was my freedom, my way out of my old world and into a whole new one. My life had been about nurturing my talent as a runner, and now I was being called names and laughed at just because of the way I was born.

My days felt empty. I was supposed to still study, to still train, to continue life as before while waiting, endlessly waiting for what the IAAF would decide to do with me. Toby, David, and the rest of the staff tried to keep me occupied, keep me motivated. But I didn't want to do anything but be alone and sleep and think.

Nights became days for me. I slept most of the day and stayed up all night staring at the walls. And I'd watch the Berlin Championship. Over and over and over again, I'd watch myself win. I studied every angle, every turn. Obsessively. I don't know why. Maybe to remind myself that I did win, that the gold medal was mine. Some would call this a depression. I didn't understand it as such at that time. My sister Olga would come to see me. She would just sit next to me in my room and not say a word. So would Violet. They would bring me food and just stay quiet and let me be.

Toby sent a psychologist to see me. Her name was Monya. She was a sweet woman but no match for what was going on inside of me. We had a few conversations, but they always went one way.

"Caster, can you tell me how you are feeling? How do you feel about what has happened?" Monya would ask, a notebook on her lap, a pen in hand ready to write.

"What feelings? What feelings are you talking about? There are no feelings here. I'm not talking to you about anything. I don't need to talk. If you want to help me, help me with my studies. You can help me structure my schooling, maybe. Other than that, I have nothing else to say."

She really tried, that poor woman. But there was no getting through to me. Especially because I saw conversations and relationships as a two-way thing. I can't sit there and tell someone my story, my feelings, while they stare at me and write shit down. I don't trust people who expect you to share and don't share back. That wasn't going to work with me. So, I didn't say shit to Monya.

What could Monya do for me? She could never understand the pain. She could never understand what was happening to me because she would never be in my shoes.

For more than a decade, I've stayed quiet about my thoughts on this thing.

What I was dealing with in that moment as an eighteen-year-old girl was a specific kind of torment. I think only the people who have faced what I experienced can understand what I am talking about. How do you explain what it feels like to have been recategorized as a human being? That one day you were a normal person living your life, and the next day you were seen as abnormal? I was

a young girl who'd been physically and emotionally violated by a system—a system that I had no choice but to exist within, yet was also beyond me.

I kept thinking, "This thing can never be undone." The girl I had been before I got on that plane to Berlin—happy, joking, innocent, eager, hopeful—she'd been disappeared on the way back. And in these early days of my exile, there was nothing to put in that empty space.

Imagine you are told one day that because of some medical this or that, you are actually not a woman. Think about it. In the eyes of the entire world, you are now something other than what you know yourself to be. And the entire world will not stop talking about you. Ever. 'Til the day you die, you will be the punchline of a joke about genitals or gender or sex or whatever.

It's hard to reveal the true nature of my feelings because I didn't even know if I was actually "feeling" anything at all at that time. I was being told I was different from the rest of society, and then my difference was tested, measured, proven, and advertised. I had no control over any of it.

Black people all over the world know this feeling well; we understand it intuitively—the feeling of being different, of being othered just by virtue of existing. Black women, we understand it on a whole other level, of course. This is why my South African people were so horrified, why my newly democratic government threatened a third world war if my medal was taken away. We had freed ourselves from a system that had legally classified people into Black, Asian, Colored, or White. A system that kept Black people uneducated, kept people apart and broke up families. Uniformed White men went around and assigned people a racial identity based on what they believed you to be; they had the power to recategorize you. What happened to me reminded my people and our political elders of a time they're still struggling to free us from.

Anger, I know. Anger, I understand. What I was feeling then wasn't just anger. It was like a hole that threatened to suck me in.

I've always prided myself on being centered and strong. Even as a young girl, I always knew the way; I have always known what needed to be done. In those first few days, weeks, and months, I felt a total loss of control. There was the loss of the success I had tasted, yes, but on a deeper level, a loss of who I had always known myself to be. A girl. A woman.

And the rejection is what people can't understand. This wasn't a "found out my husband or my wife is leaving me for another person," or "my best friend has betrayed me" type of rejection. This was a rejection by the world of my very existence. That you are not a human being in the way the world understands human beings to be. It was feeling like you were being wiped off the map of humanity. I did not have the language then to explain that. I barely have it now.

I couldn't talk to a psychologist about these things. I just wanted to be alone. I believed I was the only person who could heal myself. But I had no control over anything except my own mind. And my mind wasn't functioning. Everyday felt like nothingness. I was just hanging in the air.

A couple of weeks after being sequestered at the HPC, I asked David to please take me home to my village. I missed my family. I wanted to feel at home; I needed a place where I knew I belonged. He got permission from Toby and we drove out early one morning, before most people were even awake. On the way, I got hungry. David pulled up to a supermarket. When he moved to get out, I stopped him.

"Let me go in, David. No one knows who I am around here." He tried to get me to change my mind, but he understood that all I wanted was to feel a little normal. I was an independent girl, and the last couple of weeks had been hell for me. The supermarket was along a remote highway, and it was still early in the day. I was convinced no one would know who I was. David came in with me. When he recounts the story, he said he was looking around, making sure things were safe, when he noticed one woman staring at me. It seemed she was trying to figure something out. He knew in that moment that the woman was trying to place my face.

I didn't notice anything. I was in my own mind. Just happy to be away from the school, happy to know that I would be seeing my family soon.

"Caster . . . that's the champion! It's really her!" the woman said loudly. I didn't hear her, but I do remember that David hurried over to me.

"We have to leave. Now." David had a panicked look on his face.

I thought he was exaggerating, but I realized people inside the supermarket were following us toward the door. By the time we got outside, crowds had gathered and were singing and shouting. We walked quickly toward the car, and David was begging people to move out of the way so we could open the doors. By the time we managed to get inside the car, David couldn't drive the car forward or backward. They had completely surrounded the car, and he'd hurt someone if he moved. We couldn't drive out for at least twenty minutes.

The only times I could leave the school was when I was invited to high-profile dinners and lunches with politicians. I didn't want to attend these things, but I knew I had to. I understood that, in many ways, my career was also in their hands. David would always come with me. We'd drive the little four-door black Toyota sedan with the HPC logo emblazoned on both sides. I felt safe in that car with David. I'd refuse the fancy large black BMWs and Mercedes Benz with uniformed drivers the politicians and other important people would offer. Most of the time, I would find a reason to sneak out before I had to make any comments or go around talking to people. I would refuse to make speeches but would allow pictures to be taken if I absolutely had to. David knew that if I said, "I have to use the bathroom," he needed to get ready to drive us back to the university.

As more and more of the gender-testing story started to unravel, the public attention became more intense. No one knew that I had been gender tested in South Africa prior to Berlin, but now inconsistencies in ASA officials' stories were starting to come out. The South African government created a task force to find the truth about what happened and to protect me; Winnie Mandela was the head of it.

I remember David told me a man somehow got onto the university's campus. He was wearing a good suit; he seemed like an educated person. Someone had told him where to find David. The man pulled out several envelopes full of rand.

"I am here to marry Caster. *Today.* I want to take that girl home with me *today.* One of these envelopes is yours if you show me where she is. The other envelopes will be part of the *lobola* for her family. And I have plenty more rand available."

David could only laugh.

"Caster is not marrying you or anyone. You will walk with me out of the school. We will forget you came here. Please go home before I call the authorities." He then escorted the man out of the university. Luckily, the man left with minimal resistance.

I wanted to be a successful athlete, to be known for my talents; I couldn't have imagined fame coming at me this way. I retreated further into myself.

My coach would do what he could to get me out of the room and back on the track. He would stand outside my bedroom window and call out to me almost every morning and evening.

I can still remember his distinct whistle and then him yelling, "Caster! Caaaaaster . . . come on down, now, eh? Let's try to work the legs today."

I couldn't do it. If he called my cell phone I'd not answer or I would tell him I had a headache.

"Look, what's the point for me to train if I won't be competing? It's useless for me to train everyday if I can't even compete. I don't see the use. Give me time on my own just to think about what I want to do," I'd say.

Everything I'd worked for seemed so far way. A world champion and now nothing. All I could do was wait. And pray.

A FEW WEEKS INTO the nothingness, Michael came to me and said Toby had received a call from two big-time lawyers based in Johannesburg—Greg Nott and Benedict Phiri. They wanted to speak with me to see if they could help me. I trusted Toby, and if he let them through to me, I would give them a chance. I didn't have anything to lose.

I remember the day of the meeting. David walked with me to a windowless room on the first floor of the HPC. Toby met me at the door. The room was bare, containing only a desk and a few chairs. I sat in this room alone for a few minutes, and I remember I heard the lawyers walk in, but I didn't look up. I just stared at my hands. They introduced themselves. Greg Nott was a White man who seemed to be somewhere in his late thirties and was the CEO of the South African arm of the law firm Dewey & Leboeuf. I would find out later he had successfully represented Oscar Pistorius. Greg was an avid runner and had been deeply involved in South Africa's democratic rebuilding after the fall of apartheid. Benedict was a young Black lawyer who'd been raised in circumstances similar to mine.

Greg told me he'd watched the championships live with his son. He told me he had been overcome with emotion at how I'd been humiliated in front of the entire world. He'd made some calls to legal peers the morning after the race and had reached out to our ministry of sport to see how they could help. Greg said their legal position was that the IAAF had violated my human rights. Their idea was to sue the IAAF; they were sure they could get me a good settlement and would represent me pro bono.

I thought about this. If they sued the IAAF and I won money, then what? They would go back to their offices in the big city with their share, and I would return to my village in Limpopo with the rest of the money, and that was the end of it. I had a family to help support. I was only eighteen years old. How long before that settlement money ran out? And anyway, I knew what I wanted. I wanted to win. I wanted to go to the Olympics. I knew I could get there. In my mind, I was already there. I was a champion.

So, I took a deep breath and finally looked up at them.

"I want to be a three-time Olympic champion. I want to be a three-time world champion. This isn't about getting money. I want to run. I want to win. That's it. That's the only thing I want. To get back on the track. If you can do that for me, then yes, I will be your client."

I could see that both Greg and Benedict were taken aback by my words. My soul felt at peace with them. I didn't sense they were there to hurt me. Greg said they would discuss the situation with their associates and get back to me.

Greg and Benedict each shook my hand and left. If they were serious about helping me, they would be back. And they were serious. Now the real work would begin, and even though I couldn't see the future, I had a glimmer of hope that with these men in my corner, surely I would be able to run again.

Chapter 16

HOPE

A FEW WEEKS LATER, IN NOVEMBER, THE IAAF finally shared the results of my test with my lawyers. Greg came to see me to discuss what had already been leaked to the entire world. I don't remember the particulars of the conversation. It all came down to what the German doctors had found—my body produced too much testosterone and I couldn't compete as a woman by the IAAF's standards, which have continued to change since the beginning of official competitions. Greg explained the scientists had determined I had typically male XY versus the typically female XX chromosomes. To be honest, I didn't care then, and I don't care now what the medical findings are. I have a vagina. I don't have a penis. I don't have this Adam's apple thing men have. I don't have a beard. I have breasts. I was born a girl and raised as a girl. That was and is the end of the argument for me. Remember, I'm a practical person.

Greg asked me if I wanted to take the papers. "What did I need to take these papers for?" I thought.

"No. Burn them. I know my body is different. I am Caster. I will forever be me. All I want to know is how I can get back on the track." I refused to even touch the folder on the table. To this day, I've never seen the medical reports. Greg did as I asked and destroyed them.

I've known my body was different before even my parents or any doctor knew it was different. I didn't know exactly how, but it didn't matter. Right now, my mind was on solving whatever medical "issue" was in my body so that I could run.

"So what now, Greg?" I sat back and looked at him.

The IAAF offered only one solution.

"Caster, they want you to have an operation called a gonadec- tomy to remove the organs that are producing the testosterone. This will bring your hormone levels down. Then you can run in IAAF-sanctioned races again. I am not advising you to do this, I am only telling you what they are saying."

"That is their offer? To cut me open? You can tell them I said to go cut their mothers. They can go cut out pieces of their mothers. These motherfuckers. What kind of nonsense is this?" I got up from the chair. I was furious. Disgusted.

By then, Greg knew me, and he knew I didn't hold my tongue. He knew I meant what I said. In my culture, operations are dan- gerous things. Who in their right mind would cut their body open unless something was wrong with them? Unless they were injured or dying, and the operation was the only thing that could save them? It was madness. If I had internal testicles or gonads or what- ever the fuck they were saying I had, they were mine. I was going to keep them for as long as I wanted. This is how I was born. I loved my body. I was healthy. My body was strong and it had made me a champion. Why must I go now and mutilate it because some German doctors said there was something wrong with me?

I know there are women who have come before me and women after me who have agreed to this solution. The IAAF is lying when they say they have never offered the operation as the only option. The girls who have gone through it are changed forever. And when they become sick, when they can no longer compete and aren't winning medals for anyone, they are abandoned. There is no "retirement plan" for these girls. They are simply discarded and forgotten about.

Annet Negesa was a promising Ugandan middle-distance run- ner. She was a three-time national champion and had qualified for the 2012 Olympics at only twenty years old. Despite having already competed in multiple IAAF races, she received a call while training for the Olympics, and was told they found elevated testosterone levels in her blood. Like with me, the IAAF says they flagged Annet because of the improvement in her running time. Improvement in times that were not abnormal in any way for the female category. Annet claims she was told by an IAAF doctor, a Dr. Stéphane Bermon, that to get back on the track was a very easy procedure. She alleges no one told her of any possible complications or that this "easy procedure" would involve surgery and how that would affect her life. Following medical tests in Nice, she returned to Uganda for the treatment and maintains she believed she was going in for an injection but woke up with deep cuts in her abdomen, having undergone a gonadectomy. She never ran competitively again. The IAAF denied Annet's claims, saying that neither they nor Dr. Bermon were involved in her treatment or recommended any course of treatment to her. There are many more runners like Annet, almost always women of color, that have undergone these procedures to keep competing.

I have run with these girls. I have seen them before and after. Some are trying to get back to where they once were, but you can see the light in their eyes has dimmed. Like me, these girls are desperate, and they would do anything to run. I think about these girls sometimes—girls with little formal education, desperately trying to understand what is "wrong" with them and how in the world they are no longer considered women enough to compete. They are scared, alone, with no one to fight for them. Many don't even speak English, and there are no proper translators—they are already intimidated by a system they cannot understand. They don't have any resources to fight for themselves. Many others do not live in communities or societies that accept these differences, and they are afraid of what will happen if such news about their bodies were to become public.

Many of these women, from impoverished backgrounds, see running as their only hope of making a life for themselves and their families. If they are told that the operation will at least give them a chance to continue in the running circuit, they will do it.

Only later do they realize the operation was a mistake. Nothing is worth violating what God has given you. No freaking way was I going to do that.

My story is different from these women's stories for many reasons. I was lucky in that I had a newly democratic country that wrapped its arms around me, I had the protection of the university system, a great legal team, and a supportive loving family. I will forever be grateful for Greg and Benedict's incredible efforts on my behalf during this time, even if I didn't truly understand the scope of the process. These people saw an injustice and stepped in to help a young village girl, free of charge. They fought like warriors. Greg and Benedict would visit me at the HPC regularly. They explained everything they were doing. Greg assembled a team, an international army, really. There were American lawyers with sports law expertise working alongside the South African team, and others who specialized in human rights law. I remember they organized a medical team to discuss the findings with the IAAF's doctors. It had come out that I had been gender tested in Pretoria. My government's sports federation was embroiled in scandal over why and how this happened, but everyone seemed to be trying to come together to help me. I even traveled to Istanbul with Greg, Benedict, and my coach Michael for more negotiations with the IAAF.

Once it was clear we weren't going to court, and the IAAF was definitely not interested in going to court and having to publicly explain how exactly they've historically dealt with women like me, it was no longer a battle of legal wills. The discussions moved to a different battlefield—our medical team versus the IAAF's medical team. The point was to prove that despite my condition, I was still a girl. That something else, besides an irreversible surgery, could be done to keep me running. A private gynecologist Toby knew in Pretoria had conducted a medical evaluation on me and joined our team in negotiations with the IAAF. She, along with others from our medical team, argued that if the issue was my testosterone levels, they could try to use estrogen to bring them down and regulate them. She warned everyone that there was no research on elite athletes with my specific physical condition taking what was essentially birth control just to run competitively.

My doctor cautioned about the immediate side effects and the possible long-term ones. Weight gain, blood clots, leg cramps, weakening of bones, vaginal bleeding, general feeling of illness, breast swelling, headaches, sweating. She advised me that I shouldn't take the medication for longer than four years. I remember her saying, "if it brings the level down, and you get to run again, you retire at age twenty-one, Caster. Four years. That's it. You get one Olympics. Anything beyond that and you could do irreparable harm to your system."

I didn't care about the side effects at that time. I was only eighteen. I was young and strong, and I thought I could get through anything. As long as I wasn't taking anything out of my body, it didn't matter to me if I added hormones. Greg and Benedict were concerned about my well-being, but they said they would offer this solution to the IAAF with the right medical data to prove it was worth a shot. They asked several times if I was sure I wanted to do this. I was sure. No lawsuit, I just wanted to get back on the track. I was too young to go through some lengthy legal battle. How long would that take? I would be wasting the best years of my running life sitting around waiting. Greg and Benedict were powerful lawyers. I knew they had a lot of resources, but the IAAF was an international organization with the power to spend years in court.

I didn't consult with anyone about my decision to take the drugs. I just told Greg and Benedict to tell the IAAF that I would take the medication and see if it worked. If it didn't work, then my running days were over. The IAAF said I would have to take it for at least six months until my levels were "normalized." They would send their people to randomly monitor me and then, once they were satisfied I had been hobbled enough, I could run again. They would also keep my medical records sealed, and no one would know what my exact condition was or how it was being managed. That was the deal. And I took it. I told no one, not even my parents. Only Violet.

We started with the medication in the form of a gel. I'd rub this gel on my arms every day. I did that for a short time, and I didn't like it because it started to melt the muscles in my arms. I was already a very thin girl, but my arms began to look weird, like twigs with no definition, so my doctor switched me to a pill.

I would do two sets of blood tests a month—one for the IAAF, one for my doctor. And the IAAF reserved the right to show up whenever they wanted, as many times as they wanted, for random blood draws. That would be my life for the next several years.

David would drive me to the hospital once a month for monitoring. I would wear a baseball hat and fold my lanky frame into the passenger seat. We'd drive straight into the hospital's underground garage. There was a private elevator that took me to the gynecologist's floor. No one ever saw me coming or going.

I started feeling sick as soon as the drug was introduced into my system. At first, it just felt like I'd eaten too much of something, I felt bloated. My muscles felt heavy, and I was always tired. I couldn't recover from workouts in the same way I had before. My head would hurt. My brain felt cloudy. I was nauseous for no reason. The foods that I normally enjoyed, I no longer enjoyed in the same way. And I would suddenly get hot and just start sweating. Particularly at night, just sweating right through my clothes and my sheets. It made it so that I would wake up in the middle of the night and have to shower. Then I couldn't fall asleep again so I'd lay on the bed wide awake, staring at the ceiling. The thirst was unbearable. I'd have a gallon of water next to me in the bed, and I would go through it desperately and then have to use the bathroom a million times. The hunger became its own challenge. Food is important for athletes; we eat more than most but this was insane. I felt like I was starving all the time. I'd eat and have to eat right away again and again. It was a constant gnawing need in my belly that lived alongside the desire to vomit. It was enough to drive anyone mad.

"I could work around it," I constantly told myself. I had no choice. I wanted to run, and this was the only way. The physical effects were there, but the medication was also messing with my mind. How could it not? I was a sleep-deprived teenaged girl. No longer my usual self. The self who cracked jokes on the track, and did her best to focus in class, the self who tried to always see the positive in things. I felt like the core of who I was, that inner strength and belief in myself, was being destroyed. This is why I would say in later years that the medication took the soul out of me. I eventually had to tell my parents and siblings what I was doing. I couldn't keep it from them any longer because they could see I wasn't the same Caster. I wasn't happy anymore. It broke their hearts.

"Why are you doing this to yourself? Just leave them," my family would say. But they could never understand. They could never be in my shoes. And I couldn't make them understand what I was feeling. I wanted to do whatever it took, outside of dismembering my body, to run. In my mind, I was already an Olympic champion. I was already the greatest 800-m runner that had ever lived. I couldn't just walk away if there was a chance I could make my dreams real.

I remember how much Violet cried when she saw me suffering because of the medication. She also begged me to stop. But I didn't care if the drugs were destroying me. If I stopped poisoning myself, then my life had no meaning. I'd have to start again from nothing. Maybe I could try to find success as a footballer, but I wasn't ready to let go of athletics. I belonged on the track.

Even if there was hope I would one day run again, I was still in the nothingness, and those close to me would try to do what they could to lift my spirits. I remember my birthday on January 7, 2010. It was my first birthday since I returned from Berlin in August. My entire family and Violet gathered at the university, and even Greg and Benedict came to see me. They had organized a party for me. I was sore and detached, but gradually I cheered up. Greg remembers this was the first time he and Benedict actually saw me smile, even though they'd been to see me at the University of Pretoria countless times. Not much could make me smile in those days.

I was happy to see those closest to me, but even my birthday didn't mean shit. I felt useless. I had come to the city to run and be successful, and I had been stopped. But these people, the ones that loved me and believed in me, they gave me hope that one day I would compete at the highest levels again.

Something shifted after my birthday. I decided something deep within myself. This was my life, and I had to live it as best as I could. I still had a chance to do something great. I would remind myself that even with the medication, this was still my body, I was still me. I knew what I was capable of. All I had to do was what I'd been doing my whole life in one way or the other—fight. I was strong enough to do it. I began training on a more consistent basis. Even with the drugs, my body was responding well in practice, and I was making competitive times. David taught me how to drive so I could occasionally drive myself to visit my family in Limpopo. I would crack open my books from time to time. But the truth is my mind couldn't focus on studies; I wanted to run competitively again more than anything. By then, Leonard Chuene had been essentially stripped of his position as president of ASA because he'd finally admitted he had known and approved my being gender tested in South Africa at the IAAF's request before traveling to Berlin. It was also revealed I went into the South African gender test without knowing what was about to happen. They placed a new man in charge of ASA, and we'd hoped he would see fit to allow me to at least run in my own country while things with the IAAF were sorted out.

The IAAF hadn't officially banned me, but it was understood I couldn't run internationally. We hoped I could run on South African soil, with the blessing of ASA, while the pills were taking effect. We tried to enter a Yellow Pages series race in Cape Town on March 10, 2010. The Yellow Pages series were run by the South African federation, not the IAAF. The new acting president, despite making a bunch of noises to the media about how "athletes were the most important" and he was there to "take care of the athletes," called Seme and told him I should not run until things were settled with the IAAF, but it didn't make sense. There was no reason for them to not let me run, considering all of the support I had gotten from the public, the government, and politicians. Greg, Benedict, and Seme flew to Stellenbosch with me and a camera crew from the BBC who were filming a documentary about me. When my coach tried to register me for the race, the organizer immediately changed the entry to "invitation only." Since I hadn't been officially "invited," I couldn't run. I was angry. My own people were afraid of the IAAF and wouldn't let me in. After this happened, I said on camera that I didn't care anymore about athletics. As of that day, running or not running didn't matter to me. It's what I was feeling in that moment, but obviously I said it because I was hurt. This here is a moment where I can fully say I was deeply hurt. I was turned away at the door by own people. I was not a quitter. It just wasn't in my nature. When I started something, I needed to see it to its completion.

When we returned to Pretoria, we put out a rare statement to the media that Greg and Benedict helped me craft:

> *I have been subjected to unwarranted and invasive scrutiny*
> *of the most intimate and private details of my being. Some*
> *of the occurrences leading up to and immediately following*
> *the Berlin World Championships have infringed on not only*
> *my rights as an athlete but also my fundamental and human*
> *rights. . . .*

Soon after this, the IAAF finally released my prize money. I remember the day Jukka called to tell me that he needed my banking information so the money could be transferred into my account. I felt an immense sense of relief and joy because it meant that things were at least moving forward.

And there was something else that had moved forward in my life. Violet. Everyone still thought she was my "best friend," but we had become lovers. Violet had broken up with her boyfriend before I went to Berlin. After I returned, while I was holed up at the HPC, I knew I was ready to tell her how I felt. I hoped she felt the same way. She admitted she did, but she was scared as she had never had romantic feelings for a woman until she met me.

At the time Violet and I got together, I can't say same-sex relationships were common or generally accepted in my country. Terms such as "corrective rape" were being used in the media during this time to describe the practice of men raping women who were in relationships with other women to "fix" them—but I wasn't aware of it. What I mean is it wasn't part of my reality. The truth is I didn't think about such things. I had never felt unsafe in my village even though I made it clear to everyone I was only interested in women. But the world was much bigger than just my village, and I would come to understand this kind of prejudice soon enough. For now, though, I loved Violet and now I knew she loved me back. Here at least was a thing that was going right in my life. Something I was sure of.

We became incredibly close. Violet saw me through my worst moments. I'm not proud of the way I sometimes treated her during the year I was sidelined. I wasn't in my right mind at that time. I didn't want to share Violet with anyone; I wanted her to be available whenever I needed her, even though she had a full-time job and a running career she was trying to save. She tolerated a lot of bullshit from me. I think she felt sorry about my situation. She saw someone she loved publicly humiliated daily. For Violet, ever the empath, this was difficult to deal with.

Violet was five years older than me, had a painful family history, and was making her way in the world, without a scholarship that covered school fees and meals. Meanwhile, I was hiding in the HPC and couldn't even walk outside school grounds without an escort. I was young and selfish and I recognize that now, but at the time Violet was the only person, besides my sister Olga, who had also moved to Pretoria for work, that I trusted and wanted to be around.

After I was humiliated and rejected from the Yellow Pages race in Stellenbosch, I went back into the nothingness. I refused to train, I'd sleep during the day and stay up all night. I was losing myself even though I was diligently taking the pills and the tests showed that my testosterone levels were going down.

I was starting to understand how the business of running worked. I could no longer make money running in IAAF-sanctioned races. I'd signed a three-year Nike contract, but I wasn't sure if that would stick. I knew that if I could win something like the IAAF Golden League, I'd be set for life. If I could keep running and winning, that would mean partnerships, it would mean business opportunities. The spotlight was on me, my country loved me, but now I was being told there was nothing I could do to keep that shine.

I couldn't accept the reality of what was happening, in the way that it was happening. Rather, to my teenage mind, it felt like the life I had just begun to live when I crossed that finish line was once again being taken away from me. Everything I'd overcome, everything I'd accomplished, everything I'd dreamed of . . . gone.

My father worked about a half hour away from the school, and I'd occasionally talk to him over the phone, but I told him to stay away. David would go for walks around the campus with me. He'd say this would pass and I would be a champion again one day. I wanted to believe him.

I locked myself in my own mind. Finally, Violet was so concerned about my behavior she called my family. She told them that it seemed I was giving up on life and they needed to come and see me. My mom, dad, and two of my uncles travelled the four hours from Limpopo all the way to Pretoria. But the way I saw things, there was really nothing they could do for me.

"Just let me handle this the way I want to handle it. I got myself into this, I'll get myself out. Please don't waste your time and money coming here. I am OK. I'll deal with things my own way," I said to them.

Even though I insisted that I was fine, my family asked that we go to church that day. They felt like I needed to hear the word of the Lord and be surrounded by the faithful. I agreed. So, we traveled to the main Christian Zion church in Limpopo for a service they'd hoped would clear me out.

AT THE TIME, we'd negotiated with the IAAF an acceptable testosterone level of no more than 10 nanomoles per liter (nmol/L). My private gynecologist would test me once a month to make sure my levels were dropping, and the IAAF would send someone to test me at least once a month—these were always surprise visits. We never knew when they would come. I remember an IAAF official showed up at the school on Christmas Eve. I was having dinner with Violet. He came with his wife, and I felt that was unprofessional, so I argued with him and refused to let him take my blood that night.

But the pills were working.

Even though I was feeling sick, what mattered was that I was alive. I didn't know when I would run again, but I tried to be my old self, even if sometimes I felt like I was falling apart on the inside. You can see it there in the BBC documentary that captured my year of exile. I was still joking with the other students, still acting, and believing I was in control of something, anything, even when I wasn't.

And then it finally happened. Six months later, in June 2010, my testosterone levels had fallen enough that the IAAF officially freed me. I remember Greg came to the HPC to tell me in person. I smiled so hard my cheeks hurt. All I had to do was continue taking the pills. Continue poisoning myself.

Chapter 17

THE COMEBACK

I WAS CLEARED TO RUN. MY FIRST RACE WAS ON JULY 15, 2010, in Lappeenranta, Finland. I won. 2:04:22. The second race was at the Savo games in Lapinlahti, and there I won in 2:02:41. Far off from where I used to be, but I was back.

My presence of course caused quite a commotion in the running world. People were asking, "What happened?" "We thought she was a hermaphrodite?" "Isn't that a man?'" "How is she here?" Whatever the other runners felt, it was their right to feel it. But I was back. And it meant the world to me. I was a competitor again. Life made sense again.

I resolved to not speak about the gender issue at all. If the media tried to bring it up, I would refer to the time I had been sidelined as being "difficult," and that was it. I knew those that controlled the running world knew what was going on. I wasn't the first to have gone through this, but I had received the most attention because of it.

The media continued to speculate about me and my "condition." Athletics South Africa and government officials were still trying to figure out who knew about the gender tests and the nature of their involvement. Investigative committees were set up. South African journalists had gotten hold of emails and letters, and explosive "revelations" were coming out every day. Everyone was pointing fingers; many were washing their hands. Most of the people working at ASA during that time would eventually lose their positions. The truth is I didn't follow any of it or care. I didn't see myself as a victim of ASA. I was a victim of something much larger than that.

I blamed no one in our athletics federation; what they did, they did to protect me; they gave me a chance to run. I still see it this way even though I walked into the initial gender test not knowing what it was. No one, not Chuene or Attlee or Wilfred or any other official there in Berlin, could have foreseen what would come next.

I was focused on my running. Whatever was happening between sports governing bodies and politicians didn't concern me. I needed only to listen to my lawyers, and they kept me informed on the things I needed to know.

I wasn't even concerned with local scandals about my situation. It wouldn't be until much later that I would come to understand just how crazy things had gotten in South Africa. I remember once getting R 20,000 from a man who owned a popular strip club called Teazers in Johannesburg. Greg handed me a nice crisp paper check I deposited into my bank account. I thought it was a contribution toward my education. To my young mind, this man wanted to give me money, and I appreciated it. Years later, I found out the money was a type of settlement. The owner of Teazers had come up with some clever advertising for his club. A giant billboard on a main highway in Johannesburg that featured a naked, blonde White woman with the words "No Gender Testing Necessary" written across the bottom half of her body. Many people found it insulting and racist. Black people understood the implication. He publicly insisted he came up with the ad before the Berlin championships and had wanted to make it clear his club only had "real" women because many of the other clubs employed women whose gender was questionable. Of course, he was lying. The man saw an opportunity and used a young African girl's public humiliation to make money. He paid for his mistake.

BY NOW, I had turned nineteen. I had to walk back out into the world with this thing hanging around my neck. I wasn't oblivious to the stares and whispers from other runners. I just refused to bow. "It is what it is," I would think to myself, "you won't shame me off the track."

I knew I was different and would have to reckon with it someday. I will not apologize for who or what I am. And I refuse to be categorized as anything other than what I believe myself to be. People have the right to identify as they see fit. I wasn't going to take on an identity that did not fit my soul because some doctors had taken my blood and images of my organs. I was not a "hermaphrodite," or an "intersex," or a "DSD" or anything other than a woman.

During the year I was exiled, while the whole world discussed my sexuality, my genitals, and my body's structure, I decided to turn inward, to love and know myself. I found myself, found my strength. I like to think I spent that time closing the channels of my weaknesses, so it was as if they'd never existed. I had to be strong if I was going to survive this. I had to mute the world and the chatter. I didn't have to answer anything if they had already put everything out there. People kept talking. I couldn't stop them from talking.

All I needed to do was be myself, contain myself, wait for the right moment, and then explode on the track. Let my running do the talking.

My first two low-level meets in Finland went well even though I wasn't feeling well. I was running seconds off the sub 2s that made me an elite athlete before I was sidelined, but that was ok with me and my coach. I just needed a chance to run against others again, to climb back up to where I used to be. Even with the drugs, I knew I could do it. I was happy to be among other athletes again, even the ones who didn't think I should be there and were talking shit about me.

Most people didn't think I'd ever see an official starting line again. I cannot say I enjoyed myself in Finland, or that I was even fully there emotionally. The medication had already begun to destroy my system, but just being on the track kept me motivated.

At the end of August, I returned to Berlin for the Internationales

Stadionfest meet held on August 22, 2010, at the same stadium, almost a year to the day since I'd won the world championships. I knew there would be lots of media attention, but things would be different. I now knew things about life and the system that I didn't know before.

I had traveled to Germany with Jukka and Michael. The plan was I would address media when I wanted; for the rest of the time, they would speak for me. Most importantly, we were not going to entertain any questions about my gender or about the IAAF's decision to sideline me for a year.

People wonder if I had any stressful feelings upon returning to the country and the very same stadium where I had had my gender questioned in front of the entire world. I didn't. I was glad I was there. I was happy to show my coach around the place where I became a champion, since he hadn't traveled with me in 2009.

Jukka and Michael did a great job of allowing only the journalists who respected my boundaries to speak with me. If a journalist cautiously referenced my year-long absence, I would say "it wasn't easy to deal with" and then redirect the conversation to how happy I was to be back. And you can see it on my face during these interviews—my smile is wide and genuine.

When the gun went off, I remained patient. As the group of runners huddled closer, I was near the back of the pack. I wanted to get a feel for the pace and get comfortable. This was the first big race I had been invited to after the two smaller ones in Finland. Once I had a good look around me, I settled in. A few runners passed me, and I pushed away the feeling of wanting to just go. Then I started to make a move around the 200-m mark. Nothing crazy, just let my legs turn a little faster. I gave it all I had in the last 50 meters and slipped through an opening between the two leading runners. I crossed the finish line first with a time of 1:59.90. This was my first official sub-2 run in a year. Despite feeling heavy, I knew my heart, legs, and lungs still had it.

Fifty thousand people were at the stadium that day. I felt welcomed by the crowd, and I was glad I gave them a good show. I'd performed well, but the media was far more interested in reporting the backlash against me from the other runners.

Right after the Berlin race, Britain's Jemma Simpson, who I didn't think much about, said she wanted to be diplomatic and she understood this was a human rights issue but that human rights were for everyone on the field and not just me. Other athletes hid their disdain a little better—"Oh, is Caster back? That's fine. Happy for her. I hope they did the right thing in letting her back."

Canada's Diane Cummins, another athlete I didn't think much about, told the media she still didn't know if I was a woman or a man. She told the journalists the other athletes were frustrated because my running seemed "effortless," and they'd heard I had a hormone issue. Cummins said it was possible I could even one day break the 800-m world record, and how would that be fair to the rest of them?

I could only shake my head. What the hell were they talking about? Elite athletes weren't supposed to break records? Wasn't that the entire point of sports? Faster, Higher, Stronger? The problem here was obvious—the other athletes didn't want the person who broke it to be me.

Once these girls stopped wagging their tongues to the cameras, they would come up and smile and shake my hand or say "good job" in the locker room. I did not care. In the end, I ran, I won, and I went back home.

My next race was in Brussels on August 27. This would be my first Diamond League event, and it featured a world-class field. Jenny Meadows, Janeth Jepkosgei, and Russia's Mariya Savinova were in the final. The runners went out quickly, and I couldn't make a move in time. I placed third with 1:59:65. But it was a sub 2. That's what mattered.

One runner told the media she just didn't know how I had managed to get back on the track and that everyone felt the secrecy was "unfair." They were all concerned about a "level playing field." She said she and the other runners would have liked some "reassurance" from the IAAF. I guess my losing and their staring at me in the women's facilities weren't enough for them. My thoughts were these foolish women needed to mind their business and train harder.

My next two meets would be in Italy. The first meet was at the Palio Città della Quercia in Rovereto on August 31. I finished seventh with a time of 2:07.16. There I was just tired. The travel and the intense training right before the race took my legs away. The medication also prevented me from recovering as a normal person would.

The media began commenting that perhaps I had "thrown" the race. This accusation follows me around to this day. I don't understand it. What would be the point? Why would I deliberately lose money when I had been sitting for an entire year and desperately wanted to make up for lost time? I guess it made for a good story. And I was getting very, very tired of these stories. Which is part of the reason why the "incident" happened.

A few days after Rovereto, I had been invited to participate in the Notturna Di Milano meet on September 9. Of course, there were plenty of media there who wanted to speak with me. Jukka and Michael did what they could to make sure I felt comfortable and could concentrate on the job I came there to do. And I did my job well, winning the 800 meters in a time of 1:58:16—dipped under 2 again. When the media asked how I was "feeling" about the things being said about me, the things they themselves said, I replied I tried not to worry about what was written; I just concentrated on running. Before we went back home, Seme told me he'd set up a dinner meeting for us with a very important person.

"The World President of all Media, Caster!"

It may have been the head of Italian media or something, I don't remember, but Seme kept stressing this was a 'most important man."

That night, Seme, Jukka, and I took a cab and arrived at a five-star hotel. It was an old-world style building. It had large windows draped with curtains overlooking a plaza, and there were statues and ancient paintings and candles everywhere. Michael's eyes were doing that spinning thing they did when he sensed there was money around. He had a big grin on his face. I wasn't impressed. These things didn't impress me. We were shown to a conference room. The table was set with flowers and candles, gold-colored plates and utensils. A White man arrived a short time later. He was wearing a fancy suit, and his blinged-out watch and rings could have paid the school fees for every villager in Limpopo.

The meeting didn't last long. Maybe ten minutes. He began by telling us how important he was and how important the media was in shaping my career. The he went west and talked about the history of the hotel and how exclusive the food we were about to enjoy was. He would look at his watch and make sure the diamonds caught the light in the right way. I knew his type—"I'm a busy man, you're lucky to be here."

"There are many journalists complaining Caster is not speaking. Caster needs to talk."

I raised my eyebrows. Jukka started to shift in his chair. Seme said, "Caster speaks in the way she needs to. We want her to concentrate on her running and we believe she will be a big star. She is a very special athlete."

Then Jukka added, "We believe Caster is the Usain Bolt of the women's 800 meters; I've already said that. But we have to be careful here that she is not distracted by things she'd rather forget and that don't matter anyway."

There were service people in the room filling our glasses with water and placing small dishes of bread around the table. I should've probably stayed silent. I couldn't.

"So, the media wants me to talk more. What is it that they want me to talk about, exactly? Talk about what?" I sat back and looked at him.

"Well," he turned to me. "Caster . . . we need you to open up.

Talk about what happened in Berlin. The gender test. It would be good for you to give us the details of the gender test there. And the one in South Africa. What happened during the gender tests?" He took a drink and set his glass down. "We also want to know your exact medical condition, and how is it that you are now back running with other women. Yes. This will be good for you. For everyone, really," he said, as he wiped his mouth.

My blood began to heat up and before I could answer, Seme jumped in.

"Eh . . . my friend. Well, ah . . . we had agreed we would not talk about this thing at this meeting. Let's be careful here, my friend. Let's us not go there. This is a very delicate situation . . ."

The man didn't even look at Seme, he just looked at me and continued, "What I am offering you here is an opportunity. There is a lot of money to be made in giving an exclusive. These things will come out anyway. Better if you speak now, Caster. Shape your own story. And we can coach you on how to speak to journalists."

This, to me, sounded like a threat. The results had already been leaked to the media a year ago. Here I was a nineteen-year-old girl trying to rebuild my life. I wanted it to be about my running, my hard work, my talent. What this man wanted was to treat me like a creature, a spectacle. And he wanted me to participate in my own humiliation. He knew my background. He thought that this African child would be easily manipulated with five-star hotels and fancy dinners. He didn't understand I'd rather eat *pap* with my family than be sitting there looking at his stupid face. He had been talking down to me from the moment he sat at the table. I wasn't going to have it.

"OK, let's end it here. I know my story. I am here to run. That's it." I remember pushing my chair away from the table as I spoke. I was ready to leave. Seme knew this wasn't going to end well and began to grab his things. Jukka was still sitting there.

"Caster." The man did that thing with his face that men do when they feel like women have said something stupid. "What happened, happened, right? This is an opportunity to get out in front of it. We understand how . . . difficult this must be. We will train you on how to speak properly. It's going to come out, anyway."

Seme tried to intervene again, but I was done. Framing this as an "opportunity," pretending to care about my "difficulties," offering to "train" me like a dog, and then, finally the threat, again, that it was all going to come out anyway. I was what they call "triggered." That's the right word. The situation took me back to my days in the village. This here was a bully. I could smell it on him.

"Ah. So you want to sell stories off my back, sell my pain and make money. You people already write whatever you want about me. You must carry on and keep on writing. That is your business. You don't need me to talk to do *your* job. My business is to run. I don't need to talk to do *my* job."

"I paid a lot of money for this room, this dinner. A. LOT. OF. MONEY."

"Who asked you to pay for this? I don't give a shit about what you paid for. I don't give a shit about your money. I can pay for my own dinner. I don't need any man to buy me anything. I make my own money. I work. I have dinner waiting for me back at my hotel."

The man's face grew red.

"How dare you speak to me like that! How dare you disrespect me?"

I was disrespecting *him*. That's how he saw it. Then the man stood up, in what I felt was an aggressive manner. A confirmation of who I believed him to be. He was breathing heavily and leaned over the table, a crazy look on his face. He wanted to intimidate me. Seme got up from his chair and put a hand on the man's shoulder.

"My friend. You told us the gender thing was not on the menu . . . this thing is in the past. Caster does not want to talk about the past. She feels like . . ."

I slowly stood up while Seme was talking. I'd been sitting the whole time. Now we were standing eye to eye with only the table between us. I am well over six feet tall.

"I don't need attention, *baba*. I don't seek fame. I'm here to do my business. I'm here to do what I love. You can go straight to hell, go to the nearest hell. You can't buy me. There is nothing you have that I want. But, if you want a taste of what I have to give, you are welcome to come and get it."

I remember Seme making a sort of sorrowful sound and putting his hands up to his mouth. Jukka was silent; I remember his mouth hung open. Jukka knew me, but he'd never seen this side.

And just in case I hadn't made myself clear about what I meant by giving him a "taste," I slowly, and very clearly, said,

"You want to fight? Is that what you want? *Because. I. Will. Beat. The. Hell. Out. Of. You. Straight. Away.* I don't give a fuck where we are right now."

And with that, the conversation was over. Somehow, we left the hotel without the fight. Seme and Jukka both apologized to me. They had thought the man would honor his word to not bring up the gender issue. I was annoyed but I knew they couldn't control that man's mouth. It was over. I put it away. I never saw or heard from this person again.

OUR NEXT PLAN was to run in the Commonwealth Games in New Delhi, which would take place in October 2010, but a back injury kept me in Pretoria. It was nothing major, just muscle strain from training. It meant I got time to heal, train, and spend time with Violet. Our connection was deepening.

My training eased up a little bit with my injury and the holiday break. I returned to the University of Pretoria in January 2011, energized from the time I spent with my family and ready for the running season, even though I struggled with the medication. By now, I'd gained weight. You could see it on my face, on my body. The media commented that my face looked "rounded" and "softer" and that my body had become "curvier" and more "feminine." Some newspapers placed markers/outlines over the supposedly new hips and breasts I'd magically sprouted and speculated on what kind of treatments I may have been taking. It was ridiculous—there were no new "curves." I was just getting fat. I couldn't put on and keep muscle the same way as before. That was all.

My first race that year was in February at a Yellow Pages series race in Potchefstroom. I won the 800, although I wasn't as fast as I'd hoped, with a time of 2:04:12. I ran a few more races in my country and then I traveled to the United States in early June. It was my first time in America and I was to run at the Prefontaine Classic Diamond League meet in Eugene, Oregon. This time, I managed to go under 2:00 with a time of 1:58.

Time. Time is the most important thing in any competitive runner's life. You can say we live by the clock. If you are a female 800-m hopeful, two laps in 2:00 makes you "world class." If your training progresses and you go sub 2:00 in an official competition, then you are now part of the "elite" club. If you can maintain sub 2:00, then on any given day, you can beat anyone on the field. You can still win with an over 2:00, but it depends on the type of meet, the competitors, the conditions, and what the pack determined the pace to be. And you have to be a good strategist—all of the speed in the world won't help if you get boxed in.

The medication made it so that one day I was fine and the next day I felt like shit, and that was the point of them. I knew I still had speed but I didn't have access to my kick in the same way as before. I had to learn to strategize, control myself, learn to win from the front or the back, learn how to get out if I got caught in the middle. I've never liked feeling runners too close to me.

A few days after Oregon, I went to the Bislett Games in Oslo, Norway. I did not run as well as I could have in this race. I ran out of steam at the 200-m mark, but I still won a bronze medal. All that mattered to me was that I was there. Each of these races would prepare me for my next and most important goal—defending my world title in Daegu, South Korea, that coming September.

Chapter 18

LOVE AND HAPPINESS

WHEN I RETURNED FROM EUROPE, I KNEW I WAS ready to leave the high-level protection of the HPC. I wanted to live as I had before, in regular housing right outside the school's grounds. I was tired of feeling trapped in what had begun to feel like a beautiful prison. All of my comings and goings were observed by multiple layers of school security and administrators. I was tired of it, and it was no longer necessary. I was racing again, so there was no need to hide from the media in the way that I had needed to the previous year. I'd gathered what I could of myself and felt strong enough to handle them.

Back then Violet and I weren't in a fully committed relationship. Violet was allowed to come see me at the HPC, and she would spend the night sometimes, but everyone, including my family, still believed she was my best friend. No matter how far I traveled or how long I was gone, I couldn't stop thinking about her. As soon as I returned from Norway, I told Violet I wanted to be in an exclusive relationship. "Just you and me, Violet. You are no longer for anyone else. Just me. And I will only be for you." I told her that I planned to move from the HPC and that we could start with her committing to stay with me a few nights a week. Violet had her own apartment near the university that she shared with my sister and one other girl. She never asked anything of me or pushed me into anything. I was the one who wanted us to have an exclusive relationship. Violet was hesitant, and I understood why.

The five-year age difference between us bothered Violet, as did the fact that she had never had these kinds of feelings for another woman. I have always known I wanted to be with women only, and the age difference didn't matter to me. I loved and trusted her. Plus, Violet saw the attention I was receiving from other girls. This was hard on her, even if I made it clear I only wanted her.

I was starting to understand how to work with social media. I'll say there were a lot of strange messages and pictures popping up on my accounts. Many people had a lot of inappropriate questions, offers, and requests for me—none of which I entertained and all of which made Violet feel uncomfortable. I had access to the world in a way I hadn't before. I had to learn to shut out the noise. It wasn't just politicians, journalists, sports officials, and academics talking about me on television or on the radio: now it was some guy or girl from America or Nigeria or Europe reaching out directly to me. After I came back from Berlin, this village girl had to learn to swim in a world that looked very different. Temptations and distractions were everywhere.

I DON'T KNOW how the rumors started. What I do remember is that a man who worked with Kobus van der Walt, who was then the director of sport at the University of Pretoria, requested a meeting with me. I was close with Kobus, and I think he sent this man because it pained him to have this kind of talk with me himself.

I had no idea what the conversation would be about. I thought it was maybe something about my studies or what the plans were for my next race. As soon as I sat down in this man's office, I sensed this was not going to be a conversation about sports.

The man seemed uncomfortable. After a few seconds of silence, he finally says, "We here at the University of Pretoria are proud of your achievements and we know you have many more ahead of you. We have discussed that perhaps now that you are back in the circuit, you . . . could maybe think about presenting yourself in a different way. . . . Maybe change things up . . . try on some different looks."

Since I prefer straight talk, I decided to help him get it out.

"Different looks? You mean more like a girl? You want me to start dressing like what you think a girl should dress like?" I sat there with my legs and arms crossed, and just stared at him.

"Well, in a way, yes. And the other thing is . . . there are rumors going around about you and another runner. They are saying you are in some kind of inappropriate relationship. We cannot have this kind of thing at the school because it doesn't look good."

"Is this about clothes or my personal life? Either way, what do my clothes or my personal life have to do with my running? I'm here to run. I'm training and that's it. I wear clothes for the track, right? Do people wear dresses on the track? And why are you bringing up my personal business?"

"Caster . . . I'm just a messenger here," the man tried to continue, but I cut him off. I wasn't having this nonsense. I respectfully, as we South Africans say, told him the way to get off.

"Maybe this person who sent you should come and have the balls to talk to me himself. Who I fuck around with, who I eat with, what clothes I wear, that's none of anyone's business. You don't buy me clothes. I came to this university wearing these clothes and I came here to study and to win medals for the program and for my country. My mommy's at home. My daddy's in Silverton. I am not your daughter. I am nothing to you."

My tone was harsh, and the guy was angry, but now he knew where I stood and could go tell everyone else. I never had a problem with Kobus, even though I knew he had sent this guy to talk to me. I'm sure Toby knew this conversation would take place, and he didn't want to have it with me himself, either. As I've said, I am a respectful person—I give respect and I expect it in return. I felt insulted by the approach.

How I lived my life had nothing to do with Kobus, Toby, or the university. There were plenty of runners in our program who were doing more than running with each other. Some would even eventually marry. The issue here was that Violet and I were two girls. My time outside of the track was mine. That was my boundary, and I wanted to make that clear.

I walked out of this man's office and immediately went to find Seme and told him what had happened. I didn't mention the rumors of a relationship between me and Violet; I only talked about the man's comments about my clothing.

"Eish, Caster. Look, I told them not to come to you with that. I told them I know my athlete. I know her personality. You're not going to change her. She's going to continue wearing her beanies and her track suits. Let's just let this go, Caster. Let's focus on the work now."

I did exactly what my coach said. I let it go, that same day, in fact. But it wasn't long before the issue came up again.

The thing is I felt like everyone knew and understood me at the school. I'd been there for two years and no one had ever discussed my clothing or my personal life, at least not to my face. What I had been given at the University of Pretoria was a proper structure, a great support system. I felt accepted. This felt like my home. I had never been judged or harassed here. I believe that if I hadn't been at the University of Pretoria, I may have turned to drugs or worse after coming back from Berlin in order to forget about my problems. But now, as I returned to running competitively, I was being asked to change.

After Berlin, it was hard for me to trust people, and the conversation about my clothes and the rumors going around about Violet and me put me on edge. I expected there would be more. I just didn't know how or when it would come up again. I could tell things had shifted in some way. My coach worked with a small group of runners—the group included myself and Violet. It felt like a good group, until it didn't.

I place trust in certain people almost immediately because my intuition tells me they deserve it. But people are human. Once that trust is broken, for me, it's over. It can never be repaired. We have a saying in Pedi that roughly translates to "you can try to catch the water you have spilled, but the soil has absorbed it."

Seme's job was to recruit and coach talent for the University of Pretoria. That was the totality of his job. But Michael crossed the line with me, and that is how things ended.

I had never discussed my sexuality with Michael. It wasn't a topic with anyone, really. Back home, everyone knew. If someone asked or the situation called for me to declare I was into girls, and I felt like it, then I did. It was my personal business. To this day, I continue to say this, whether it is about my body or my marriage or my family—I am not obligated to explain or declare anything to anyone. Period.

The beginning of the end of my relationship with Seme happened when he chose to interfere in my personal life. He was one of the best coaches I have ever had, but at that time, in 2011, Michael seemed to have lost control of his athletes. The runners were gossipy, jealous of each other. Those are natural dynamics in any team, but they are usually managed and redirected by a coach. It should have been about running, not who is dating whom. I had noticed that Seme would deliberately attempt to pit runners against each other, create issues between people. He knew Violet and I were close, so if Violet was running well, and I was running poorly, he would stress on this in a way that didn't feel normal. He wasn't trying to create "friendly competition."

I remember the day Violet told me Michael had pulled her aside and said the other runners in the group were uncomfortable with the way she and I were communicating. He'd heard there was something "not right" between us. He said if this were so, she was too old to be involved with someone my age. He told her that it seemed as if she was controlling me, taking advantage of my situation, and that maybe she was the one "teaching" me about things I shouldn't be doing. He also told her one of the male runners in the group was interested in dating her and that she should look to that side of things.

Because Violet and I had been spending more time together after Berlin, I knew it was inevitable that people would know. I just didn't think it was anyone's business. I was the one who was selfish about Violet; I wanted her around me even when I knew she had other responsibilities.

Seme helped me become a great athlete, but he was not entitled to my feelings. He was an old-school Zulu man; they had their own beliefs about same-sex relationships. Even if I had a deep affection for him, at the end of the day, I was an athlete. I never once cared or thought about Seme's personal life—he should not have interfered in mine.

I went straight to Michael and told him what Violet had said. Michael didn't deny it, and he told me that he did it for my own good. He said Violet was dating men, and I had to concentrate on defending my title at the upcoming world championships.

"Let this thing with this woman go, Caster."

I knew Violet wasn't dating men. I knew he was trying to set her up with one of the other male runners. We exchanged more words until, finally, out of frustration, he said that if I didn't stop whatever was happening with Violet, he would call my father and tell him.

My response was simple—"Call him. I don't care. What is it that my father and mother are going to do? What do you think that would change, anyway? Violet and I are together. Now you know. It's not a rumor anymore. And we will stay together. My relationship has not gotten in the way of my work for you. We are all making money. I am who I am. You don't need to threaten me. I will call my father and tell him myself." I walked away from Seme. We both knew there was no coming back from this.

The South African media picked up a story about how I wasn't running well enough and that I was distracted and that Michael didn't want to work with me anymore. I never answered or defended myself. The truth is the end came because he put personal things in front of our working relationship.

Once I was cleared to compete, I had never missed a training session. Seme knew I was on the medication. He knew how hard I was working to get back in shape. I was giving him everything I had. Violet did not get in the way of my performance. Violet made me happy; we made each other happy. After everything I'd been through that past year, it was hard to believe the same man I looked upon as a father would go behind my back and try to separate me from a person who brought me joy.

After my conversation with Seme, I went back to my room at the HPC. David, as always, was there waiting for me.

"If you've been hearing things about me and Violet . . . I'm sure you've only heard half-truths, anyway, but I am confirming that Violet and I are together, David."

He was surprised. He hadn't heard any rumors, but he'd spent a lot of time with me and Violet, and he hadn't noticed it.

I told him I'd been protecting myself, protecting my relationship, but now it was out and things would change. David did what he always did. He told me everything was going to be ok and asked if I needed anything from him.

Now I had to call my father. I wanted to do it before Seme did. It would be better if he heard it from his daughter than get whatever version my coach was going to spin up for him.

"Dad. Look, these people are going to call you or maybe they already have, I don't know. Violet and I are in a relationship. We are more than friends. We have been for a long time. It's my personal business and it does not get in the way of my running. And I will not allow anyone to interfere."

This might be what Americans call "coming out of the closet" but I didn't see it that way. My family had always known where I stood, now they would just know who I stood with.

Violet had been in my life for about three years. She'd been to my parents' home numerous times. They knew she was a very close friend. I'm sure they also knew there was more to our friendship, but they never asked. What they knew was that she was a good person, and she was always welcomed.

My father didn't sound surprised. He reminded us that we were Christians and that God told us not to judge. He added, "As your parent, Caster, all I want is for you to be happy. For you to be safe. You have been through a lot. That is all that matters to me."

Then we agreed I would come home so we could all talk as a family. I went home a few days later.

On some level, I knew my parents wouldn't have a problem. But I also understood it wasn't eight-year-old Caster telling them that one day I was going to marry a woman—this was their twenty-year old daughter, a girl whose life had been turned upside-down the past year, telling them she was in love with another woman. This daughter whose body had become the topic of conversation around the world. I had brought a lot of attention to our village and the Semenya clan. And now I would bring even more.

I remember my mother did not speak; she simply listened as the words spilled out of me.

"And I don't care about what other family thinks about this. Uncles, aunts, who are these people anyway? They have their own yards. Their own kids to worry about. I want to know where you stand, in this household, the household that matters to me. Because I don't want to hear from other people that you don't accept me. If you have a problem with me or with Violet then I will no longer come stay in a place where I am not welcomed."

I told them if it was difficult for them to live with me such as I was, then I would leave the country, I would start my life all over again somewhere else. That's how much I loved Violet. How much I wanted to be with her. When I was finished, my mother said,

"Mokgadi. We know who you are. You have been good to us and you are blessed. What makes you happy makes us happy. Who are we to question other's people's relations? This will always be your home."

My parents were not worldly people, but they knew my romantic life was a concern and an issue for many. At least South Africa's government had moved the country's thinking forward in terms of policy. To this day, South Africa is the only African country to formally legalize same-sex marriage. This happened in 2006, the year Violet and I first met, when she mistook me for a boy in the women's locker room.

I went back to the university and knew I would end my relationship with Seme after I defended my title at the world championships. I was ready to go. Ready to take on the world. I was enough. I was twenty years old now. I felt myself whole.

The South African national team traveled to South Korea in late August 2011. The field was competitive—Kenya's Jepkosgei would be there, as would Russia's Mariya Savinova and America's Alysia Montaño. The media, of course, tried to get me to talk about my year off, but I deflected. I said every human has ups and downs, and I was there to compete.

That 800-m final was crazy. The pace was insane from the beginning. I thought I had it on the straightaway but somehow Savinova ran me down in the last 75 meters or so. When that woman flew by me, I knew it was over. Whatever that woman did, it was massive—it was like a rocket passed next to me. She took the life out of my legs. Like in one of those WWF matches when the guy gets hit with a table or a chair or something. He can see it coming but there's nothing he can do about it.

I had the momentum. I could see that gold medal but then I felt Maria right next to me with 40 meters to go. Where the hell had this woman come from? I thought I was running alone, leading the pack, but suddenly she was there. There was a split second when I was going to try do something, but my legs said, "*Noooo, my girl, not today. We don't have it today. Stay in your lane. Stay where you are, just maintain, before you break something here. Just hang on . . .*"

If I had tried to fight Mariya at that point, I would have fallen on my face before I even got to the finish line. Savinova passed me with a smile on her face and got to the line in 1:55.89. I was dying right behind her and got the silver in 1:56.35.

I remember thinking, "how the hell is this woman smiling and running a 1:55?! What the hell is this?!" It didn't matter. She beat me that day. I knew I'd get a chance to kick her ass at some later point. Even when Mariya was later accused of doping, even when it was confirmed she was doping, and I would receive two upgraded gold medals for the 2011 World Championships and the 2012 Olympics, it didn't matter to me. It doesn't change the fact that she whipped my ass that day. The way I see things—whether the drugs I was being forced to take had slowed me down or the drugs she'd taken had speeded her up—a win is a win. That was the first time in my life that I felt like I truly got hit by another runner. I respected her for that win. I still do.

I didn't defend my world championship, but I had a silver medal. I was satisfied with my performance. Mariya—the same runner who told the camera to "just look" at me in 2009—gave me a warm hug. Jepkosgei, who'd earned a bronze, made it a three-way hug. There's always warmth when others win. But when I went to congratulate the American, Alysia Montaño, she ignored me. She purposefully didn't acknowledge my presence on national television. I always say I'm not bothered by these things. The truth is this one stung. Alysia is African-American. I considered her an ancestral sister. I don't know if someone on her management team talked to her about her behavior or if she had a good talk with herself, but from that moment forward, Alysia behaved with more kindness toward me.

I have spoken publicly about the lack of support from other women—both off and on the track. Some of it is jealousy, obviously. People want to win. No one likes to lose, and they don't like to see the same person win over and over again. But we praise people who constantly win if there is a consensus that they are "deserving" of it. And many of my fellow runners felt I wasn't deserving of it. They didn't even think I belonged in the same gender category. Many, if not most, of the women I run with fail to see me as someone whose fight to run free actually includes them. They are wrong about this. They will see it in due time.

I walked away from Daegu feeling even stronger. More capable. Now I had to get back to my country and walk away from the people and, eventually, the place that had become a second home to me.

PART IV

THE REDEMPTION

Chapter 19

ROAD TO LONDON 2012

S EME WAS SURPRISED WHEN I TOLD HIM I WAS leaving the group. I appreciated everything he'd done for me in bringing me to the university, but I did not owe him my heart or my body. Those were mine.

I would still run for the university's system but I would no longer live inside school grounds. Now I was ready to face the world in a different way. I didn't want to ask permission anymore. And that's what it felt like to live in the HPC—I felt like a child. Toby and David and everyone else at the school did well in taking care of me. But I wasn't a child anymore. I was a woman. I needed to be independent.

The option now was to continue training on my own as I'd done before coming to the school or find another coach. Fate would have it that one of the best 800-m runners in history was living in South Africa.

Maria Mutola was one of my heroes. If there ever was a runner I wanted to be like, it was Maria. She was a powerfully built middle-distance runner who had dominated the 800-m distance for over two decades. She was a fellow African, from a small village in Mozambique. Maria had won everything—every major title along with an Olympic gold and multiple world championships. I'd dreamt of running against her, but Maria had been born in 1972, so we had an almost twenty-year age difference, and she'd retired by the time I got to the elite level.

And she loved soccer. In 2010, Maria had moved to Johannesburg to play for Luso Africa, a top women's soccer club. There had been rumors about her gender, too, but that's where those have stayed—as rumors. As far as the world knows, Maria had not been subjected to anything close to what had happened to me. But people did talk about her looks, the shape of her body. Sports insiders and those who ran against her would often comment that she wasn't feminine enough, that she wasn't "pretty" in whatever way women were supposed to be while still being able to run faster than most humans ever could.

I admired her running style and her longevity. She was a winner. The best. I needed to be pushed in a different way. I wanted to work with someone who understood the physical pain of training, someone who had been a runner, someone who could demonstrate techniques. Seme was a great coach, but he was an old man set in his ways. And unlike Seme, Maria would understand that sexuality does not interfere with performance.

After Michael and I fell out, I'd been training alone the last few weeks before heading to South Korea for the championships. I reached out to Maria during that time, and she gave me some great technical advice. She agreed to coach me when I returned, and we began training at the end of 2011. The ultimate goal was the 2012 Olympics.

I didn't tell Maria I was on the medication. We had traveled to Düsseldorf, Germany, for a couple of races and my performances were so up and down Maria didn't understand what was going on. I was over my natural weight, and I was sick, but I still looked to be in great shape. She knew I was capable of going under 1:55, but since we began working together, I hadn't even gone sub 2. I'd have a great first lap and then blow the second one. I couldn't do a negative split. Nothing made sense to her.

After another terrible run in Germany, I finally came clean.

"Maria, I have to tell you. They are making me take these drugs. I can't run without them. We're not going to get the results we wanted from this program, and you deserve to know because we are working hard but maybe this thing is not going to happen."

Maria did something I wasn't expecting. She started crying. Big tears came down her face right there as we both stood on the track. Seeing this strong woman cry broke my heart.

"This will not be an easy road, Caster. You may never achieve these dreams of yours. I am sorry for you. I am sorry this is how it has to be."

Perhaps a different coach would have left me, but Maria stayed.

The South African sports media published stories about how terribly I was running, and ASA officials would make statements on how unimpressive I was in the lead-up to the Olympics. It would have been demoralizing to many, but I didn't worry about it. I learned from every race, regardless of the times. The point was to show up, put on my spikes, and run.

Maria's coaching style was brutal. She accepted nothing less than perfection and consistency. I had to follow her program. No alterations. She pushed me to my limit, and despite the drugs, the extra weight, and generally feeling unwell, I qualified for the July 2012 London Olympics at the trials in Pretoria with a 1:59.58. It was the first time I'd gone sub 2 on South African soil. The qualifying time was a concern for many people, since the women I'd be running against in London had posted much faster times. The talk was that it was going to be difficult for me to run against Jelimo and Jepkosgei and Russia's Savinova. And the talk also went that even those established stars were going to have problems against an exciting new young girl who'd been running incredibly well that year. Her name was Fantu Magiso.

Magiso was twenty years old and had posted some impressive times. She hadn't qualified in the semifinal at the South Korea Championships, but Magiso had been steadily improving. She was a favorite to challenge and maybe even win the 800-m gold medal in London 2012 because of her performance at the Rome Diamond League meet in June that year. People were surprised when she'd outkicked Jepkosgei to the finish line. The girl ran away from the pack and threw down a 1:57.57, an Ethiopian national record. I was there, too, but I was not feeling well and came in eighth with a 2:00.7.

MARIA TRAVELED WITH ME to London. And so did my parents—after all these years of watching me on a television screen, my parents boarded an airplane for the first time and traveled overseas. They would get to see their daughter run in person. The company Proctor & Gamble had created a "Thank You, Mom" campaign and was sponsoring trips for the mothers of Olympic athletes. I remember I told them I would participate but that I had not been born of one person and they needed to sponsor my father, too. I also had the great honor of being chosen as South Africa's flag bearer at the opening ceremonies.

I knew even before I got to London that something was wrong. I couldn't feel my body. I did my job and made it through to the final, but I felt dead.

The lineup would be stacked with pure speed—Kenya's Janeth Jepkosgei and Pamela Jelimo, America's Alysia Montaño, an exciting nineteen-year-old Burundian named Francine Niyonsaba, who had already kicked my ass in prior races, and three Russians, the strongest of which was Savinova.

Fantu Magiso, the up-and-coming Ethiopian girl whose times had been so impressive, was a DNS. Did Not Start. Fantu had traveled to London but had been removed from the lineup. Ethiopia's officials told the media she'd suffered a leg injury. She'd been walking around just fine and hadn't even run in a heat but . . . sudden mysterious leg injury. All I know is when I saw Fantu the following year, she was not the same runner. I never saw her in the running circuits again after that.

When the warm-up time came for the final run, I went over to my coach.

"Maria, I can't do it. I'm tired. I don't think I can run this thing."

Those were my exact words. Whatever I had to give, I'd given it in the heat and the semi. I was finished.

Maria wouldn't hear of it. She just looked at me and said, "You'll be fine. Just do your thing." And with that she walked away from me toward her seat in the stands. She wasn't the kind of person to entertain this foolishness from me.

I went back to the track. Here is where I usually work out any nerves, I come into myself, I do my drills. This is where usually the other runners watch me and take themselves out of the race. Instead, I stretched and . . . fell asleep. On the field. At the Olympics. The place I'd dreamt of being since I started running.

We'd been given the final call to line up, and I was snoring.

"Semenya! Semenya! Come on, girl. It's time. SEMENYA!" It was the great Kenyan, Janeth Jepkosgei, shaking me awake.

"What?! What?!" For a moment I had no idea where I was. I didn't even remember falling asleep.

Jepkosgei shook her head and looked at me like I was crazy. I turned over and grabbed my spikes. I tried to put myself together. "Whatever is going on, I don't know, but we will see," I thought.

I tried to do my final run-through. My thoughts were not connecting. "What the hell is happening?" I asked myself.

We got to the line. I couldn't quiet my mind.

The gun went off.

I was in the back of the pack. Fighting for my life. You could see the strain and disbelief on my face. I remember thinking, "What am I doing here?"

I look in front of me. Jelimo, Savinova, Jepkosgei . . . everybody is up there. . . . What is going on?

And that was the other thing, I couldn't focus. My normally quiet racing mind wasn't quiet at all. Talking. Chattering to myself. I was moving, but it was like a still picture. Nothing was flowing.

When the bell rang for the final lap, I thought, "Fuck, this is over." I was dead last, with Niyonsaba right in front of me. I just couldn't gain speed.

Maria told me she'd been so saddened by the sight of me dragging on the track, she started to leave the stadium. She couldn't bear to watch what she knew was going to happen. And then she heard a collective gasp.

I have never admitted this publicly, but when I heard the bell signaling the halfway mark, I was going to jump out.

I have never quit a race in my life.

My mind was on a loop. *"Jump out. Get out. You're going to be last. End it now. Now . . . get out, girl. Jump out . . ."* I had made it all the way to the Olympic 800-m final, and I was going to eliminate myself.

Now we're at 300 meters to go, I feel something in the body. Savinova is gone. Way out. No way to run that woman down, but something in me just kept saying, *"One step at a time, Semenya. One step at a time, girl,"* my legs were saying.

I passed Niyonsaba and Montaño and some others. I thought about my mother and father in the stands, watching their child. They'd traveled to the other side of the world to see me. These people who'd spent most of their lives in a village, these people who loved and nurtured and supported me. I could not jump out in front of my parents.

Despite everything that had happened, I had made it to the Olympics. My country had chosen me as the flag bearer. My people, my journey . . . all those who'd supported me . . . there was no way in fucking hell . . . I had to keep going.

Something reconnected between my mind and my body, some energy began to flow. I remember I started to really move. 200 meters. 150 meters. I passed more bodies. I'm looking. I'm looking, and thinking, *"There has to be a way to get up there . . . keep going, girl, there's a bronze right over there. Get there and you're on the podium."*

"OK . . . we're at the straightaway now, girl. Let's hit it," the legs talking again.

And then I ran like I've never run in my life. Ever. It felt like I was running *for* my entire life.

When I got through the line, I had won the Olympic silver medal in 1:57.23.

On the podium, I remember I kissed that silver medal. It wasn't a gold, but it might as well have been. I had worked so hard for that one. I remember that moment, looking at the medal and still being amazed that I had almost given up halfway through the race.

When I play the film back, I believe that had my body reacted right at the bell, the world would have gotten to see something they had never seen before. I would have broken the world record. I just kicked too late and ran out of track.

While we were still in London, I told Maria something didn't feel right with my knee. There wasn't pain or anything like that, but I knew. Because we work with our bodies, athletes sometimes have a sixth sense about these things—it's more like a premonition that something is about to go wrong.

"Ag. It will be fine," Maria said, "let's just go." Maria was like that. Caring but tough. She didn't want to hear about these things. For her, it was always push forward.

I HAD MY Olympic medal. I would continue training with Maria and prepare for the 2013 season.

Things went wrong almost right away. A week after we returned from London, during speedwork training at the university, there was that damn click in my right knee. The same leg and injury that had put me in a hospital when I was seven.

I said to Maria, "Remember what I said in London? I felt the click just now."

"Does it hurt? If it doesn't hurt, finish the workout." Maria had the stopwatch in her hand.

I knew I shouldn't have, but I kept going. And by the time I finished, my knee had blown up to three times its size.

Maria's eyes popped out of her head. She knew it was over.

My first thought was how my private gynecologist said I needed
to retire right after I went to the Olympics.

"Four years, Caster. You can take the medication for four
years, go to the Olympics, get your medal, and you retire in 2012.
After that, you may be doing irreparable harm to your body." I
hadn't listened to her. And now my leg was shot. I knew my season
was over.

Maria couldn't believe it. She was an excellent coach, exactly
what I needed to get where I wanted at that time, but sometimes
the mistake athletes-turned-coaches make is treating the athletes
they're training as if they are an extension of them. Maria only
wanted to implement what had worked for her on me. And, like I
said, Maria was a beast. We were similar athletes, but we weren't
the same. Maria was about perfection, hitting whatever the plan
was for that day, no matter what. That had worked for her. I was
more intuitive when it came to workouts.

I went to SASCOC, the South African Sports Confederation
and Olympic Committee, and told them I'd hurt my knee. They
assured me I would continue to receive funding and that they were
proud I'd brought home the silver medal. In May 2013, while I was
recovering, they removed me from their bursary program. I had no
idea until a friend called to say he heard on the news that I'd been
taken off the roster. The committee reported they'd heard from
ASA that I was "sitting" and would not make it to championships
in Moscow, so they couldn't fund me unless they knew I was training. Basically, neither SASCOC nor ASA believed I'd make it back,
so they didn't want to spend their funds on me.

I didn't see it coming. I brought them an Olympic silver medal
and had injured myself. They said I had their support and then they
abandoned me after just a few months. I'd bought a home in Pretoria not far from the university when I returned from London, and

Violet and I had moved in together. I'd saved and invested much of the money I'd made, so even after buying the home, I could afford to pay for my own medical expenses. I don't know what would have happened if I didn't have anything. I remember thinking—"Ok. So this is how it works. SASCOC is not to be trusted."

The years 2013 and 2014 were the two worst of my running career. Despite physio and rehab therapies, my leg constantly bothered me. I could run through the pain and discomfort, but my times were shit.

Then I lost my coach. As often happens in our world, someone Maria thought she could trust was embezzling funds from her foundation, and she'd already lost almost a million dollars. She had to leave South Africa and return to Mozambique to settle her affairs. I still wanted to work with her, so we agreed she would continue coaching me remotely for a year. Being in a long-distance relationship is difficult. Maria couldn't see the pain I was in; she couldn't help me adjust in real time.

My training did not progress well enough to qualify for the August 2013 World Championships in Moscow. The trials were held earlier in the summer in Belgium, and I clocked in at 2:01, but I needed a flat 2 for the national team. I continued trying. On September 7 I managed to dip under 2 at the World Challenge meet in Rieti, Italy. I was feeling so ill that I don't know how I managed a 1:58.92. The truth is at that point, I was running for Nike. They had remained loyal throughout the years—not taking away their support even when I was sidelined in 2009. I felt like I owed it to them to at least try.

By then, it wasn't just my leg that was holding me back. My theory is that my intense training regimen helped lessen the side effects of the drugs. Once I was injured and couldn't push myself in the same way, the side effects became worse.

It was hard for Violet to watch me suffer. We would often sleep in different bedrooms because of my night sweats and panic attacks and because I would frequently get up in the middle of the night to drink water, use the bathroom, and eat. I had constant nausea, and my stomach would turn all day and night. This thing was bending me inside.

I had to deal with my physical ailments and the constant media attention. South African media had started following Violet and me around. They had sensed something had shifted in our relationship. Whereas before there were just "rumors" about my long-time friend, now tabloid pictures of us wearing matching-colored clothes, holding hands, and driving cars with "CASVIO" license plates would confirm things. Our home was in a gated community, so they couldn't follow us inside, but it was clear we lived in the same place. We didn't care about any of it. We were going to be together.

By mid-2014, I realized I couldn't even run a 2-minute 800 meters, much less dip under it. I could not make a team.

One day, I came home from training and went straight to our couch. I held my head in my hands.

"Caster?" Violet came over and sat next to me. I took a deep breath.

"I'm done, Violet. I'm not going to do this anymore. I need a break."

"A break? The Caster I know needs a break?" I know Violet was trying to encourage me in this moment, to remind me of my fighting spirit. But I was done. Sometimes the right thing is to just sit still.

"I'm going to call Jukka. I can't finish out the season."

Once I said this out loud, all I felt was relief.

My last 800-m race was the World Challenge meet in Madrid on July 19, 2014. I came in last of eleven runners, time 2:06. Britain's Lynsey Sharp won that meet.

I reached out to Jukka immediately after the race. "I need you to cancel the rest of the season. I need to rest." Jukka didn't believe me.

"What? No. No, Caster, you just need to think about this. No need to make such a decision now. You will come out of this. You always have," he said.

"I have thought about it, my friend. It's over for me right now. If I continue like this, coming in last at these races, I'm going to lose all hope. My leg is killing me. I don't feel well, Jukka. I'm sorry. I can't. This is the right decision for me."

This period of my life taught me a lot. Sometimes quitting is the right thing to do. There are times when "powering through" really does more harm than good. By then, Maria and I had had a conversation and both decided it was best to end the coaching relationship. I needed more than she could give, but we both agreed to maintain our friendship.

I returned to Pretoria after Madrid, and the news went out that I had ended my season. Things felt very quiet. No major news media picked up on it. There was barely a blip about it on social media. My disappearing from the running circuit didn't cause major waves. I got a few messages from some athletes, but that was about it. I'm sure the IAAF was relieved. In their minds, they'd finally gotten rid of the Caster Semenya issue.

I spent the winter at home, weighing my options. I was no longer running for the University of Pretoria. I remember Toby and I had a long talk. He'd always done right by me, but he agreed it was time for me to fly. Every bird has to leave the nest. He said I would always be welcome at the school, and he'd cleared things so I was authorized to train on their grounds.

Now I was free—completely independent. I thought about soccer, of course. Maybe when I felt better, I could join a women's league. My right leg may have had a forever injury, but I could kick equally as well with my left and use my size and power to defend. I didn't actually plan to quit running, but maybe soccer could help me get back in shape. It would be a change of pace.

I spent my days resting, recovering, eating. I gained even more weight. I needed the rest, but Violet had a few other things in mind.

We both knew we wanted to eventually get married and have

kids. I'd already asked her to marry me and bought her a ring, but we hadn't told our families yet. We'd been so sure of our future together that we'd even visited an IVF clinic soon after I returned from the London Olympics. They could have just taken our money, but they ran us out of that clinic. The doctor said we were too young and should go home and think about it. We had time.

And now time seemed to be all I had.

I was feeling so ill that I went to see my gynecologist. She ran some tests and the news was not good. The drugs were causing my twenty-three-year-old body to behave like I was a middle-aged menopausal woman. The hot flashes, night sweats, panic attacks, sleeplessness, and loss of concentration were getting worse. She reminded me the medication could also be weakening my bones, making me more prone to injuries.

"You were only supposed to do this for four years, Caster. That was it. I am telling you as a medical professional. You will continue to deteriorate."

I was stubborn. I told her I was going to keep running. I would know when it was time to end it. I was physically and mentally breaking down, but I refused to give up. "There is a way back," I thought, even as I just lay around the house unable to do much of anything.

Violet came home from work one day and said some words that hurt me deeply but that needed to be said. Violet was one of those people whose soft demeanor and quiet voice could give people the wrong impression. Her kindness was not a weakness. She always told me the truth, even when I didn't want to hear it.

"I never thought I'd see you, Caster, behaving like a person who is done with life. You're just like all those people out there with no drive, no ambition. I told you a long time ago this running is not everything. It will be over one day. You know that. Look what happened to me. And now all you do is sit. You don't have an education. You never finished your degree at UP. Where are you going to work? Who will hire you? Let me tell you this . . . I am not going to marry an illiterate. I will not share my life with a person who had opportunities and just threw them away."

I will never forget Violet's face as she said these things. She was sad and furious with me. She was right. I had no drive. I wasn't me anymore. If I didn't at least get a diploma, how could I motivate other girls and women? I had become something more than a runner to my people. People loved and looked up to me. We could barely go to the mall or a restaurant without strangers asking if they could shake my hand, wanting to hug me, talking about how my strength inspired them. And if Violet and I ever had children, how would I push them to get an education if their own mother never got one? Violet never recovered from her injury and had had no choice but to give up running competitively. That did not stop her from studying and working.

Here, I must say, I cried. I cried like a child. Those tears were hot. I felt pure shame. I thought of my parents. How hard they worked to make sure my siblings and I ate and had decent shelter over our heads. Everything they'd sacrificed just so that we could continue to draw breath on this earth. They'd never had a chance to get an education. I was better than this. The first thing I did was enroll in a sports management program with the University of South Africa. It was a short course, but at least it was a start and I needed to reactivate my brains, to get back into the rhythm of being a student.

And I wasn't done with running. I was still an athlete, and I wanted to give it one more chance. I just needed a new environment, a new coach.

Around September 2014, I decided to call Jean Verster. He was a South African coach who had studied in the United States and had been an elite middle-distance runner in his day. He was known as one of the best coaches in the country and was working at the North-West University in Potchefstroom. He ran the university's high-performance center and was the point man when the Spanish men's soccer team stayed at NWU before their 2010 World Cup win.

"Why, Caster," he laughed when he heard me introduce myself. "What a pleasure and a surprise." He sounded happy to hear from me and I got straight to the point.

"I would like to train with you. I don't think my career is over. I want to learn and I want to run. I still have it. I just need a place where I can find it again."

Jean told me that he'd admired my career and that he knew I'd been having some troubles. He said I'd done the right thing canceling my season, that my body was telling me to rest and I had to listen to it. Jean asked me to meet with the head of the NWU sports program the following week to see how we could work together.

I knew I wasn't the same Caster. I was still nursing my injured leg and I was grossly overweight, but all I needed was a chance. The director offered me a three-year scholarship. I would study sports science. Soon after, I met with Jean in person. Even seeing how out of shape I was, he believed in me.

Potch was about 180 kilometers away from Pretoria. Violet wasn't happy about the distance, but I would no longer be sitting. I moved to Potch in late October 2014. It was exactly what I needed—small and rural, almost like my own birth village. There were no distractions there—not much else to do but eat, study, train, and sleep, which is all I wanted.

Jean was a soft-spoken and deliberate man. He had a calming presence. He did not push me. What we needed, he said, was to get me back to basics. More than anything, Jean wanted me to rediscover my love of running. He believed I understood my body better than anyone else. If he knew I was on the IAAF's drug regimen, he didn't let on. We never discussed it. Jean treated me like he treated everyone else in the group.

I trained and studied sports science with a passion I didn't know I could have. I allowed a few media interviews once word got out that I was trying to run again. I told myself to be happy, to stay positive, to salvage the feeling of hope I'd begun to have while there. I was determined to go to the Olympics in 2016, and I wanted another world championship. People may have thought I was delusional. The IAAF certainly thought I was done—they were still monitoring me and taking my blood, but they weren't as hectic, and they weren't showing up multiple times in a month.

I often say my journey feels predetermined because somehow it feels like a higher power has moved things in ways that have kept me going. The backlash about my treatment at the Berlin championships had made the IAAF revisit their sex testing and gender policies. Prior to my ordeal, they were used to more or less quietly getting women like me off the track. But the international scandal and political fallout that came after Berlin 2009 forced the IAAF to have to publicly state their position. After the negotiations with my legal team and the back and forth between medical experts in 2010, the IAAF officially announced their regulations for "hyper-androgenic women"—or women with naturally elevated levels of testosterone—in 2011. They set a testosterone level limit of 10 nmol/L. Lamine Diack was still head of the IAAF when the deal that allowed me to keep running was made. I remember there was a Dr. Stéphane Bermon and a female doctor, Dr. Angelica Lindén Hirschberg, who were also part of the IAAF's medical team for those negotiations.

All I had to do to run was be at 10 nmol/L or below to participate in any IAAF-sanctioned race. That's it. And that's what I always did. My belief was that given my still being competitive on the track for several years while on the medication, the IAAF thought 10 nmol/L was still too high. They needed to find medical evidence to prove this. I had refused the surgery they knew would have quickly gotten me off the field, so I believe the IAAF went out searching for other girls like me and began experimenting on them. They wanted to get the data they needed to revisit their 2011 regulations and eliminate me.

Sometime in 2012, Dr. Bermon was part of a group of doctors at the Department of Reproductive Endocrinology at the University Hospital in Nice, France. They performed gonadectomies on four young women, all considered elite athletes at the time. The paper was published in a medical journal in 2013. It reads like a horror movie to me. I remembered that doctor's name—this Dr. Stéphane Bermon was the same person back in 2009 who told my legal team their method of dealing with my condition was surgery.

These girls were all from "rural or mountainous regions in developing countries"—meaning they were all probably coming from a place with little resources. Developing countries meant they were definitely not European. The girls were between the ages of eighteen and twenty. They were all unnamed, although Annet Negesa, the Ugandan girl, has publicly said she believes she was one of the girls used in the study. And I believe I ran with one of the other girls in this unfortunate group—a young girl who was a fantastic runner, then suddenly couldn't make good times and disappeared from the circuit. She is one of the runners you could see had lost the light in her eyes.

I think any human would find what happened here sickening. One of the girls was referred to the hospital because the antidoping officer noticed she had a large clitoris, another girl was referred to the IAAF's medical department by her own federation's doctor, and the other two girls were picked because they showed a higher-than-normal endogenous testosterone levels during routine blood and urine draws for their athletic biological passports, which is supposed to be an antidoping tool. After confirming all of the girls had a DSD, the doctors proposed gonadectomies with clitoridectomy—the surgical alteration of their clitoris—and some future "vaginoplasty" so their vaginas would look more like whatever a vagina is supposed to look like to these people. The study says they told the girls the surgeries "would likely decrease their performance" but that sports authorities would allow them to compete in the female category after one year.

The study went on to say, "In contrast to the tendency to request a gender change, our four athletes wished to maintain their female identity and had many questions about menstruation, sexual activity, and child-bearing."

"In contrast to the tendency to request a gender change." What tendency? Where is this tendency? Where did these doctors come up with this idea? I was not surprised all four athletes wished to "maintain their female identity." They were women. Why would their hormone levels or the way their privates looked change that? The paper doesn't explain this. It is just assumed that women who have a certain testosterone level don't want to be women.

The girls were told their performance *would likely decrease* due to the surgeries. I am sure not one of these girls ever saw an elite-level competition again. The heartbreaking part was how the study detailed how they'd had many questions about child-bearing and menstruation and sex. Like me, they were probably all thinking about their future families and had no idea of their medical condition. The message was that something was "wrong" with them—inside and outside. Not only would they not be able to make a living by running in any IAAF-sanctioned races and would possibly be losing educational scholarships, but they were also being told that society did not consider them women. The implication was that their bodies were lacking and damaged while the truth was that they were strong and perfectly healthy.

In the summer of 2014, while I was sitting at home injured, physically ill, and unsure of my future, an eighteen year old Indian sprinter named Dutee Chand had been flagged for gender verification after winning two gold medals at the Asian Junior Athletics Championship. Her story was similar to mine. The IAAF said they had received an anonymous complaint from another athlete about her physique and running style. When she received a call from her country's sports federation asking her to come in for a test, she assumed it was for doping. She described a series of demeaning tests where doctors probed, measured, and photographed her privates and breasts and took blood and urine samples. It was then leaked to the media that she'd "failed" a gender test and she was pulled from her national team. As would eventually happen with me, the IAAF blamed her country's sports federation for the leak, and she was told she couldn't compete unless she had surgery or took medication to lower her testosterone level.

Dutee was an innocent girl from a village in India—like me, she had already started helping her family with her earnings. Her times were nothing out of the ordinary for the female category, but it was the way she looked that seemed to be a problem. Dutee described feeling embarrassed, depressed, and confused. She refused both the solutions offered to her. She did not understand why they were saying she needed a surgery and medication if she wanted to run with girls. With the help of a journalist who was also an academician in gender matters, Dutee announced she would bring a legal challenge to the IAAF's hyperandrogenism regulations at the Court of Arbitration for Sport that winter. The case eventually went to CAS in March 2015.

I was not aware of Dutee, or even aware of the IAAF's medical study on the four young runners, until much later. The IAAF's position was that women with high testosterone levels had an unfair advantage equal to the advantage that male athletes had over female athletes. On its face, this is ridiculous. We are not men. I am a great runner, and I train with men, some of whom I can maybe give a hard time to on my best day, just like any other elite female athlete could, but I have never been able to even approach an elite male runner's times. Likewise, there are plenty of men with normal "male" testosterone levels whose only hope of beating a female athlete with "female" levels is in their dreams.

While Dutee's case was winding its way through the court, I continued to take the poison and train. Jean and I created a beautiful relationship; we trusted each other, and I was slowly starting to climb back up mentally and physically. On August 1, 2015, I surprised myself by qualifying for the Beijing World Championship with a 2:00 800 meter at the trials in Lynz, Austria. I wasn't feeling well and I still didn't have my form, but I would be back on the world stage after more than two years. The Beijing World Championship would be taking place at the end of August, which meant I only had around three weeks to train.

I remember I was still packing my things in Austria to return home when I received a call from Greg.

"Hey Caster! How are you, my dear? How are things? How is the leg?"

I was glad to hear Greg's voice. Throughout the years, he'd never given up on me. By then, we were more like daughter and father than lawyer and client.

"Greg, my man. I'm good. I'm happy. I just qualified for Beijing. I'm figuring things out but I'm feeling better."

"Well, I have news that will make you feel even better, Caster," Greg said. "The IAAF lost a case about their hyperandrogenism regulations. You can stop taking the medication immediately. As of today. Right this second. They have two years to come up with scientific evidence that testosterone gives women an unfair advantage. You're free now, Caster." I could hear the overwhelming emotion in his voice. Greg was so happy for me.

I wasn't sure what to say.

I may have said something like, "OK, Greg. Thank you. I'll call you when I get back home." And I hung up. I didn't really know what to think. I wasn't sure I'd heard him correctly. I didn't get excited. I had lost the ability to be excited about things at that point in my life. I don't think I believed what I'd just heard. But then my phone rang again.

The next call was from Jukka, my manager.

"Caster, dear girl, did you hear? Did you hear about what's happened? . . . The IAAF dropped the regulations. HAHA!!! My girl . . . you know what this means, eh?" I could imagine Jukka's smiling face, his hands probably waving around excitedly.

"Hey. . . . Yes. Thanks, Jukka. I heard something about this today, but . . . I don't know . . ." This news was hard to process for me. Like you are drowning and see someone coming to save you, but you don't know if they are real and even if they are, you wonder if they will get to you in time.

"Caster. Listen to me, it's real. You don't have to take the medication anymore. Now, my girl, you know what to do. . . . *Let's go kill these motherfuckers.*" I can still hear Jukka's laugh when he said this. I couldn't help but laugh a little, too.

After so many years of struggle and loss and sickness, I just didn't know what to think. Jukka asked me if I was happy. I told him I didn't know. I didn't know what I was feeling. The truth is I didn't trust the IAAF. We would have to see if the decision meant anything.

But I stopped taking the medication that day. I threw the pills I had with me in the trash.

I felt the first stirrings of hope in my chest.

Chapter 20

GOLD IN RIO

W E WERE TRAINING ON SCHOOL GROUNDS WHEN it suddenly began to rain. It was just me, my pacer, and Verster.

My coach wanted to end the session.

"Is it raining blood?" I asked him.

"What?" Jean looked at me like I was crazy.

"Is it raining blood here, my man? My session isn't over. I am training. You stay here and watch me. If you leave, you can never come back. You can go get an umbrella, do whatever you need to, but I'm training here. And I want my times. Give me my times." By then the rain was heavy, coming down in sheets. There was no wind, no thunder. Just a steady pour. My pacer stood there, soaked, looking back and forth between me and Verster.

And Verster shook his head, smiled to himself, and stayed. And here is where I believe he truly began to know me as the athlete that I could be, as the athlete that I am. I wanted to show him I was worth his time; worth the spot they'd given me at the school. We were training for the Beijing World Championship.

I was determined to be a winner again.

I WOULD SAY 2015 and 2016 were years of renewal. I rebuilt myself at Potch with Verster and his athletes. It was a strong group, and I would eventually become a sort of mentor and mother figure to the younger athletes. I didn't look like the rest of them, meaning I wasn't in shape and I was still limping around. But I had a single-minded focus and complete and total determination. I was going to be a champion again. I was going to find my way to the Olympics again. I was going to win gold medals. That was it.

I'd stopped the medication in early August. My plan was to heal my body and mind. I drank as much water and electrolytes as my body could take and I sweated and peed like nobody's business. The pause in regulations seemed real, and I wanted to flush out as much of the poison as quickly as I could. SASCOC began calling me but I refused to answer them. I'm sure they had heard I was training again, and they smelled an Olympic medal in the future. When they couldn't get in touch with me, they sent an official to see me at NWU. I remember a middle-aged Black woman with glasses carrying a briefcase who met me on the track. She was wearing her official SASCOC identification. The conversation did not go well. I started talking before she even introduced herself.

"Why are you here?"

"I am here to discuss your relationship with SASCOC," the official said.

"I have no relationship with SASCOC. They dropped their support right after I won an Olympic silver medal and injured my knee. They didn't even call me so I could make preparations for my family. Don't you know what was done to me?"

"No," she said. I didn't think she was telling me the truth. "I wasn't in the office at that time so I have no idea about what happened. We'd like to discuss your future."

"OK. Please tell whoever sent you that I don't give a fuck about SASCOC. They didn't care about me when I was in need. I have to go now before I say more I will regret." And I walked away from this person.

SASCOC continued trying to reach out to me. They sent emails. They still called my phone and the school. They even sent a fellow athlete and close friend of mine, Kgothatso "KG" Montjane, to try and convince me. She knew they were never going to change my mind. As far as I was concerned, I didn't need them. If I qualified for the Olympics, then I qualified, and they would place me on the team. These people wanted medals. I didn't need favors from them, and I didn't need to be nice. I would always sacrifice myself for my country, but not for any federation or organization. I would run for myself, my friends, my family. Not for them.

I traveled to the World Championships in Beijing in August 2015. This time, Jukka and Masilo from Nike traveled with me. I remember a journalist asked me about Dutee Chand, and I told them, "I'm here to run. I'm not here to talk about such stuff. I'm not an IAAF spokesperson."

It felt great to be back among top athletes, but after the first heat on August 26, I knew I wasn't going to make it to the final. I managed a 1:59.59, which qualified me for the 2016 Rio Olympics, but I went back to my room and just collapsed on the bed. The semifinals were the next day. I did not sleep well, and I didn't wake up feeling any better. As soon as I got to the stadium, I told both Jukka and Masilo I wasn't going to make it. The other women were just too fast, and my body was tired.

Jukka did not take it well.

"If you want to quit running, Caster, then just quit. Better than hearing you say such things like this. This is not who you are. I'd rather you just get off the field now and don't even try." I said nothing to Jukka. He walked away from me. Jukka respected me, and I know he was saying it to motivate me, but I knew my body.

Masilo just put his arm around my shoulder and said, "you are fine, Mokgadi. Just go out there and give it what you can. Don't worry. Just be you."

I remember I lined up and the gun went off and I came in last with a time of 2:03.18. I dug deep for that run . . . I don't even know how I was able to walk back to the locker room. It was all I had. I can't say I was disappointed. You can never be disappointed when you know you gave everything. I remember I saw Masilo again later that day.

"I told you I wasn't going to make it this time, uncle. But I'm going to get you and the Nike people a gold medal at the Olympics next year."

Masilo smiled. He'd become a great friend by this point, more like a member of my family than the executive responsible for my sponsorship at a global company. "You do your thing, Caster. Rest now and you come back stronger next year. We are here for you. We believe in you."

And they had. Throughout it all, Nike had never abandoned me. For now, it was all about me training and getting healthy.

I sat in Jean's office after Beijing to have a conversation about my progress, what I wanted, what I believed I needed. Jean was not one of those "it's my way or there's the door" kind of coaches. He allowed me to combine everything I'd learned from Seme and Maria and create my own program, what I felt would work for me.

I've had only three coaches in my life—Seme, Maria, and now Verster. Seme's and Maria's approach to coaching was night and day. Where Seme was soft, Maria was a hammer. Michael's program improved upon whatever I'd built running barefoot and alone on those dusty grounds in Limpopo as a teenager. His philosophy was, "If it isn't broke, don't fix it." "We'll just keep doing what you've been doing, Caster," he would say. He believed in stretching things out, moving along slowly, conditioning, and then when the body was ready, you hit it. He didn't rush things; he didn't push until he was absolutely sure. Michael was one of those coaches who didn't believe in pain; he believed in slow buildups. Maria's style was hardcore. If the plan for the day was to run 200s in 27s, then that is all we were doing, no matter what. Maria did not rest me well, but she made me a beast, she recreated in me an image of herself.

Verster was different from them. Verster believed in gut feelings. Before every session, he would ask me how I felt that day. It was an interesting thing for me. And I could be honest with him. If I said, "I don't feel like training hard today," he would honor that. I would say he wore my edges down; on some level, he must have known how much I'd suffered trying to conform to the IAAF's regulations, even if we never discussed it. If I wanted to spend an entire training session on weights or sprints or stretching, then I was free to do that. What he wanted was to see me regain the joy of running.

And I was doing it. I could feel it coming back to me.

I took everything I'd learned until that point and combined it with Jean's program. I sat in his office and showed him what I wanted to do, how I wanted to prepare for the 2016 season—especially the Olympics and every major race after that. I'd been studying anatomy, studying physiology, even psychology. The more I learned at Potch, the more I saw what had been missing with Michael and Maria and where I needed to add. At this point, I had been on the drugs since 2009. For more than six years, the majority of my professional life, I had been running in a body that wasn't my own. This time, things would be different.

"Jean, I love you. I love your coaching style. But I think I must do this on my own. You can come and see me whenever you want. You know where I will be. The group will be over there." I pointed left. "And I'll be over there." I pointed right. "I need to focus on myself. You can focus on the other athletes. I don't want you to worry about me. I have to worry about me and I have to worry about this leg."

Jean sat there and listened. Even if he didn't agree with certain things, he was going to let me be me. Finally, he smiled.

"Do it, Caster."

While I was returning to my natural state of being, the World Anti-Doping Agency had discovered that some of my peers were purposely altering theirs. After a thorough investigation, they recommended Mariya Savinova and other Russian athletes be given a lifetime ban and be stripped of all their medals dating back to 2010. The Russian federation had been bribing IAAF officials for years to look the other way while they illegally drugged their athletes. And this is why I say that the IAAF is first and foremost a political organization. For them, it isn't about the beauty of sport, developing and rewarding natural talents—it's about money and influence and power. Doped athletes like Savinova had been winning medals and prizes, yet despite the IAAF's talk about cleaning the sport of illegal drugs, it was people like me and Dutee whose natural bodies were seen as abnormal and were being targeted and shamed out of the sport. We were the ones enduring public humiliation when people who had taken illegal drugs were portrayed as just victims of their own government's thirst for medals.

Around the time the Russian doping scandal was exposed, in November 2015, Lamine Diack was removed as president of the IAAF. I remember that back in 2009, Diack agreed to come to South Africa, sit down with our government's sports federation, and speak directly with me about the IAAF's mishandling of my case. But he canceled his South Africa trip in October 2009 and traveled instead to meet with Russia's president for a sports and economics conference. I did not care that he went to Russia to do whatever he needed to line his pockets, but I believe he should have kept his commitment to meeting with us. Years later, Diack, along with his son, would be convicted of accepting bribes and turning a blind eye to Russia's doping program. As the Americans say, karma is a bitch.

I was not focused on IAAF politics at the time. My focus was on winning and maintaining my home life. I had officially moved to Potch full-time in October 2015, but I was going back to Pretoria every weekend so I could spend time with Violet.

Violet and I knew we were going to spend our lives together and had decided we were going to do it the right way. It was important to us that we honor our customs, our ancestors, in the way our families had been doing for generations. We planned to marry at the end of the year.

Violet and I are from the same tribe, but she was raised by a Tsonga family. The wedding customs are similar regardless of which tribe you're born into. I first consulted with my ancestors,

I visited their graves, I prayed for guidance, and hoped for their blessing. I remember my grandfather came to me in a dream soon after. He told me the Semenyas were happy with my choice and would accept Violet into the family. Once I had this confirmation, I sat with my parents and my siblings and told them I wanted to marry Violet, and that I'd had our ancestors' blessing. My family was happy.

Now the process would begin. It is a complicated one to outsiders' eyes, but it is one we are proud of. Violet and I believed that by following our tribal traditions and honoring our ancestors, our marriage would be blessed for the rest of our days.

My family first sent a letter to Violet's home. It essentially said the Semenyas had seen a rose in their yard, and we wanted to bring it home with us and nurture it there. Violet's family sent a letter back saying they had received our letter of intent and would like to hear more. This is how the negotiation for *lobola* begins. The *lobola* isn't about "buying" a person, even if that's what it looks like to foreigners' eyes. It is just a practical and respectful exchange of resources that cements a lifelong union between two families. And it isn't just money—it could be cattle, household items, clothing.

These negotiations can feel almost like a game of chess; and even if you know the outcome, it can still be very suspenseful. Only the elders and family representatives may speak. If the families are not seeing eye to eye, there is usually a big show of walking away and trying again another day. Thankfully, we came to an agreement that same day. I had brought everything with me, and then the fun began.

We spent hours singing and dancing and eating. Violet came back with us to my birth village at the end of the festivities, and she spent the weekend at my parents' home fulfilling the customary duties of a new daughter-in-law. We were officially married in the eyes of our tribal law.

The pictures of us in our traditional wedding clothes dancing in

Violet's village were leaked almost immediately. That moment was ours, and we wished it had remained private, but we were not hiding our relationship. I found it interesting that people to this day still comment on my dressing "like a man" at the ceremony. People made a big deal of me paying *lobola* to Violet's family, probably because men are traditionally the ones who give *lobola* to the woman's family. It didn't matter to me. They pointed out I had taken on the traditional man's role in our partnership, and somehow this was proof I should not be running with women. To that, I say, so what? And where's the surprise? When have I made a secret that I dress like a man? When did I ever say I wasn't masculine? A shock would have been if I'd done the opposite. But there would be no point to my putting on women's wedding attire. Our ancestors never said two women couldn't get married, and they never said anything about what those women were supposed to wear or who should offer *lobola* to whom. When we married again in early 2017, in the Western "white wedding" tradition, Violet wore a white bridal dress and I wore a mens' suit. It was a beautiful event that we spent an entire year planning. People talked, and again, we did not care. I am what I am.

In any case, my life was good. I felt blessed. In 2015, I had a coach I trusted and a system where I was allowed to be myself; my body was coming back to me, and now I was a happily married woman.

THE SOUTH AFRICAN National Championships were to be held in Stellenbosch in April 2016. I told Jean that I wanted to treble and he should sign me up for three races—I was going to run the 400-m, 800-m, and 1500-m events. He thought I was insane. "You can't do that, Caster." I did it. I became the first woman, the first human, to run and win all three races in a four-hour timespan.

Soon after, I traveled to the African Championships in Durban on June 26. I won the gold in the 800 meter and 1500 meter, and anchored the winning team in the 4 × 400 meter relay. Everything was clicking for me. I remember I didn't like the way my ankle felt after the relay. I limped a little when I was going to get my medals, but it was nothing to worry about. When the races were over, an ASA official asked if I would greet the new president of the IAAF, a man named Sebastian Coe. I don't remember specifics; all I remember is a White man in a black suit. I said, "Nice to meet you, sir," shook his hand, and then told him I had somewhere I needed to rush off to. It wasn't until years later that I realized I had met Sebastian Coe in person. I hope he got the show he was looking for when he came to the event.

I should have stayed home and rested after I came back from Durban, but I pushed on. My next big race would be a Diamond League meet in Monaco on July 15. I wanted to make a fast time, make it clear to everyone I was back in form. And I set a new 800-m national record there with a 1:55.33 run.

And then my ankle . . .

Violet came to pick me up at the airport, and I could barely walk. My ankle was huge, as big as a baby's head. I'd broken my navicular bone playing baseball when I was a teenager, and it had never healed properly. I knew I'd aggravated the same injury. We were one month away from the Olympics.

I had several MRI scans done in South Africa, and Jukka sent them to Dr. Hans-Wilhem Müller-Wohlfahrt in Germany, a famous orthopedist known for helping elite athletes get back on their feet. He called and said that in his expert opinion I was out of the Olympics. It was a stress fracture.

"This girl will not run," he'd told Jukka.

When Jukka called me with the news, I said, "Respectfully, Jukka, fuck him. He doesn't know me." I refused to accept or even entertain the idea that I would miss the Olympics. I had a chance to win a gold medal. Not silver, not bronze. Gold. And that medal was mine.

My thinking was that if I was going to break my ankle for good, if I never ran again after the 2016 Olympics, then let it be so. I know I've said I am a practical girl; I should have been thinking of my future, but that's how I felt. After everything I'd been through, for me, it was an Olympic gold medal now or never.

I went to my favorite physiotherapist, Anita van der Lingen. My ankle was huge—you couldn't see any bones in it at all. Jean was stressed because he knew he had allowed me to do my own training programs. Everyone, including Violet, felt I had overtrained and run in too many races.

I didn't want to stress people out more than they were. I told Jean he was officially off the clock when it came to me. He could rest himself and I would call him if I needed him.

Above all, I didn't want it to get out I was injured. Competitors smell blood in the water when they find out about these things. I asked Jean to please not alert any of the school officials. I would do my best to walk normally whenever I came across people at the school or on the street. It was easy because I had a distinct limp from my knee injury when I walked anyway. The moment I was out of their eyesight, I would have to stop myself from screaming in pain.

Anita was incredibly talented, and she tried her best, but she could not bring the swelling down.

That's when I decided to open the journey for her.

There are times Western medicine is fine, and there are times when we need to do things in the way of our ancestors.

So, just like I'd seen my grandmother do for those she treated, I grabbed a razor and I cut myself. Many times. There was bad blood in that ankle. It needed to come out. You can still see the razor marks on my leg today.

As soon as I let the bad blood out, the swelling came down. You could now see the veins at the surface of my skin. Anita was shocked when she saw me again. We kept working on the ankle, and about two or three weeks before the Olympics, we heard a click. My ankle wasn't back to normal, and it still hurt, but something had snapped back into place. We began strapping the ankle while I continued to train, mostly in the gym. I was using a machine that worked my entire body; it allowed me to swing my legs and put the same kind of stress on them as if I were pounding the ground but without the force of gravity. I couldn't run, so I'd have my pacer next to me using a similar machine. I went out to the track and realized I could now run straight, but I couldn't run the bends. I made the decision to do only the straightaway and attempt to bends once I got to Rio.

I delayed my trip until one week before the games started. I wanted to stay home for as long as possible and avoid the craziness I knew would be waiting for me in Rio.

I'd hoped to run in the 400 and the 800 meter. I knew it would piss off a lot of people if I participated in both distances, but given the state of my leg, it was best to just keep it to the 800 meter.

Verster wanted to go over our plans for the race, but I remained quiet. We had an unspoken understanding and trust.

"You will have to trust me, Coach," I said the night before the race. "You just have to trust me because I am trusting my body."

By now, everyone knew that Dutee's win against the IAAF meant that I, along with anyone else suspected of having a DSD, would be running free. Anyone connected or interested in the sports world, analysts and sports scientists, academicians, even athletes who weren't in the same events or even competing anymore, were talking about it on television, radio, social media.

My win in the 800 meter seemed "inevitable," not because I'd been training and running well, but because people felt I had something that made my winning unfair. Yet they thought nothing of cheering on the seeming inevitability of wins by genetically gifted athletes like Usain Bolt, who boasted millions more fast-twitch muscle fibers and a stride that was several inches longer than his peers. No one suggested Michael Phelps's dominance was unfair and he should take medication so he produces just as much lactic acid as his competitors or have surgery to fix his hypermobile joints. Swimmer Katie Ledecky was never accused of being a man because she smashed multiple world records, and her ever-improving times in several events would actually qualify her for the men's Olympic team. But it mattered if I won because I represented something that was abnormal.

The implication everywhere was that I wasn't a woman. There were people speculating on how many "gender benders" would be at the Olympics, and some even raised the horror of there being an all "intersex" 800-m winners' podium.

I remember Paula Radcliffe, a long-retired marathoner who'd held the world record, went on various major news outlets. She had testified against Dutee's right to run and in support of the IAAF in the landmark case. Her view was that if women like us—meaning women with differences in sexual development—were allowed to run, then the women's category would be destroyed. Radcliffe saw a risk that coaches would start traveling to certain communities where hyperandrogenism is more prevalent, searching for girls who would be able to perform and "looked fast," and train them to win.

It seemed to me from the reports, though, that in Radcliffe's mind, my performance had very little to do with my training, my dedication, my mental strength. It all came down to my natural hormone levels, even though Western science still does not have conclusive evidence that testosterone is the definitive marker of the performance difference between men and women. A lot of people agreed with her concerns. But there were many people who would identify discrimination in her statement too. Paula Radcliffe was talking from a position of privilege, and in my opinion, utter pettiness too.

There was so much abuse coming at me from everywhere. Things got so crazy that Olympic officials feared I would be physically harmed, and they hired armed guards to protect me at the stadium. It didn't matter to me. I focused on training and getting used to the conditions. I tried to shut out as much of the noise as I could.

The day before the opening ceremonies, new IAAF president Sebastian Coe stated they were surprised at the Court of Arbitration for Sport's ruling striking down the testosterone regulations. He told the media they would revisit the hyperandrogenism issue in the next year. He then tried to make himself look good by adding that it was important to remember that "these are human beings . . . athletes" and that the issue needed to be treated "sensitively." Bullshit. If he wanted to treat it sensitively, the right thing to do was remind the media the Olympics were about sport, to please keep their focus on that and enjoy the show. He should have set the tone as the leader of the world's most powerful athletic organization. Instead, his comments heightened the media frenzy. His talk made the other runners feel like there was injustice in my presence, and I shouldered the brunt of it.

Journalists tried their best to get me to comment, hounding me the entire week before my heats. I mostly just ignored them. They reported I was "hiding" at the Olympics. I wasn't hiding. I was there. I would look at them and walk right by. I just didn't want to talk. What was the point? People wanted to know if I'd met with Dutee. I did see Dutee out on the track during an evening training session. I went over and we talked for a few minutes. I wished her luck in her event and told her she must stay strong and focus on her goal. She was trying to qualify for the 100-m final. We never discussed the gender issue or her case. That wasn't necessary. We were athletes first and foremost, but I did have an immense feeling of gratitude. Dutee had chosen to fight in court, and she had won. I was at the Olympics in the natural body God gave me because of her courage and will to fight.

No more night sweats, panic attacks, or nausea. I felt stable, my system strong and healthy. I felt whole; physically better than I had in years, even though I arrived at the Maracaña Stadium with only one good leg. The only people who knew my ankle was a potential issue were Verster, Jukka, Violet, Masilo, and my physio, Anita.

Two hours before the 800-m final run, Sebastian Coe made a second public statement vowing the IAAF would go back to CAS with the proper evidence and have their regulations reinstated. To me, it was just another bullying tactic. And it felt very, very personal. This was the same thing that happened in 2009, when a few hours before my run, the IAAF told the media there were questions about my gender. The point was to shame me and wind things up. Once again, they were telling the world and the other athletes that women like me didn't belong there. I didn't care what he said. My business was to run and to win. I wanted my gold medal.

I remember how nervous Verster was. He was pacing in the warm-up area.

"Chill, Coach. We've got this," I told him. "I'm going to go there and run my race. Everything is going to be OK." I put my hands on his shoulders and smiled.

"OK, Caster. I can tell you're feeling good. Just go out there and float. This is what you've been waiting for." He took a deep breath. . . . "Enjoy your final."

We hugged, and I walked away.

The chatter about the 800-m final was brutal. I didn't give a shit, but there were also rumors going around about two other young runners who would be in the final with me—Burundi's Francine Niyonsaba and Kenya's Margaret Wambui. We happened to be the only three women of color in the lineup, and we were all African. This was the first Olympics for both of those girls, and I felt bad they had to deal with this. My only hope was the talk wasn't affecting their mindset and they would go out there and give it their best. Some of the other female athletes were busy getting in front of cameras and lamenting they would be running for "bronze" or anonymously giving quotes about how "unfair" the situation in the final was going to be.

I had long ago learned to use people's nonsense to fuel my performance. "Keep talking, motherfuckers," I thought, "keep watching me." I did my thing during the warm-ups. I made sure each athlete and their managers and coaches saw me. Whatever direction my competitors were coming from on that track, they would see me preparing and know I was there to conquer. I was

THE RACE TO BE MYSELF 255

there to win. I wanted what I had been dreaming of since I started this journey—an Olympic gold medal. I didn't really give a fuck then or now what they were talking about.

I remember I stood in lane three going over my plan in my head. It wasn't different from what I'd done in the past, but I had a different kind of determination this time. I was prepared for this to be the last race I'd ever run. My body and mind were fully connected. I was present and ready.

The gun fired, and off we went. No one broke out in front. After the first bend, my ankle was still good, and I settled in on the inside. I took the lead, but not by much. I didn't want to get ahead of myself.

Don't kick too early.

I couldn't see anything beyond the track in front of me, but I could hear the steady pounding of the other runners just behind me.

I glanced quickly over my right shoulder and there was Niyonsaba. That girl was putting on a show. She was quickly gaining pace. I stared straight ahead. Run your race. Steady.

"OK, Semenya, get ready for it, girl . . ."

Fifteen more seconds and there was the bell for the final lap. Francine wanted to move to the inside, and she was running faster than I wanted to, so I let her pass. I didn't want to mess her up. No collisions. She was the leader now. And that girl was flying.

Francine had beaten me a few times before. She was working it. But I didn't think the young girl could sustain her surge. I could hear her breathing. I resisted the urge to get in front of her again.

"Hold yourself . . . wait for it . . ."

I was just behind her, feeling comfortable where I was. My chest was high, my arms pumped rhythmically, I controlled my breaths and just let her carry me along. It was a good position. I knew she was the only person I needed to beat. The rest of the pack was now chasing us.

And then it was time. The straightaway. Pure speed now. No strategizing.

I planted my feet a little more firmly, asked my body for more, and it responded right away.

I was in the zone now, everywhere and nowhere at the same time.

You can get there, girl. Keep going. It's yours. That gold is yours.

I am sure in the moment I thought of nothing. But now when I think back to that race, I feel that perhaps images would have come and gone in my mind.

Me running barefoot in the rain, my legs and feet caked with mud. I could see myself back in our yard caring for our animals.

Run like a madwoman. Let's go, girl . . .

I could see my mother and father in our village and how in this moment they would be sitting in front of the television, holding each other, hearts beating as one, screaming at this daughter of theirs to GO!

And my friend and now wife. How back in 2009 Violet had given me the South African flag to carry with me to Berlin. How she'd told me to get off my ass and get an education.

I was sprinting now. The last gear. After this, I would have nothing left. Now I could hear the crowd roaring. I knew I'd left Niyonsaba behind.

There it is, girl . . .

I saw the line.

I crossed it.

I'd won the gold. 1:55:28. A new national record.

Niyonsaba came in second, and Wambui had come out the winner in a hard-fought battle for bronze with Canada's Melissa Bishop.

Just like the Beijing 2008 Olympics, this was a clean sweep for the continent of Africa. I was so proud of us in that moment.

Right after, I did the Cobra and went to congratulate the other runners. It had been a great race. There hadn't been any falls or jostling, and several of the women also set NRs and PBs.

And then Britain's Lynsey Sharp happened. There is an infamous picture of Linsey holding on to a sobbing Melissa Bishop while I tapped her back to congratulate them. Both ignored me, but it was Lynsey whose back I had touched. Her lack of acknowl-edgment on the biggest sports stage was crude. Bad sportsman-ship. Sore loser. And she wasn't done yet.

Sharp then made a spectacle of herself when she went on to cry during a live interview about how she and Melissa Bishop and Joanna Jóźwick "all knew how each other felt" and they were hop-ing something would be done "at the top" about the "issue." She said "the public can see how difficult it is with the change of rule" and that if you "take away the obvious ones it's really competi-tive." Linsey had beaten me in a few races in prior years. When she won, the race was fair. When she lost, she turned on the tears. She had come in sixth in Rio and set a PB but she, and whatever caucus she had formed, felt like they deserved the medals.

Canada's Melissa Bishop, whose dramatic sobbing about los-ing the bronze medal you could probably hear outside the sta-dium, had won a silver medal at the Beijing World Championship the previous year and had set a Canadian national record here. Poland's Joanna Jóźwick, who came in fifth and also had a PB, went on to disgrace herself, her country, and the entire games by declaring herself the "true silver medalist," and said she was glad she was the "first European" and the "second White" to cross the line. The racism was blatant with that idiot. Most people at least had the decency to soften their ignorance for the public, but not that one. The idea of an all-African winners' podium, with women who looked different than the norm, just made people crazy.

Some wonder why I still congratulate my peers after a race when I know how they feel and what they have said about me. I consider myself a true sportswoman. For me, once the business of the race is over, things shift. It's about more than running, more than win-ning. It truly is about the idea that sport unites people. When we are done with the race, everyone should congratulate each other to honor the moment when we were all there struggling and breath-ing together; we should congratulate each other because we all started and completed the mission. People don't understand that.

They don't know when something is bigger than their individual smallness. I am human; I remind myself of this constantly—I can be petty, disgruntled, even annoyed by a competitor. I can enjoy the fact that the person who annoyed or talked shit about me had to look at my ass during the entire race, and I never had to see theirs because I beat them. But when the race is over, I have no hard feelings for anyone. It's about our shared humanity.

Wambui, Niyonsaba, and I went straight to the winners' press conference after the race, and the first question asked was about our gender and whether the IAAF had made all of us take hormone treatments and what effect it had on our running. Neither Wambui nor Niyonsaba had ever even uttered the word "gender" in public.

I was tired. Just tired of all of this. I'd dealt with it for almost a decade. I'd swallowed my poison. I had suffered enough, and I could see in that moment how my suffering would be passed on to a whole new generation of young girls who'd done nothing but work hard and left it all on the track. Like me, they would run their hearts out and be reduced to their genitals and whatever biological issue others thought they had.

"Excuse me, my friend," I said to the journalist, "We are not here for that. Ask questions about the race. Don't ask us about the IAAF. Ask us how it went, how we're feeling, talk about splits. Ask us about our performance. This press conference is all about the 800 meters that we ran today. That's it. That's what matters." The room went silent. I sucked the air out of it. Our body language was such that if the media didn't straighten themselves out, we would all just get up and walk out. I remember looking at my coach in the audience, and his eyes were very, very wide. No one expected that statement from me, given that I had spent all those years mostly staying quiet.

With that, I hoped I set the tone that people like Sebastian Coe and other IAAF officials should have.

South Africa was bringing home ten medals—two gold, six

silver, and two bronze. I was thrilled my teammate Wayde van Niekerk had not only won the gold in the men's 400 meters, but he had also smashed the world record. South Africa had just a fraction of the resources of some of these other countries, and we'd performed well and made our people proud.

I'd brought a bottle of Amarula, a creamy South African liqueur, in my suitcase. If I won the gold, I remember thinking, I'm going to bring this out and have an adult beverage with my team. The national team headed back to the Athletes' Village, and I surprised everyone with the bottle in the cafeteria. Everyone was shocked because they'd never seen me drink anything other than water, juice, and energy drinks. We mixed the Amarula with ice cream and stayed up late, talking about the games, our performances, the obstacles we each overcame to be where we were.

I called my family as soon as I went back to my room. I never took the medal off. It was still around my neck when I got into bed. I remember I wrapped a blanket tightly around myself and held on to that gold medal like you would your own child. I remember running my fingers over the front of the medal, which featured Nike, the goddess of victory. The 2016 Olympic medals were huge. Bigger than the palm of a hand. Much bigger than the ones from London in 2012. My friend Masilo, the Nike executive, had also traveled to Rio. I'd promised him and the Nike people a gold medal the previous year, and I'd delivered.

Right before I fell asleep, I briefly entertained the thought of someone breaking into my room and trying to steal my medal.

"Ehh," I thought, "I'd kick their ass . . ."

I dreamt of being home with my family.

When I got back to South Africa the next day, I handed the gold medal to my Violet right then and there in front of everyone at OR Tambo International Airport. No one deserved it more than her.

Chapter 21

RETURN OF THE IAAF

SEB COE HAD MADE IT CLEAR AT THE RIO OLYM-
pics that the IAAF would find a way to reinstate the testosterone regulations. From the moment I won the 800-m gold, I sensed
a giant clock had materialized over my career and that I was running against it.

The IAAF is a powerful organization, so I knew they would
find a way to get me out. Until then, my job was to continue to
mind my business and run.

I had already begun to test my legs out in the 400 meter and the
1500 meter in official competitions. Right after the Olympics, I
traveled to Brussels and set a new personal best in the 400 meters,
my first major competition at that distance. I had mastered the 800
meters. I wanted to learn how to dominate the other distances, to
see how far I could push my body while I was still in my prime.
And I wanted to break the 800-m world record. The truth is I hun-
gered for it. Like any elite athlete, I wanted to have a world record
on my list of accomplishments.

The IAAF would make sure I would never have the opportunity. My feeling is they sensed I was getting close to breaking
the record, and they had to stop me. They didn't think I was a
woman, so they didn't want me to be the standard-bearer for the
800-m distance.

In 2015, the Court of Arbitration for Sport had given the IAAF
two years to come back with evidence that women with hyperandrogenism had an unfair performance advantage. The IAAF com-
missioned another testosterone study by their own Dr. Stéphane

Bermon. He was the same doctor who back in 2009 told my team the IAAF's "preferred method" of dealing with women like me was a gonadectomy. Bermon had published that study in 2013 in which he was part of a team of doctors who took four healthy elite athletes and removed their organs and surgically altered their genitals.

The IAAF published their new study in the *British Journal of Sports Medicine* in May 2017. They used elite athletes competing in the 2011 and 2013 IAAF World Championships and compared natural testosterone levels of elite females and elite males in various events to come up with the results that women with higher testosterone outperformed other women. It was total bullshit. Prominent doctors, scientists, and academicians pointed out the study was full of errors. Bermon had used running times from athletes who didn't exist, they had used multiple repeats of the same times from real athletes, and they even used times from athletes who had already been found doping.

The IAAF hadn't officially changed the rules yet, but I knew the point of first publishing the study in a science journal was to test the waters, to see what the public reaction would be before announcing new regulations. The 2017 study didn't seem to have been peer reviewed, and the IAAF wouldn't let anyone see the data. Is that how science is supposed to work? It was shameful. That is how those in power operate. They hadn't been able to use their "preferred method" on me back in 2009, but they used their money, and their influence, to find a different solution.

At the time, I didn't care about the specifics of what the IAAF was doing, but I could sense them behind me in the same way I can sense a competitor's movements during a race. And whether I wanted to think about it or not, journalists would constantly remind me that my career as an elite competitive runner was uncertain. I became more direct about expressing my feelings. When asked by a South African newspaper that July how I felt about the testosterone study, I replied that I didn't have time for idiots. I was busy studying for my sports science degree, and I was preparing to run my next big race.

The 2017 World Championships were held in London from August 4th to the 11th. Seb Coe, just as he'd done the previous year at the 2016 Olympics, chose to direct the media's attention toward me, instead of to the runners and our athleticism. He once again made a big show of stating the IAAF would return to court later in the year to reinstate the testosterone regulations. The man couldn't help himself. Coe has always struck me as a small man, unsure of himself. One of those men who needed to wrap themselves in the sense of their own importance. To me, there are people who are born leaders, who become leaders through circumstance, and then there are people who seek to be seen as leaders. Sebastian Coe was a seeker, and he would do anything to maintain that sense of importance. Coe had been a great middle-distance runner in the '80s, even breaking the 800-m and 1500-m world records. Then he'd been some kind of politician. No surprise. Then he sold himself as the "savior" of our sport and became president of the IAAF in 2015 during the doping turmoil.

I WOULD MEDAL in the 1500-m event in London. I came away with bronze; Kenya's Faith Kipyegon won gold, and America's Jenny Simpson, silver. It was an amazing race to be in and an even better one to watch. Although I became famous for mastering the 800 meter, the 1500 meter, the "thou-five" as I call it, is actually my favorite race. The 1500 meter allows a runner to sit longer; you don't have to go as hard right out of the gate as you do in the shorter middle distance. And it is more of a tactical race, there's more time to look around, more time to jostle for position, and these create more opportunities for mistakes and surprises, which makes it very exciting to run and to watch. I was so proud that I'd medaled in the race.

Almost immediately after my win, before I could even get to

the locker room, reporters began asking how I felt about the IAAF "bringing back gender testing." I told them these questions were like listening to the same song for the past nine years. I told them I was quite bored with the whole thing. I wanted to focus on the future, I said, not the past.

This had been my entire life as an elite athlete. I'd go out there, give it my all, and be asked questions about my gender, questions about the IAAF. The official 1500m winners' presser, unfortunately, would be more of the same. I remember the conference started off great. But, of course, that didn't last long.

It has been said I responded "angrily" to a male journalist who asked how I could be thinking about the future when the IAAF would soon shut me down. I didn't. I responded with the same grace and respect I sometimes wish the media gave me. I told him that whatever the IAAF was planning on doing wasn't my business, that my business was to run. The journalist cut me off and went further, "It may not be your business, but it could become your problem."

I had already been called "sports thorniest problem," and that's what I had come to represent in many people's eyes. A problem. I told him that even if they felt my career would be over soon, I had already achieved so much of what I'd wanted. I reminded them I was a human being, a student who would be graduating the following year. I told them I had also become a businesswoman in my country. In other words, the IAAF didn't define me as a person and they weren't going to stop the life I had already built. I wanted everyone to know I was determined to make the most of the time I had left on the track and my life wasn't just about running.

There would be a few days to go until the 800m championship final and I spent them doing what I always do at competitions. I trained, kept to myself, stayed in touch with my family and friends. The 800m race would feature most of the women I'd run with in Rio. My plan was to stay patient. When the gun went off, I was in no hurry. I stayed in the middle of the pack for most of the race and kept my eyes up front. All I wanted was to see who I needed to beat. A few seconds into it, I knew Burundi's Francine Niyonsaba was going for it. She took the lead and was aiming to keep it. The only other girl willing to stay near her was America's Ajeé Wilson. On the backstretch, the entire race was between those two and they were fighting hard. I made sure to settle in, keep calm, so that when I saw a chance, I'd take over. By the time we were 150 meters away from the finish, Ajeé and Francine were running with everything they had and nearing the end of their supply. I'd been holding myself. All I had to do was stay and time things so there was enough track left to let my kick get to work. Right around the 100-m mark, I saw it and felt it. I dug deep and ran past them to the finish line. I won the 800-m gold medal in 1:55.16. It was a personal best, a world-leading time, and a new national record. All eight competitors ran under 1:59, so the audience got a great show. I'd now won three world championships. The 800-m gold medal was especially meaningful as it felt like I had finally defended my 2009 World Championship.

I remember the comments the announcers made that day—it was more of the same. They said things like "Looks like two different races out there" and "No effort at all from Semenya," "Caster just cruises past these women." I was used to it. My effort didn't seem like an effort. Such is my talent, I suppose. I make something that is torture look easy.

Running is my freedom and my joy, but my body bears the marks of doing this thing I love. I endure the pain during endless training sessions. The actual race happens only once. You are now sharing that pain with your peers, you are now surrounded and lifted by those who have come to see you do what you do. It still hurts like hell. Just because you are used to the pain doesn't mean you can't feel it. Elite runners lean into pain and transform it. A normal person's brain will tell you to stop doing the thing that is hurting your body. For athletes, who work with their body, the brain tells you the same thing, but there's another part that pushes you to keep going, to just get to the other side of it, because above all, we want to win.

Look, it may not be "nice" or "proper" to say this, but I think some female athletes are accustomed to flopping around on the track because that's what the powers-that-be like to see us do. I'm not just talking about running here, I'm talking about everything. And the truth is that seeing people hurt in sports makes some people happy. What those people want to see is the struggle, they want vivid images of humanity pushed beyond its limits. For women, especially, we're supposed to be so weak that even when we accomplish something physically difficult, we must fall and gasp and flop around.

I remember reading how women were barred from running in the early days of organized sports because men thought their body parts would fall out and that it was "unseemly" for women to sweat in public. Well, look closely at professional women's races. Most of us run, cross the line, congratulate each other, and go on with the rest of our business. We may take a few deep breaths, maybe we're dealing with a shin splint or a stitch or some injury, but we're fine. If you're an elite athlete and you really can't breathe and you fall down when you're done with a race, train harder.

What I'm saying is that at the end of a race, women aren't any more or less winded than male runners. The intense focus on my behavior after crossing the finish line, the constant critique of my performance as "effortless," was just a continuation of the narrative that I wasn't a woman. It was their way of saying that something else, besides training and talent, was responsible for my seeming lack of effort. I suppose I could've made a big show of gasping for air and thrashing around on the track after I crossed the finish line just to show how much it hurt, but that wasn't my style.

In any case, the 800-m race at the 2017 London World Championships would be the last one I'd ever run.

In February 2018, I finally graduated with a diploma in sports science from North-West University in Potchefstroom. I'd done it. Come what may, no one could take that accomplishment away from me. I was now officially an educated woman. My time with Verster had come to an end. He'd been a great coach, a fantastic mentor, a gentle guiding force, but it was time for me to go.

I celebrated this great accomplishment back home, in the village of my birth, with my entire family and friends. When I returned to my home in Pretoria, there were some things I was sure of, and continuing my education was one of them. I enrolled at the Tshwane University of Technology's sports management program. I knew having both a sports science and a sports management degree would prepare me for the future. I'd also be a sports ambassador for them and run local races in their colors. Violet and I had plans to eventually open our own athletic club. We both wanted to nurture young athletes who, like us, were coming from places without a lot of resources. I'd mostly trained myself when I was a kid, but now I could pass along everything I'd learned. I sometimes thought of myself as that little girl again, desperate to learn, looking for attention, wishing for guidance. I remembered how I used to run in the bush alone, how I'd watch others train and copy whatever they were doing. I'd accomplished so much in my career, I met some good people eventually, but maybe some things would have been different had there been someone or some kind of organization that could have guided me. Maybe I could have avoided some injuries, maybe healed better from others that continued to plague me.

I was twenty-seven years old. IAAF or no IAAF, I was preparing for the inevitable time in every athlete's life—when the clock stopped running.

On March 8, 2018, I ran the 1000 meter in 2:35.45 at the Liquid Telecom Athletix Grand Prix at Tuks Athletics Stadium and set a new national record. A couple of weeks later, I ran the Grand Prix's 1500 meter with a goal of breaking famed South African runner Zola Budd's national record of 4:01.80, which had stood for more than thirty years. I got close with a 4:02.41 but the conditions were windy and rainy and not right for the kind of performance I wanted to give.

The following month, I traveled to the Commonwealth Games in Australia for the first time in my career. There I'd win gold in both the 800- and 1500-m races, and I'd finally break Zola's record with a 4:00.71 run. My body was in peak form. I'd always known that I was capable of one day breaking the 800-m world record, but now I knew I would do it. I was ready. I had a single-minded focus about it. Then a week or two later, the IAAF announced their new testosterone regulations. They didn't need to go back to court and address the Chand case because the IAAF had come up with a new strategy that went around it.

The regulations would now only apply to athletes with what they called "differences in sexual development" (DSD) and only to those competing in the 400-, 800-, and 1500-m distances. Since Dutee Chand was a 100-m runner, she would not be affected by these rules. The IAAF didn't need to address her case. The testosterone limit would need to be lowered from the original 10 nmol/L they'd announced in 2011 down to 5 nmol/L for a period of six months before an affected athlete was eligible to compete. And it would need to stay at 5 nmol/L or below whether in or out of competition, even if an athlete was resting or injured. There would be no respite from the poison.

The new rules would come into effect in November 2018. They were giving me seven months to comply. I knew it would affect several other runners who were competing at the time, but to me, this was personal. I had become the face of this thing, I was the runner closest to the 800-m world record, and they wanted to shut me down. Even though Dutee had challenged the IAAF and won in court, she had not made it past the heats at the 2016 Olympics and hadn't won any international competitions since. Dutee wasn't a threat to the IAAF in the same way I was.

I wasn't the only person to see the new regulations as being aimed directly at me. If having a higher level of testosterone was some kind of insurmountable advantage, according to the IAAF, most rational people couldn't make sense of why the regulations would only cover three events in track and field. I would have had more respect for the IAAF if Seb Coe had just called me directly and said, "Look, we don't want you to run anymore." Instead, they did this.

For the next few months, I participated in as many major events as I was physically capable of—I traveled to Doha, Eugene, Oslo, Paris, Monaco, and Zurich. I continued to set national and track records. When journalists asked about the new IAAF regulations, I said I didn't speak about nonsense. As the clock wound down, I understood the options: go back to poisoning myself (only poison myself twice as hard), agree to irreversible, life-altering surgery and then spend the rest of my days taking pills anyway to regulate my body's hormones, change my events, or walk away from athletics. I wasn't going to comply with the medication. That, I knew. There was not a single moment where I even considered doing that to myself again.

I wasn't going to put the drugs back in my body. It did not matter to me whether they wanted the levels back up to 10, down to 5, or 0. I was no longer an eighteen-year-old girl desperate to run. I was a world champion, an Olympic champion. I had achieved my dreams. I had brought joy and stability to my family and pride to my country. I had an education that would allow me to make a living and contribute to society. And I was happily married to the love of my life and dreaming of building a family one day. I could not put myself through the mental anguish and physical torture of the poison.

The IAAF also offered women with DSDs who refused the medication, but still wanted to compete, what they felt was a generous and sympathetic offer—we could run any distance we wanted in the male category or run in some future "intersex" category should it ever become available. Both of these suggestions were insulting. I am not a man. Women like me are not men. The IAAF knew that not one woman with a confirmed DSD diagnosis had ever even approached the running times of male elite runners. As for the "intersex" category—I would never run in such. For me, participating in a third category of human gender identity would be accepting being othered, accepting the discrimination I was fighting against. If I ever agreed to that, it would mean I would give up the identity I'd been born with and had never questioned to take on a new one I didn't believe myself to be. Even though I understand that those in the medical community call me an "intersex" person because of the way my internal organs are structured, I do not call myself "intersex." That identity doesn't fit me, it doesn't fit my soul. Even calling myself a "lesbian" doesn't fit my soul. I think of myself as a woman who loves another woman. I have always resisted categorizations.

I THOUGHT ABOUT the young women who would be finding out for the first time that they fell under the regulations. I thought about the runners who already knew but because of the Dutee Chand case had never had to take the poison to run. They would be spared the public trauma I endured as an eighteen-year-old back in 2009, but I'm sure the sport would be seeing a few sudden injuries and retirements. These girls would quit rather than risk the possibility of their medical information being made public. Even those who decided to change events knew they would be doing so under a cloud of suspicion. The IAAF had made it so specific—400, 800, 1500 meters—that any runner who suddenly moved up or down in distance would be seen as intersex, someone with a testosterone or hormone issue, whether they had one or not. I received calls and messages from a few athletes, and each interaction was heartbreaking. These girls were not in a good place mentally. Most came from places and families that would not support them, communities where they would be shunned, possibly even hurt. Running had not just been their joy but also a way to get an education. Running was their only source of income, and most were already financially supporting their families. Their sports federations weren't going to stand up for them—with words or anything else.

I had another option. Someone had to fight the IAAF. I was the athlete best prepared to do so. Even if I'd never actually publicly confirmed my medical situation, people knew about it, and I was seen by many as a sympathetic figure. I'd remained mostly silent about things for a decade. I'd held my head high during my career, wanting only to be seen as a woman and a great athlete. Now, it felt like it was about more than that. I needed them to see me as a human being.

GREG AND I HAD a long talk. As my lawyer, Greg had stood beside an eighteen-year-old me back in 2009, and he was ready to do it again. I spoke with my wife and manager, Becky Motumo. I remember that Becky, who I'd first met and hired in 2016 after I'd won the Olympic gold medal, sat and listened to me while I figured out this moment in my life. Becky, like Greg, had become like family at this point. I was not an easy person to manage, but she had shown me nothing but compassion and support. I knew no matter what I decided to do, she would stand by me. Going up against the IAAF would not be easy. It would be a distraction from training, and it would interfere with the precious little time I got to spend with my family. It would require others to give up their time for this cause. The way I saw things, I had no other choice but to fight. I never entertained the thought of quitting. I never backed down from bullies as a kid and I wasn't about to do so now. I was at the top of my career, in peak physical shape. I felt like I had more to give. And I would fight not just for me but for everyone else who would be caught in the web. In early June 2018, my team and I announced we would challenge the IAAF at the Court of Arbitration for Sport. I received many messages of love and support in social media as well as plenty of hatred and ignorance.

Soon after the announcement, I traveled to Paris for the Stade Sébastien Charléty Diamond League event on June 30th. There I won the 800 meter in 1:54.25. It was a new Diamond League meet record and a new national record. I'd broken the 1:55 barrier and was closer to the world record than I'd ever been before. The media, as always, wanted to know how I felt now that the IAAF had officially reinstated the regulations. I responded that I wanted to be an inspiration to the world and to the youth and that I would not focus on negative things. Those reporters knew this would eventually play out in court and that every time I stepped on the track could be the last.

By early July, Dr. Bermon and the IAAF knew the data they had used in the testosterone study was flawed, so they quietly published corrections in the same medical journal and hoped people would look the other way. They also refused to turn over their research in full—only partial data was disclosed—which meant that other scientists could duplicate their study. They knew whatever data they had would not hold up in court in a science-focused, evidence-based trial. They didn't have proof that showed natural testosterone, as my body used it, was the determining factor in my success, and they didn't have research that proved women like me had an unfair advantage over other women. To me, all they had was a study where they mutilated young girls and some data from elite athletes who thought they were just following the antidoping sample collection requirements.

The only thing they really had to stop women like me from running the 400-, 800-, and 1500-m distances was my success and the exposure that came with it—whether I'd wanted that or not. It is my belief the IAAF did not want to see another 800-m winners' podium like the one at the 2016 Rio Olympics, where the African continent swept the medals. It did not matter to me that the two other women who'd taken the silver and bronze medals, Wambui and Niyonsaba, would also eventually announce they had higher levels of natural testosterone and would fall under the new regulations. To me, the 2016 Rio Olympics 800-m podium was no different than the all-African winners' podium at the 2008 Beijing Olympics, where Jelimo, Jepkosgei, and Hasna Benhassi had won. There was nothing out of the ordinary in our running times. What the IAAF had, in my view, given everything I had been through and seen from them, was their ignorance and bigotry and racism, their belief that I and women like me were cheaters who didn't belong.

I traveled to Nigeria in August for the African Championships, and there I won the 400-m race in 49.96 seconds and set a new South African national record. I won the 800 meter in 1:56.06, a championship record. By this point, I held the South African national records in the 400-, 800-, 1000-, and 1500-m distances. Because of my performance in Nigeria, I was chosen to represent team Africa the following month at the IAAF's Continental Cup in Ostrava, Czech Republic. I won the 800-m gold in 1:54.77 and the 400-m silver in 49.62. The 400 meter is the shortest of what is still considered a "middle-distance" event—practically a sprint from start to finish. It was hard on the body but it was over quickly, and there wasn't much strategizing. I just ran as hard as I could until the finish line.

One of the meets' organizers caught up to me after the events and told me that Jarmila Kratochvilová, the famed 800-m world record holder, was there and wanted to speak with me. Kratochvilová had been whispered about for years. She'd been suspected of doping because she was part of the Soviet Union's infamous special programs list back in the '80s, but there had never been any proof, and she'd tested negative on a random blood draw. Jarmila's gender hadn't been questioned in the same way mine had been. What happened to me didn't happen to her. As far as I knew, Jarmila had never been subjected to gender testing despite her imposing physique. Anyway, what Jarmila looked like didn't matter to me, and whether she had taken drugs didn't either. Doped or not, at the end of the day, she was the one who held the record.

I remember someone had pointed her out to me in the audience at a race back in 2011 but now, almost a decade later, she actually wanted to meet me. Only Pamela Jelimo and I had ever gotten within a second of Jarmila's 800-m record. That day, the organizer led me to a spot right outside the track where Jarmila was standing. I remember she had a warm smile and said, "I've never seen anyone run the 800 meter like you, Caster. I know you're ready now. I believe you're the only one who can break my record." I thanked her for her encouragement and told her I wanted it but that I was not going to rush it and would just let my body do its thing. We had a quick embrace and I went off to the locker room.

It felt good to hear Jarmila say these words directly to me. It felt good to hear what sounded like full, genuine support from another female athlete instead of one of those two-faced runners who congratulated me on a win and then went and talked shit behind my back or boo-hooed in front of cameras.

I knew I was ready to break the record. I told myself I would break it the following year. My body was in the best shape it had ever been. That September in Ostrava marked the official end of my 2018 running season. I returned to South Africa to rest and get ready for war with the IAAF, but I was not going to let that interfere in my personal happiness.

Near the end of the year, Violet and I opened the doors to our youth program, the Masai Athletics Club, where we would eventually house and train young South African athletes. God had blessed us, and we'd both felt a responsibility to help future generations. Soon after, Violet and I were told the IVF treatment had worked and Violet was pregnant. My future as an elite athlete may have been uncertain, but I had so many beautiful and positive things to look forward to. That's how I've always been—I can't control what I can't control, but I have conditioned myself to concentrate on the good things in life. And here was something both of us had dreamt of for so many years. I was going to be a mother; I was going to have a family of my own.

Chapter 22

INSIDE THE COURT

M Y CASE AGAINST THE IAAF WAS SCHEDULED TO begin on February 25, 2019, at the Court of Arbitration for Sport in Lausanne, Switzerland. The court was supposed to be an independent body created to settle sports disputes between athletes and sports federations. The media set it up as the "Sports Case of the Century." The arguments would be about gender, medical ethics, and the very idea of "fairness" in sports. Greg would be teaming up with Patrick Bracher and two Canadian lawyers, James Bunting and Carlos Sayao. We had assembled a team of expert witnesses, including two of the doctors who had negotiated the estrogen treatment with the IAAF back in 2009 that had allowed me to run again without having my body dismembered.

From the beginning, there were issues with the case. It was supposed to be Caster Semenya vs. IAAF, but Athletics South Africa wanted to join us. That was a problem for me. I didn't want ASA anywhere near my case. When they first began to make noises about being a part of it, I told Greg it was not a good idea. I didn't believe ASA were there to support me as an athlete. I'm not stupid. The South African sports federation eats at the IAAF's table. Why would ASA risk losing their place at the table for one athlete? ASA were my people, yes, they represent South African athletes, yes, but ASA cares about money first and athletes second.

When Greg and Benedict and I came up against the IAAF back in 2009, we went at it alone. We did not have help from ASA. There were words of support but not much else. In the fallout from Berlin, ASA officials had been busy deflecting blame, pointing fingers at each other about who was at fault for the Caster Semenya saga. Everybody talking shit about everyone else in the newspapers or on TV. It quickly became about politics, about people keeping their jobs. All while an eighteen-year-old me sat in a room waiting, not knowing if or when I would ever run again. All while the world talked about me like I was an alien or a monster.

Back in 2010, ASA was bankrupt. Everyone knew it. There had been accusations over the years that funds were being mismanaged at that organization. Even Leonard Chuene, who'd been the president when I ran in Berlin, had been accused of misappropriating funds, along with a bunch of other people. Things hadn't gotten better over the years. I think ASA saw my case as a way to balance their accounts.

The South African government had given R25 million to ASA to fund my case, which is about 1.8 million US dollars. I had no knowledge of this money; my case was being funded privately. We did not need any money from the government or ASA. This is what happens when you get to a certain level of fame. People smell money around you, and they want some of it. It doesn't matter how they get it or whether it's good for you.

Which is why, one evening, when Greg and I were sitting together discussing preparations for the case, I said, "If ASA really wants to help, they should give us the money they say the government released for me and let us do what we do. They say they have experts; they should let us see if the experts they have will help our case. That's it. They don't need to join our claim."

Greg was a great lawyer and an even better man. But he didn't know the things I did from having dealt with these federations. I spent a lot of time in the bush. You don't play nice with snakes. The way I saw things, ASA would be there if they needed you to win medals, but when you couldn't win anymore, they would forget you. When an athlete couldn't perform, there was no one there to pick up a phone. They wouldn't even tell an athlete they were going to stop funding them while they were injured. I felt the same way about many of the politicians in my country. They did a lot of talking. Lots of mouths opening and closing, tongues moving around and sounds coming out. But you would be forgotten as soon as you walked out of their office and your story didn't get them votes.

People from ASA wanted information from my legal team before they would submit any documentation to the court, but they wouldn't tell us what their plan was or who they were bringing. If you're coming to fight for me, then why aren't you sharing? What was it that they could or would do to help me? This did not feel like a team effort.

My lawyer didn't want it to seem like he was blocking the South African officials. I understood Greg's way of thinking. The more people we seemed to have on our side, the better. And the media was all over my case. Any hint of conflict or tension between me and ASA would blow up into another scandal.

"Let's give them a chance, Caster," Greg said.

"You are taking a big risk allowing them in. You are the leader here and I trust you. But I don't trust them. We would be operating with liars and opportunists. We will be operating with people who are only thinking about their own interests."

We would be operating with a national organization that was basically controlled by the IAAF.

ASA filed their own separate claim with the Court of Arbitration for Sport. There were some disagreements between my team and ASA over what they requested from the court and what my team wanted—including not seeing eye to eye on which three judges should be on the arbitration panel—but in the end, even though they were a separate entity, we would collectively be considered "the claimants" against the IAAF.

I'd hoped things would go our way, but I also knew we were dealing with a rigged system. I told Greg I was prepared to lose. But I wasn't going down without a fight. Even if a part of me felt the outcome would not be in my favor. That was the most important thing. I was a fighter. It is how I'd always seen myself, and it was how others had come to see me.

Greg and I flew to Geneva. I remember that the night before the trial, I went for a run alone to clear my thoughts. I was so far away from home. So far away from my pregnant wife and my family and my beloved South Africa. I came back to the hotel and saw Greg pacing around our small room. He was on his phone, talking with various people on the legal team. We'd been friends for ten years. I trusted him, and I knew we were ready for whatever was coming. I ironed my suit. I was going to wear all black. I felt calm. All I had to do the next day was tell the truth and let God handle the rest. Win or lose, it would be my opportunity to finally tell the world what I'd been through. The professors, the medical doctors, the this-or-that expert on both sides of the table could say whatever they wanted. I knew I had to sit there and hear these people talk about my "condition" and what I was or wasn't. I have never focused on their terms for women like me anyway. Fuck them. I am Caster.

THAT MORNING, Greg and I walked through a crowd of media into the Château de Béthusy building. I held my head high and flashed the cameras a peace sign. My team consisted of my lawyers and the five experts we had assembled. I noticed ASA came with a crowd of people. I had no idea who they were or what they were doing there, and most were never in the court room.

Once inside, we were directed to a main room where the arguments would take place. There was a long, rectangular wooden table surrounded by chairs. The three arbitrators would sit at the head of the table. Our team had one side of the table and the IAAF's team sat directly across. It was not a courtroom in the way most people imagine it. It gave you the sense of a round-table discussion. My lawyers and I would be present every day, but the experts for both sides would be in the room only on the day of their testimony.

Our argument was that I was a woman, even with my body's differences, that the rules were discriminatory because they only applied to women. Men didn't have to physically prove they were in the right category because of a rumor. They didn't have a testosterone range they had to adhere to. In fact, the IAAF is aware there are elite male athletes whose natural testosterone levels are actually in the female range. We argued the rules were both physically and psychologically harmful to all women and that the regulations should be thrown out because they lacked scientific evidence proving my body's differences gave me any kind of "unfair" advantage in my sport.

The IAAF claimed it was a private organization, and as such, they were not subject to human rights laws. They could discriminate at will. They claimed the identity of athletes who fell under their new DSD regulations would be kept confidential. This was a lie. They claimed their new regulations would not ensnare athletes arbitrarily based on rumors and allegations, as their previous regulations had. This time, they said, only an IAAF medical manager would be allowed to open an investigation into an athlete, only when acting in "good faith" and on "reasonable grounds," based on "tips" from a "reliable source." In other words, the same racist, sexist shit. We all know what kind of women are usually considered "suspicious" for being too muscular or not looking womanly enough. Black women. Women of color. And "tips" from "reliable sources" still meant any female athlete could be subjected to gender investigations based on rumors and people's biased assumptions of just how masculine was *too* much.

The IAAF had changed tactics from the Chand case. They told the court that in the Chand case, they had discussed "biological females with high testosterone" but these new enhanced regulations would only apply to "46 XY DSD" athletes, who they considered "biological males with a female gender identity."

I have to say hearing this troubled me. The IAAF argued that allowing me to compete in my natural body was the same as allowing a man who believed he was a woman to compete with women. That was nonsense. The difference in running performance between an elite male and an elite female athlete is 10 percent to 12 percent. Despite my fast times, I hadn't even broken the world record. I am the fourth fastest 800-m runner in the history of the sport. And as far as I know, not one of the women who have run the 800 meter faster than me had my condition. I had differences in my body, yes, but it should be common sense that whatever my testosterone level may be, it does not make me male. And if speed was all about testosterone, then why wasn't I as fast as my male colleagues? An elite male athlete with natural testosterone levels in the accepted female range would still outrun me by the 10 percent to 12 percent performance gap.

The IAAF argued I'd been so successful as an athlete because I'd been hiding how fast I actually was. The treatment that—according to their medical research—was supposed to slow me down, had not worked as expected because I hadn't taken it in the way I was supposed to.

Ridiculous. I was a woman who had been violated. And they were arguing I was a man and a fraud.

The trial started with me introducing myself and my story. I didn't feel nervous. I felt determined. I told the panel where I came from, how I'd become an elite runner. I told them about the 2009 Berlin incident and how the way I was treated in front of the world continued to haunt me. I told them I agreed to take the drugs because at that time I was desperate to run but that it had caused me great physical and mental anguish.

The IAAF's lawyer, Jonathan Taylor, cross-examined me. He began by accusing me of manipulating my hormone levels during the time I was taking the drugs.

I sat there listening and staring at this boy—that's what he looked like to me, an overweight, puffy-faced boy. When it was my turn to speak, I told him he wasn't around when I made the original deal with the IAAF. Neither was his Lord Coe. My lawyers and my team made a deal with the IAAF back in 2009, and the agreement was simple—I could run whatever race I wanted to run as long as my testosterone level was at 10 nmol/L or below. That was it. Whether it went up or down, or how or why it went up or down, was no one's business. I'd never missed a drug test, so why even bring this up? It was stupid.

Taylor bizarrely tried to suggest I was hiding from a blood test during the 2012 London Olympics when I had been eating in the Athlete's Village. I committed the crime of putting food in my mouth at the cafeteria in full view of all the other athletes during the Olympics. If the IAAF's officials came to my hotel room to take blood and I wasn't in the room, they could have found me. Trust me, if they really want them, those doping officials will get their fluids one way or the other. Taylor knew that. He wanted the suggestion out there that I had done something wrong. He made himself look like a fool with that one.

"Eating, Mr. Taylor. I was eating. In public."

"You were cheating," Taylor said dramatically.

"*Excuse me*? Cheating who?" I asked him.

"You were cheating the medication, Ms. Semenya. You had testosterone spikes." Taylor answered pointing at some paper he was holding.

I shook my head. Let's talk facts.

Our original agreement with the IAAF was that I was to have two monthly blood draws, but the IAAF could, and often would, show up more than twice a month and at random times. That had been my life from 2009 to 2015. I would stop whatever I was doing, dinner with family, a gathering with friends, training, reading, studying, whatever it was, just to give them my blood. All elite athletes deal with random blood and urine tests, that's part of the job. But that's not what I was going through. These other athletes still get to enjoy their life. Go on vacations. Live as normal people. I couldn't. I told the court I didn't feel like a human being during those years. I felt like a science experiment. Like the IAAF's lab rat.

Taylor kept making sounds and waving around a piece of paper with numbers on it. The IAAF had not only humiliated me in front of millions of people when I was eighteen but now, they were also giving the world even more of my private medical information. Now I was a "46 XY biological male" who thought she was a female, cheating by running slower than I was capable of. And I hadn't swallowed enough of their poison, or I hadn't swallowed it well enough for their research papers.

I looked at Taylor straight in the eyes and said, "The IAAF has tested me and tested me all of these years. Before every race I had to prove I complied. They allowed me to run in those championships. Why would the IAAF allow me to run if I was cheating? They had the same information then you're waving around now."

My agreement with the people who were at the IAAF in 2009 was 10 or below to run a race. It was none of their business if I ran with a level 1 or a level 4 or a level 9.7. The bottom line was that the IAAF's data showed my hormones were never above a level 10 when I ran in an official capacity. And whatever level my testosterone was at when I wasn't running was none of their fucking business. I was never in breach of the contract we had negotiated. I stayed silent about their "preferred" surgical method and medication. They had agreed to seal my medical records, and now they had told the world about my chromosomes. If anyone had broken agreements, it was the IAAF's incompetent officials.

They were the ones who had cheated *me*. They had cheated me out of my young adulthood; they had almost cheated me of my own sanity, my mental and physical well-being.

"How I feel about all of this is that the IAAF confiscated my life. They confiscated my rights as a human being. I was a child then. Look at what was done to me." I stared at Jonathan. I hoped he was shamed down to his core. Even if he was the IAAF's lawyer, he was still a human, and he still had the ability to understand how wrong this all was.

But Taylor wasn't done with the stupidity yet. He sucked in his breath and then said it was suspicious I had "never lost a race."

"Now, you're confusing yourself, Mr. Taylor. I haven't lost the 800 meters since 2016 because I have mastered the distance. It is my specialty, and whether people like it or not, that one is mine. It's my race. That one, I've been running since I was a teenager. Put it to the side. I have lost a lot of 400 meters and thou-fives throughout my career. Check my record."

Then this lawyer, who I don't think had ever run across a street, much less gotten near a track, accused me of running negative splits, as if it was something no other runner had ever done. Then he made an issue of how I never ran on the inside lane. It was really dodgy to his client that I never "hugged the rail."

Was this man serious? I wanted to laugh. These people really were crazy.

"I don't understand what it is you are talking about, Mr. Taylor. Sebastian Coe here ran negative splits. Paula Radcliffe ran negative splits. Bekele, Gebrselassie, Dibaba. All these famous runners run negative splits. Middle- and long-distance runners run negative splits. Why are you pointing at me running negative splits as if that's something that's never been done?"

And what did it matter to them where I sat during a race? If I wanted to hug the rail, or run on an outside lane? It was frustrating to listen to this boy talk about things he didn't seem or pretended to not understand, using nonsense to make me look bad as an athlete and as a person. I sat at the table and spent the rest of the week listening to more of the same from the IAAF's experts. Not one of them looked me in the eyes when they were speaking.

When it was Dr. Bermon's turn, he talked about how his medical background led him to *believe* I could run faster. I'd heard this "theory" throughout my career—that I was not running as fast as I could have. Sometimes I would watch my races and hear the announcers say some variation of "Here she goes. . . . Semenya *effortlessly* wins again. It's frustrating to watch her, really. You can just feel that she's got so much more to give."

Let me be clear.

I cannot run any faster than I have. If I could, why wouldn't I go out there and break the world record when I knew the IAAF was going to find a way to ban me? I could have cashed in—world records come with bonuses. I could have secured more endorsements that would have supported my family's future. I would have an even bigger legacy than I already have. Why not?

The answer is simple.

Because I can't run any faster than I have. And that is the problem with the "science" these people have concocted. Whatever role testosterone plays in the shape of my body, in my musculature, in my skeletal frame, it does not actually make me a man. Whatever medical condition they say I have, it does not give me the same speed advantage on the track as a man. If testosterone worked in my body the same way it does in a man, I'd have been born with a penis and then I wouldn't have to tell this story.

No matter what the IAAF says, my times are well within the women's category. No matter what they say, I pushed my body to the limit and beyond on every run and training session. I'm just better than a lot of the women I was running against. And that was the problem for the IAAF and whatever notions of femaleness they have.

A witness on our team testified he was present when, during what was supposed to be a medical presentation, Bermon said he didn't understand why, if women like me were really women, we wouldn't want to have a treatment that made us appear less masculine. It seemed to me that Bermon was obsessed with "masculinity." I don't know, maybe Bermon had some kind of deeper issue with testosterone and having too much or not enough of it. Bermon said he took great offense at the suggestion the IAAF required women to have genital surgery to compete in the female category.

He said it was a lie. Except he and the IAAF were playing with words. He did it, and he wrote about doing it right there in his published 2013 study. Now he was "offended" and wanted to clear his and his employer's name. He went on to say gonadectomies were the generally accepted treatment for individuals with DSDs who wanted to stop virilization and that none of the medical experts he'd spoken to had any evidence it had negative effects. Bermon would later admit in court that not every athlete with a so-called 46 XY DSD condition who underwent testosterone-reducing treatment like mine returned to the track. This is why, to me, the IAAF's treatments aren't about leveling the playing field—they're about getting a certain type of women off the field completely.

I remember Dr. Hirschberg's testimony. Hirschberg was a Swedish professor who cowrote a follow-up with Bermon to the 2017 testosterone study attempting to prove that androgen levels were responsible for performance. I'd met her in 2010 or 2011 after I had been reinstated by the IAAF. I was in Stockholm for a race, and I was told to go to her practice for a blood test. I didn't give a fuck what this woman had to say except I was glad our lawyer had her admit in court none of her birth control pill research involved women with my specific medical condition, and none of her patients were even professional athletes. She was just treating women with hormonal imbalances who ran a couple of times a week for exercise.

Then the IAAF brought out a Doriane Lambelet Coleman, an American law professor, who had been an elite 800-m runner in the '80s. Her role was showing how the regulations were legally sound, even if they were discriminatory. She kept using the IAAF's newest term—"biological males with DSD"—and went on about how female athletes were being bullied into silence about their fears that our side of things would be overrun by men if I was allowed to compete. She could not have been talking about the same women who had been laughing at me, boldly calling me a man for years and crying on camera about how unfair it all was?

And then, as if to make the point clear, the IAAF brought out their next expert.

I remember I was sitting between Greg and Jim when a pale, fragile looking, very tall woman walked to the expert's chair. She didn't look healthy to me. I used my elbows to nudge my lawyers on either side of me.

She said her name was Joanna Harper. She introduced herself as a transgendered woman, a long-distance runner and a medical something who for some reason came to testify about her transition and how she'd done a study using several other transgendered runners.

"What. The. Fuck. Is. This?" I thought.

Joanna had been born and lived and ran as a man for forty-something years before she transitioned. She told the court the side effects of the hormone pills were not as bad as I'd claimed. To her, I was lying about my pain. Joanna said she'd gained "significant benefits" from taking the pills in her transition, with barely-there negative side effects, and that these pills were the generally accepted medical treatment for "women with high testosterone and a female gender identity."

I noticed she referred to herself as "a woman with high testosterone," and not a "biological male with a female gender identity." She said both she and her transgender women subjects had experienced a loss of speed of between 10 percent and 12 percent after taking estrogen, which proved they'd leveled any competitive advantage they had over other women. So, according to Joanna, the IAAF's testosterone requirement was reasonable, and I should have leapt at the chance to swallow the drugs.

I remember I turned to look at Greg while Joanna was testifying. This was some shit, right here.

Joanna's choice to take the pill for her transition was her business. That had nothing to do with me and my right to run in my body. When I made a deal with the IAAF back in 2009, the treatment wasn't supposed to change any aspect of my body outside of lowering my testosterone. I used the hormone to compete.

Harper admitted on cross examination that she was not a medical doctor and had no experience in any scientific field relevant to my case. None of the transgender women athletes whose testosterone level she'd been measuring were elite or even professional athletes—they were all middle-aged amateur long-distance runners. All had been born and lived and competed as men for the majority of their lives. Again, their business. It has got nothing to do with me. And no matter how many people tried to put me in that box, that was not my box.

As far as I'm concerned, Joanna was a tool for the IAAF. She willingly made herself the face of the whole "transgender panic"— the fear that if women like me were allowed to run free, then women like Joanna were coming. The IAAF wanted to tell the world that if elite female athletes were crying about how unfair it was to run against Caster Semenya now, wait until a younger generation of Joanna and her friends put their spikes on, and some of these ladies may not even want to take their prescriptions. Eventually, men wouldn't even transition, they would just announce they were women and take over women's sports because for some reason that's what men have been planning on doing.

The bottom line is the IAAF has no real research concerning elite athletes with my condition and the side effects of the drug they were planning on forcing us to take. We are elite athletes, not people who run a few times a week to stay in shape. Forcing me to take estrogen is not the same as other women taking the same pill to regulate a hormonal imbalance. It is not the same as a transgender woman taking the medication to aid in a physical transition that affirms her gender identity.

As far as I know, or as far as the IAAF will allow us to know, I am the first, and one of the only, athletes who has ever taken the drug to compete. Whatever research they have is coming from my body and the way I took the pills from 2009 to 2015. And it bothered them that even with the pills, which were supposed to slow me down the way it had for Joanna and her friends, I still performed well in those years. I still managed to win.

The IAAF has no evidence to show what would happen if I lowered my testosterone level from 10 nmol/L to 5. We're talking about medication they know weakens bones, which makes people more injury prone. Medication that could cause blood clots in addition to all the other terrible physical symptoms I'd experienced. I don't know, maybe the IAAF hoped I'd agree to go back to the poison, bring my levels to 5 nmol/L, and then drop dead on live television during an 800-m race. In any case, I was a woman—I didn't care about their Xs and Ys and what their manmade data and machines showed. I sit down to pee just like their mothers. Always have. Call me whatever you want, but the sporting world will just have to deal with that reality.

I sat there throughout the week listening as the IAAF brought out more of their "experts." All bought by the IAAF in some way or other. I heard the judges and lawyers and experts talking and arguing with each other. At some point it all just became noise to me. And, suddenly, at times I could hear laughter coming from another room, the room where the IAAF's people were. I felt like to them this was just a game. Just a trip to Switzerland they could write off and add to their resumes. To me, this was a fight for my life, my identity, my livelihood. The IAAF's case was nonsense, and I called it nonsense and "fiction" during my closing statement.

When the trial was over, I knew things wouldn't go in my favor. My lawyers and our experts had done a great job. But there was only so much they could do. ASA didn't help shit and even asked the court to be compensated for their costs by the IAAF should the court find in my favor. So basically, if I won, they would get paid. See? Money. Our side hadn't even asked for compensation from the IAAF.

I remember walking down the corridor on my way out of the building on the last day of testimony. I was glad it was over. All I wanted then was to rest and get to the airport and back home so I could see Violet. Then a White woman walked up to me. She looked a little familiar but I couldn't place her immediately. She had this pained look on her face.

"Caster. I am sorry for my testimony. I really am. I am so sorry." She held her hands together in front of her.

Now I realized who she was. The IAAF's expert, the American law professor who kept calling me a biological male.

I knew her need to apologize to me came because something in her soul wasn't sitting right. She was remorseful, but what the hell did she want me to do now? Did she want me to make her feel better? Should I have said, "It's OK, my dear. I know how it is. You had to do it. No worries. I appreciate your apology."

Please. I have no time for that shit.

I nodded and walked past her and left the building.

Chapter 23

THE AFTERMATH

I CONTINUED TO RUN WHILE WAITING FOR THE VER-
dict from the Court of Arbitration for Sport. On April 25th, I
won a national title in a 5000-m race in Germiston. Time 16:05.97.
Reports say I was taunting the IAAF. No. I was preparing for
the future.

In the end, what I knew would happen did. On May 1, 2019,
CAS handed down the ruling. They agreed the rules were discriminatory, but that they were reasonable and proportionate enough
for the IAAF to protect the female category. Greg called me and
read their decision to me over the phone. They said I had done nothing wrong and praised my character throughout the proceedings.
The panel agreed the science was not conclusive and suggested the
IAAF take some more time to do research before implementing
the regulations. I knew the IAAF wouldn't waste any time. They
imposed the new rules one week later. Seb Coe went to the media
crowing about how thrilled they were with CAS's decision.

Shortly afterward, the World Medical Association issued a
statement condemning the decision and asked medical doctors
to not prescribe medication or perform any tests or surgeries on
athletes, given that the IAAF's regulations were based on a single
study. It was unjust and against the Hippocratic oath to force people without medical need to take drugs or have medical procedures
to compete in a sport.

I decided to travel to Doha to run in the Diamond League season opener on May 3rd. It would be the last race before the regulations came into effect. I won the 800 meter in 1:54.98. It was my

thirtieth consecutive win in the 800-m event, the fastest time of the year, and a meeting record.

Right afterward, a journalist from BBC Sport approached me for an interview. The journalist wanted to know how I was feeling about my future in sports. Among many other things, I said, "It's up to God. God has decided my life, God will end my life; God has decided my career, God will end my career. No man, or any other human, can stop me from running." At the end of the day, I said, I would find a way to keep going. Everything I was doing, I was doing for my country, for the people who loved me, and for those who would come after me. "Confuse the enemy," I told the journalist. "They'll be relaxed, and I'll still be working."

On May 29, my team appealed the CAS verdict to the Swiss Supreme Court on the grounds that it was discriminatory, and I put out a public statement: "I am a woman and I am a world-class athlete. The IAAF will not drug me or stop me from being who I am." This fight had gone beyond me proving I had no physiological advantage on the field over other women. This fight was about human rights. It was wrong to compel perfectly healthy people to harm themselves to participate in a sport based on manufactured evidence.

A few days later, on June 3rd, the Swiss Court suspended the CAS ruling. The temporary rule suspension meant I could still run my 800 meters while the Swiss Court decided on my appeal, but it applied only to me. None of the other women affected would be allowed to run. At first, I thought not to run in any of the restricted distances in solidarity with women like Niyonsaba and Wambui, but I changed my mind. The best thing to do was run. Keep myself and the fight in the public's eye for as long as I could. Running was fighting at this point. My job was to continue to be a thorn in the IAAF's side.

My next 800-m race would be at the Rabat Diamond League event in Morocco on June 13th. The day before I was to fly to Morocco, the Rabat meet organizers called Jukka and told him

I was no longer welcome. They gave him no reason. I'm sure the IAAF was not happy about my public statement and had to do something about it. They insisted they had nothing to do with this decision and said Diamond League events are not organized by the IAAF. A bunch of shit is what that was. Sebastian Coe's IAAF had everything to do with it. I listen closely to what he says. "Organized" being the key word. The IAAF didn't organize the Diamond Leagues, but they wanted to show me who had the power over them. They wanted me to know they could just make a call and I would no longer be welcome to run. This is how the IAAF operates.

I RAN MY last IAAF-sanctioned 800-m race on June 30, 2019. It was the Diamond League Prefontaine Classic in Stanford, California. I knew, even before I arrived, that it would be my last time running the 800 meter on an international stage. We had no idea what the Swiss Court would decide, but I no longer heard the clock ticking. It had stopped. It was a forced retirement on this part of my career.

That day, I walked to the starting line. The last thing I remember thinking before I quieted my mind was, "You will not lose this race."

When they announced my name to the crowd, I lifted my fist in a power salute. I received a very warm reception. My fans knew it would be the last one. I won in 1:55.69, the fastest time on US soil, and I set a new national record.

I returned to my beloved South Africa. I'd planned to take several weeks off because Violet would be having our first child the following month. It was God's timing. He'd given me a certain amount of time in which to do as much as I could with this body, and I had no regrets. I did not waste the talent and the opportunity God and my ancestors bestowed upon me. I'd conquered. No one can take my accomplishments away. I won thirty-one straight

800-m races. Sebastian Coe will just have to deal with the fact that this will stay in the history books. I'll always be the greatest runner of my generation.

OUR DAUGHTER WAS born in July. I had become a mom. As I watched Violet's body change and grow to accommodate a new soul, I remember how lucky, how blessed I felt to be able to experience this with my wife. I will never be able to carry a child, but God had seen to it that my partner could. Life completely changed in that moment. I remember when I first held my daughter in my arms. I knew I would spend the rest of my days making sure she was safe and happy. I felt the same way when our second daughter was born in July 2021.

Becoming a parent for the first time changed my perspective and my priorities. I recognized that much of my life had been centered on myself, that there is a sort of selfishness in the single-minded pursuit of your talents. Even though I believe God has used me for a higher purpose on this earth, I had been, for the most part, completely and totally focused on myself, on performing, on winning. My career had cost me a lot of personal relationships, including the closeness I used to have with my parents and siblings. From 2009 until the moment my daughter was born, I had concentrated on training, performing, on possible business opportunities. I didn't have to do anything that didn't benefit my running. Before I became a mother, my life was structured around what I needed to be an elite athlete—train hard and sleep when and as much as I needed to. I ate whatever and whenever I wanted. I could shut out the world at will. I could no longer do those things. I was a mother now. Our lives revolved around diapers and feeding and sleeping schedules, cleaning and organizing, and then, eventually, school and swimming lessons. Violet and I were determined to give our daughters the tools and advantages we never had. There is nothing like having a child to remind you that you are not the center of the world.

I remember that soon after we brought our daughter home, Violet and I went into town for something or other. My sister Nico had moved in with us and was looking after our daughter. A young man began to film us while we were in an internet cafe. Violet politely asked him to stop, and instead of respecting the request, he became aggressive. At first, I stayed out of it because I knew Violet could handle herself. But as things became louder, I realized this boy was going to hit my wife. I knew this kind of kid. I'd grown up with the likes of him, so I knew what he was going to do. I walked over and made my presence known. The boy turned and immediately took a swipe at me. He wanted to cause a scene, and it was working. I used my arm to block him; I didn't do anything else. I didn't throw a punch or shove him. I used the move to let him know things weren't going to be easy for him if he tried anything more. In a different world, in a different time, I would have felt the need to teach this young man a lesson the same way I'd done with the boys I grew up with. But I was a new mom, with different priorities. The most important thing was getting back home to our infant daughter. We left without further incident, but he later told police I had slapped him and he wanted me arrested. They told my lawyer the whole thing would go away at a price. I refused, and we ended up in court, where the case was eventually dismissed. The incident was picked up in local and some national media. I wasn't embarrassed, and I wasn't worried. What I wanted was to make it clear to people—I was not going to allow myself or my family to be extorted or violated in any way. As much love as I have for my people and my country, the incident reminded me to never get too comfortable in public.

ON JULY 30TH, the Swiss Supreme Court reversed the decision that allowed me to run and ruled that the IAAF could enforce the testosterone regulations while they considered my appeal. The change meant I could not run the 800- or 1500-m races at the Doha World Championships that September. Had I been able to compete, that is where I believe I would have broken the 800-m world record. My fitness, the weather, the altitude conditions, everything was right.

I can't lie. This was a blow. A hard one. I'd made a statement that the case had destroyed me mentally and physically. It was a huge loss because of the plans I had for my future—I knew I would not be able to defend my world championship or Olympic titles. I had no choice but to make peace with it. The strange thing is I also felt relieved. It was finally over. The clock hanging over my career had stopped ticking. In its place I sensed the nothingness again, but in a different way than I'd known it when I'd returned from Berlin in 2009. Once again, I had to walk away and find a way to gather myself. It had been ten long years of insults, speculations, outright lies, and fighting. At the end of the day, nothing is permanent in this world. We are living on borrowed time. I wasn't going to waste the minutes I had left on this earth on ignorant people like Sebastian Coe and his lawyers and his doctors and the rest of the experts who did their dirty work.

THE MORE INFORMATION that came out about the IAAF's regulations and the fiction behind their research, the more support I received from women's groups, international and South African media, and female athletes who had weathered sexism, racism, and controversies about their looks, like Serena Williams, Billie Jean King, and so many others. Athlete Ally, an organization that championed the rights of athletes regardless of their sexual and gender expression, put out a letter signed by over sixty elite female athletes against the IAAF's regulations. Nike, the first company that believed in me, created a beautiful campaign about the resilience of women and celebrating and accepting our differences. I'd been chosen as one of *Time Magazine*'s 100 Most Influential People.

I'm sure all of this empathy and support bothered Coe, who couldn't stand being questioned about the regulations or me in particular. He could barely say my name in interviews. With me and Sebastian, it's personal. He has something against me—that's how I feel, and no one can change my mind. Coe, more than most, knows what it takes to run the 800 meter at an elite level. He knows the pain, or rather the utter torture, I should say. I think that is why he is so invested in the middle distances.

Coe said the regulations weren't about an "individual" or a "country" or a "continent," they were about the "integrity of women's sports." Sure, Seb. I could see how Lord Coe imagines himself as some white knight, a protector and savior of women and "women's sports." One only need to see the way his face reddens and he puffs his chest out when he talks about the "women's category." My thoughts are that he should concentrate on doing the job he said he would do. Clean up the sport. Clean it up on both sides of the aisle—the men's and women's categories. Everybody knows there is a systemic doping issue in athletics, and the IAAF has made a mess of dealing with it. One athlete can get a positive test and be back on the track the next day, while another athlete could end up banned for four years for the same substance. It would be better for athletics and athletes if Sebastian Coe focused on real cheaters instead of focusing on rare but completely natural biological variations in women or the transgendered athletes who are supposedly waiting to take women's medals. It would be even better if the sporting powers focused on the things that women really need to become better athletes—they can start with equitable pay, making sure we can do our jobs without being harassed physically and mentally, creating a system where resources are distributed fairly.

IN ANY CASE, I appreciated the love and support, and I did feel hopeful, although, as I've said, I am a practical girl. Once I knew the Swiss Court had closed the door on my favored events pending the outcome of the appeal, I discussed the future with my team.

I wanted to go to the 2020 Tokyo Olympics, I wanted to defend my 800-m title, but the reality was the only way to compete was to move down to 200 meter or move up to the 5000. That was a decision I would have to make almost immediately. It takes an athlete around two years to properly train their body for a specific event. I had been training my entire life for the middle-sprint distances—I could run the 400, 800, and 1500 meter, but 800 was where I excelled; it was the distance I had mastered. For anything below a 400 meter or above a 1500 meter, I would need to start all over again. And I was no longer a teenager. I was nearing the age of thirty. The body is an incredible gift, but it has a limit. Your late twenties through the early thirties, in most physically demanding sports, is called the prime, when most athletes give their greatest performances, but it is also where things start to break down permanently. I had to make a decision.

I began training for Tokyo in November 2019. There was a chance the Swiss Court would overturn the regulations before the start of the Olympics, but I had to be prepared in case it didn't happen. At first, the plan was to drop down to the 200 meter. I thought of myself as a natural sprinter, but sprinting wasn't in the cards when I was starting out as a teenager. Sprinting requires coaching because of its physical demands. I did not have access to coaches or a system in which to train for sprints when I was growing up in Ga-Masehlong. Middle- and long-distance running need little coaching, so it made sense someone like me would focus on them. Sometime in March, I publicly stated I would attempt the 200 meter in order to continue competing at the highest levels and hopefully get to the Olympics. That same month, I won a 200-m race at the North Gauteng Championships meeting in 23.49. A massive personal best. The Olympic standard was 22.8, but this showed I had the capabilities. Despite my age, I was a solid athlete, and perhaps I could quickly retrain my body for pure speed.

The Olympics were scheduled to be held in July 2020 but were postponed for a year because of the COVID-19 pandemic. If the Olympics had been held in 2020, I would have had access to the explosive power needed for speed in the 200. I believe I would have qualified with a good time. I don't know if I would have made it past the heats, but I feel like I would have at least been on South Africa's team. I was the one who decided to try the 200, and I was the one who decided to stop. I could do it, I could run a good time, but for how long? A season? Maybe two, at best? What would be the point? Break myself down and then never recover? I would rather do something I could still do even at the age of forty-five. That's what I want people to understand—when I study something, when I dedicate myself to something, I want to continue at it until I master it. That's my goal. Once the Olympics were moved to summer 2021, it gave me clarity. I would move up in distance. I would attempt to qualify for the 5000 meter. It was the right choice, given my age and physical condition. I needed to take care of myself, take care of my body, and prepare for longevity. I wasn't going to tear up my muscles to sprint—I'm a sports scientist; I know my body's limitations. In September 2020, the Swiss Court officially refused to overturn the IAAF's regulations. I would not be defending my 800-m race.

I began training in earnest for the 5000 meter. I knew the Olympic qualifying time was around 15:10, and I wasn't anywhere near it. By April 2021, I was running the 5000 in 15:52:28, and by May I had dropped the time down to 15:32:15. That June, I finally had a physical graduation with a cap and gown for the sports management degree I'd earned from Tshwane University of Technology in 2020. I was incredibly proud, as were my parents and Violet. Later that month, I traveled to Europe to see if I could qualify for the Olympics. I hadn't traveled in a long time and I had just gotten my COVID vaccine. I went to Belgium, Austria, Germany—but my body just didn't feel right. In all the qualifying races I tried, the first 3 kilometers would be fine but not great, and the last 2 kilometers would just be awful. My body was tired. I knew I was done and called off the season. There would be no Olympics for me. As they say, God gives and God takes away. I returned to South Africa just in time for the birth of my second daughter.

In April 2022, I went to the Portland, Oregon, World Championships. I'd maintained my long-distance training regimen, and I was steadily improving my times. As fate would have it, a few South African long-distance female athletes had been injured, so I was one of the runners added to our national team. I hadn't been to a world championship since London in 2017. I didn't expect to be back at one so soon. This time, I would be attempting to qualify for the 5000 meter. My time was nowhere near where it needed to be. Still, I was so happy to be there. To be back on the track, wearing my country's colors. I loved to be around other competitors again, surrounded by the warmth of the crowd.

When I first arrived at Oregon's Hayward Field, I saw Seb Coe in the registration area. He was standing in the middle of the room, making sure people noticed him. I know he recognized me. When he saw me, it was as if he'd seen a ghost or a witch, and he quickly ran away. I smiled and shook my head. "He still has some 800-m speed in those legs," I thought. Once I finished my initial paperwork, I went to the medical registration desk and had to hand over my medical clearance to none other than Dr. Stéphane Bermon. He, too, looked shocked and like a man lost.

I didn't advance in the 5000-m heats, but that was to be expected. I came in thirteenth with a time of 15:46:12. A good 14 seconds slower than my personal best, but it was a beautiful sunny day and hotter than hell. Win or lose, what mattered to me was that I was present. I remember the sound of the audience. They appreciated me being there and that I'd given it everything I could. As I always had and always will.

Later that day, when asked about my presence, Seb Coe told the media that "Caster Semenya has every right to be here and get treated and serviced like any other athlete, but . . ." and then crowed about how the regulations could impact other distances in the future and how he wasn't going to be lectured about his testosterone decisions by second-rate sociologists and scientists. Same old Seb. He didn't have the decency to just shut up and let it be about the sport and the athletes. It had to be about his power to control people's futures.

True to his word, on March 23, 2023, Seb Coe announced the IAAF had new regulations based on ten years of "research." The announcement took everyone by surprise. They would still allow women with DSDs to compete, but they would now have to lower their testosterone from 5 nmol/L to 2.5 nmol/L or below for a continuous twenty-four months, whether training or resting, to compete in any discipline. For those who are currently running in the 400-, 800-, and 1500-m distances and taking the drugs under the regulations set in 2019, they graciously lowered the time threshold to a continuous six months. This means none of these girls will be able to compete in the upcoming 2023 Budapest World Championships, nor, most likely, the 2024 Paris Olympics. Which was the point, of course. The IAAF also banned all transgendered athletes who had experienced puberty past the age of twelve years old across all disciplines.

For women like me, it is a complete ban under the guise of a new regulation. Seb Coe and the IAAF know that no human can maintain the same level of any hormone from one day to the next, even from sunup to sundown. The body doesn't work that way. Life doesn't work that way; it would be hard for any person to even take a medication at the exact same time every day. He announced that as more scientific evidence becomes available over the coming years, they may revisit the policy. I'm sure they will be gathering and misreporting data from the girls who feel like they have no other choice and desperately try to comply.

I will not take the drugs. This means I will no longer be able to run in any IAAF-sanctioned event. So, I will enter a different stage in my life now. I will always be a runner, IAAF or no IAAF. And

I will always be here, nurturing and protecting young talent. You may see me there on the track coaching the next world champion or Olympian, or simply sitting in the stands enjoying the show. The IAAF can't get rid of me.

I realize that every time I've experienced a great loss in my career, God and my ancestors have seen fit to give me something greater. That something is love. Even when I closed myself off to the world, when the nothingness has threatened to swallow me, I was given love—from my family, my wife, my friends, even strangers. I was given new life to love and foster in my daughters. I've never really thought about it that way until now.

I think of marathoner Eliud Kipchoge's words on his success: "Learn to say no, learn self-discipline, avoid complaining." You can take away all my material things, but I say No about me, about my soul. No one can take my sense of self-worth. Kipchoge says that it is the disciplined people who are truly free because they can do anything they want without asking for permission. I agree. I feel a sense of freedom today, because of the way I have led my life until now, that I have never felt before. I don't worry about people. They worry about me. I sleep well at night. I stay positive. Like time, I only move forward. There are certain people in this world, no matter what you do, you can't crush them. I am one of those people.

I have only one true competitor now. It's not me against the world. I'm not Tupac. It's me against the clock. In a different way than it used to be. Time for us is finite. We are only given so much of it, and only God knows when the final clock stops.

I plan to do as much as I can with this life I was given. Whatever the future holds for me, I am not afraid; I know I am strong enough to carry it. In the end, I won the race that truly mattered.

THE COBRA

SOME WILL CALL THIS THE END; I WILL CALL IT THE beginning of a new chapter. The story may not have been what you thought it would be. Maybe it was. Either way, it's mine.

I believe we are each born with something that no one else can touch. That only belongs to and can be defined by you. No one can measure it. No one can take it away from you. And you must be strong enough to fight for it when they try. I am still fighting, so I am not *in* peace, but I have *made* peace with whatever cross this is I have to bear. I will never be *in* peace until I and every other woman like me can run free.

I was never the same after Berlin. I was no longer the Caster that my parents knew and raised. My childhood friends, they didn't know who I became, either. I had to switch off emotions, focus on goals. Once you sacrifice yourself, life is totally different. It doesn't have the same meaning it did before I boarded the plane to Germany. I had to watch everything I said, watch where I was going, even count the steps of those around me. My life has been completely programmed. I can do this; I can't do that. Life never felt normal after Berlin, but I don't even know what that is anymore. That's what I've lost—the idea of normalcy. I became like a neutral person. No one could see if I was happy or sad. No one could see what was in my heart.

I no longer move freely through the world. I don't just go out. Everything is intentional and timed—a trip to the supermarket, a restaurant, the movies . . . not because I am so famous that people will recognize and surround me. I avoid it because I am wary of the outside world. I prefer to be in my own space. In my own home. At home, with my family, I can be happy. I can be vulnerable.

It has been difficult to carry the hopes of millions; it has been equally hard to carry the cruelty, too. There is a certain ability to detach and shield yourself that this requires. This has made me look like an arrogant person to outsiders' eyes. You can call me whatever you want. I'm still human.

This journey has cost me a certain kind of life, even as I feel that it has given me much more than it has taken away. I have wanted to be recognized for my sporting talent since I pointed at the sky when I was eight years old. I have helped my family with this talent. Now I must live the life I created based on what I went through; I can't live life the way I wanted it to be.

I think of the price sometimes, even though I don't like to dwell on negative things. For years, I took drugs I didn't need to take. I don't know what the long-term effects will be on my health. To many, I will forever be some kind of biological error, a mistake of nature. The fact is I can post a picture of myself with my children and there will be people who write, "Those are not your children. You are barren. You are not a real woman." But there will always be those who say, "I am happy for you, Caster. Your family is beautiful."

It is true 2009 haunts me; there is trauma here. I admit that. And I tell my wife and my family sometimes, when I am feeling pensive, that I hope this does not affect me later in life. I can't turn back time, I can't wish myself back to the day before Berlin. No psychologist, no doctor, no one can change what happened to me. I was a child who had to behave like an adult. I became suspicious of everything and everyone. I felt myself to be an eighteen-year-old girl who turned one thousand years old on her next birthday. I wasn't able to make the carefree mistakes normal people make and learn and grow from. There were no parties for me. No wild nights. Instead, I was silent and still. I have led a rigid, structured life. The life of a soldier.

People have committed suicide because they can't find a way out of how the world has defined and treated them. What many find amazing about my journey is that I have picked myself up from this. I continue to face the world, and I fight. It's because I accept myself, I understand myself. I won't let others define me—not a politician, not a scientist, not an athletics federation.

I DO NOT ASK for pity. I have never begged. I can't say I have ever felt sorry for myself. What I have searched for, since I was a little girl, is freedom and belonging. I found that in running, even when I was told I wasn't free to run and that I didn't belong.

I told Violet one day that the IAAF may hold the power, but I sanctioned the show. I wanted to run that final in Berlin in 2009. I was just a young village girl, but I was the master of my own destiny in some ways. I controlled the narrative, and I did so by not speaking. I had to be smart. I had to keep my head low. Stay focused. I didn't judge myself. My existence on this earth was never about proving others wrong or right. I live here, just like everyone else.

I didn't have a choice about how I was born or how I was raised. I didn't have a choice but to be a woman. So, I am a different kind of woman. The science of gender isn't set in stone. The more we study, the more we learn. I believe it's wrong to force women like me into surgery or medication to compete. Maybe the hormonal makeup of my body does give me an advantage. Then, so what? It's mine.

I believe I'm a living testimony of God to show that when you are given life, never take it for granted. I was given a body, I was given a soul, I was given a brain, a heart, and all the organs in my body. I am using them each and every day. And I love being different, I love when I'm walking around and people think I'm a man and then realize I'm a woman. I'm present. I'm alive.

Because I am a masculine woman, people have asked if I had

ever just wished I'd been born a man. Wouldn't it have been better for me? The thing is, I don't want to be a man. If my body's makeup makes me "intersex," as they say, then I'm intersex. There's nothing to be done about that. The terms will change as the years go by. They always do. To me, they're just words.

Even if I did this or that to fit some people's idea of what a woman or a man is supposed to look like, my soul would remain the same. My body is mine, and I will not change it for anyone. That is what saved my career; it is the reason you know who I am. And I feel sorry for the sisters who agreed to the surgery, for their road to inner peace may be harder and longer than mine.

My soul feels right in my body. I believe it always will.

But if one day I change my mind about that, it's my business. Mind yours.

I MAY FEEL THAT something was taken away from me back when I was an eighteen-year-old girl, but I don't feel I am owed or "deserve" anything. I have worked for everything I have. I am not a cheater.

I am writing to you from my home in Pretoria. That I bought with my blood, sweat, and sometimes, rarely, my tears. I am surrounded by the love of my wife and family, and I find comfort in the sounds of my children laughing and playing. My almost four-year-old daughter told me she wants to be like me one day. That means more to me than anything.

This story has many roads, some are winding, others are straight, some are wide, others narrow—all led to my becoming Caster Semenya, the Daughter of South Africa. My story isn't about running so much as it is about what it means to be a human. In the beginning, I was just a runner. Today, I have become a symbol of resistance and freedom and self-acceptance. It's no longer about winning a race, it's about the struggle for universal human rights.

The IAAF thought they could shame me off the track back

in 2009, but things didn't turn out the way they usually did. We may have lost the legal battles, but I won where it matters—I still became a champion, and the IAAF exposed their true nature. This thing is no longer about secret conversations and secret surgeries and secret medication. Now the world knows more about what they have done and what they want to continue to do.

We have now taken the fight to the European Court of Human Rights. It has been given priority status. I hope there is a favorable outcome for the young girls who are now and will be subject to the regulations. I hope there is a favorable outcome for all women, for they will come to see that these regulations will affect them, too.

I will run as long as my body allows me to, and then I will walk away with my head held high, with my dignity intact. At the end of the day, I live for those I love, I live for the people who believe in the work I do. I mind my business, and I don't back down from any challenge. I stand strong, and I stay in control. I am Caster. I will always be myself. No one can rule over my life. That is what I call the Cobra Mentality. That is the code I have lived and will continue to live by.

One day, this part of my life will be over. There will be no more speeches asked of me, no events I need to attend. Everyone will stop talking. All the noise will be silenced. It will just be me and mine. And when I think of that future, I think of myself back where I started. Back in the village of my birth. I will have my own farm. I will tend to my plants and my animals. There will be a facility where the youth can feel safe to train after school. I imagine a running track surrounding my property, and I imagine myself with a whistle and a stopwatch, urging the young runners to be better than they were the day before.

To all those who have loved and supported me, I thank you from the bottom of my heart. To my fellow competitors, my sisters from all continents, especially those women who didn't think I belonged with them—I hope my presence made you train harder, I hope having me on the track pushed you to run faster, I hope I inspired you all to personal bests and beyond. We all have a purpose in this life, and perhaps that was one of mine.

I am Mokgadi Caster Semenya. Remember the meaning of my name—I am the one who gives up what they want so that others may have what they need. I am the one who seeks, I am the one who guides.

ACKNOWLEDGMENTS

THERE ARE MANY PEOPLE TO THANK FOR THIS journey. I know it will seem like I have forgotten many of you. To those who have not been named, just know you are in my heart and mind, and circumstances did not allow me the time and space to properly address you.

To my mother, father, and ancestors, I thank you for giving me life. It is a blessing to be on this earth and I will cherish every breath for the rest of my days.

To my siblings, cousins, and entire family, I thank you for loving and appreciating me just as I am. For never judging and criticizing me, for accepting the will of my life. Without your love and support, I would not be the person I am today.

To Violet, my wife and friend—my all—thank you for being there, for your patience, love, and constant care. For letting me be myself for you. You have understood me more than I understood myself. You are my soulmate. We ride together, we die together.

To Maseko, Ezekiel, Principal Perhaps, and many more during my early days as a runner. You all saw the potential for greatness in this little girl and allowed me to go out there and showcase my talent. You made sure I got to all the competitions I needed to be at. If it wasn't for these men, I wouldn't be here. I will never in my life forget it.

To the University of Pretoria, especially Toby Sutcliffe, coach Michael, and my protector David—you opened the doors for this rural girl with dreams of living in the city. Thank you for showing me light, giving me guidance and protection. I would not have become a world champion without your support system. You will always remain in my heart.

To Greg Nott—may God bless you for coming to the aid of a

little girl who just wanted to run. I am forever grateful for your continued love, kindness, patience, and understanding.

To all the lawyers, doctors, experts, and activists who rallied to my cause, who fight every day for universal human rights, I thank you from the bottom of my heart.

To everyone at the Tshwane University of Technology, especially Drs. Pen and Given, thank you for believing in me and helping me to achieve things academically I could never imagine. Thank you for pushing me and making a space for me in a place I didn't think I could fit into. The genuine love and time you continue to give me is priceless.

To Northwest University, especially coach Jean Verster and athletics manager Terseus Liebenberg: I thank you from the bottom of my heart for the opportunity you gave me to find my inner peace, to reactivate and rebuild myself in body and mind. You saw I still had the potential for greatness and I am happy I was able to deliver on the promise I made.

To my Nike family, especially Masilo—thank you for never giving up on me no matter what, thank you for accepting and celebrating me through the good and bad, thick and thin. I am eternally grateful for the time, effort, support, and patience throughout my career.

To my Wiphold family, you've being there since day one. I cannot thank you enough for protecting, appreciating, and accepting me for who I am.

To my Discovery family, I thank you for your unwavering support and unconditional love throughout this journey. It is a joy to work with all of you.

To Juuka, Masilo, Maria, and Becky—you have all played a massive role in my life and career. You have all made sure I achieved the best possible outcome in everything I did. Thank you for never judging or criticizing me and picking me up when I faced what seemed like insurmountable challenges. I am grateful for your presence in my life. May God bless you all.

To my physios, especially Anita Van der Lingen—thank you for healing my body and helping me stay on the track. Thank you for the great work you've done to make sure my body is in shape, and that it always recovers well. Know that I appreciate the time you've sacrificed with your families to travel around the world with me.

To my strengthening coach, Jacus Coetzee—you are one in a million. You have helped me understand my body and helped me become the great athlete I am today. Because of you, I was able to discover the strength in me, what I could truly achieve. All you have wanted was for me to be great. Know that you are always in my thoughts.

To every pacer I've run with—thank you for doing a great job, for allowing me to explore the world with you, helping me run consistent times, getting me to where I needed to be. Without your work, no runner can reach their full potential.

To Peter McGuigan at Ultra Literary Agency, Norm Aladjem at Mainstay Entertainment, Tom Mayer and Nneoma Amadi-obi and everyone at W. W. Norton, Lemara Lindsay-Prince and all the Penguin Random House UK staff, Sibongile Machika and Annie Olivier and everyone at Jonathan Ball Publishers, and Sulay Hernandez at Unveiled Ink—thank you for allowing me to tell my story, for giving me this opportunity to connect with the world, and bringing the world closer to me so that I could be understood better not only as a great athlete but as a humble human being. Thank you all for your patience. I have truly enjoyed this experience and appreciated learning about the publishing business.

And finally, my eternal gratitude to the South African Nation, for your unconditional love, support, and respect, despite my flaws and through my ups and downs. Thank you for celebrating my achievements and resilience in sports without judgement. Thank you for standing beside me, wrapping your arms around me, and lifting me up. May God bless you all.

With love,

Mogkadi Caster Semenya